Critical Praise for *L*

"[A] riveting account. . . . Dillon p[...] cessful) search for the solution to [the] mystery mas[...], [...] the reader through the various dead ends and wildcat theories with an even, nonjudgmental, but always curious voice."

—Bruce Barcott, *Newsday*

"Pulitzer Prize–winning journalist Patrick Dillon explores the disaster with obvious admiration for the men who suffered it and compassion for those they left behind. . . . [His] re-creation of the final voyages of the *Altair* and *Americus* builds a palpable sense of the dangers in commercial fishing."

—Stephen Shapiro, *The Wall Street Journal*

"Gripping . . . widely acclaimed. . . . At its heart, *Lost at Sea* is a book about how commercial fishing in the area was like a modern-day gold rush." —Ken Garcia, *San Francisco Chronicle*

"There are wrenching moments in *Lost at Sea*. . . . [Dillon's] story focuses on the investigation to determine why the two vessels had been lost and the ensuing effort to pass safety legislation."

—Michael Kenney, *The Boston Globe*

"It's a tribute to [Dillon's] skill as a reporter that he makes of this book a sensitive memorial to young men needlessly killed in their prime." —W. D. Wetherell, *San Jose Mercury News*

"The heart and tears of the story are in Anacortes. [Dillon] moved into the town for months. He ran into the players in his history at the gas station and supermarket. He drew out people whom reporters had spooked ten years earlier."

—Scott Sunde, *Seattle Post-Intelligencer*

"Dillon tells this grim story in admirable journalistic fashion. . . . [His] account of the tragedy that struck a small town is well told . . . interesting . . . sometimes heartbreaking. When he tells how the news of the lost boats trickles uncertainly back to the community, we can feel the sadness that grips the survivors. It's as if a clinging winter fog has covered the town."

—G. William Gray, *The Tampa Tribune*

"[Dillon's] descriptions of work on a crabbing vessel are riveting and frightening." —Phil Green, *Fort Worth Star-Telegram*

"A taut, heartbreaking story. . . . Dillon's fine book tells us it's the same as it ever was: men at sea equals men at supreme risk." —*Kirkus Reviews*

"His prose is poetic. . . . This is a story of individuals, but it is also the story of an old, traditional industry pushed farther and farther offshore by heavy demand from top restaurants paying high prices." —*Publishers Weekly*

"With acute prose, Dillon constructs the sinkings and the fatalism of the fishing culture. . . . The compelling portions are the sea story and the effects of tragedy on a small town." —Gilbert Taylor, *Booklist*

"Delving into the mysterious tragedy of the *Americus* and *Altair,* acclaimed journalist Patrick Dillon creates a moving portrait of courage and love." —*The Lima News* (Lima, OH)

"Daunting mysteries tend to make very good reading. Dillon tells this very real story as well as most novelists could. He develops the characters and gets the reader interested in their lives and empathetic of their plight. . . . *Lost at Sea* brings you as close as you'll ever want to go to that experience." —*The Sun Newspaper* (Bremerton, WA)

"The author . . . recounts vividly the region's disastrous storms and freezing temperatures, the financial pressures and high stakes the ship captains face. This book will appeal especially to the fans of the popular *Working on the Edge,* a tale of the terrors of Alaska crab fishing by Spike Walker, and Sebastian Junger's gripping tale, *The Perfect Storm.*" —Sara Jameson, *Grants Pass Daily Courier*

LOST
AT SEA

AN AMERICAN TRAGEDY

PATRICK DILLON

A TOUCHSTONE BOOK
Published by Simon & Schuster
New York   London   Toronto   Sydney   Singapore

TOUCHSTONE
Rockefeller Center
1230 Avenue of the Americas
New York, NY 10020

First Touchstone Edition 2000
Published by arrangement with The Dial Press,
an imprint of The Bantam/Dell Publishing Group.

Manufactured in the United States of America

3   5   7   9   10   8   6   4   2

Library of Congress Cataloging-in-Publication Data is available.

ISBN 0-684-86909-8 (Pbk)

*For those who've waited at the dock
and all who ever will*

THE *AMERICUS*
Crew List, February 1983

George C. Nations, Captain
Age: 43
Experience: 13 years
Next of kin: Janice Nations, wife

Brent Boles, relief captain
Age: 24
Experience: 4 years, 10 months
Next of kin: George Boles, father

Victor Bass, deckhand
Age: 19
Experience: first voyage
Next of kin: Lloyd and Jean Bass,
  parents

Larry Littlefield, engineer
Age: 29
Experience: 9 years, 2 months
Next of kin: Al and Judy Littlefield,
  parents

Jeff Nations, deckhand
Age: 19
Experience: 5 months
Next of kin: Janice Nations, mother

Rich Awes, deckhand
Age: 20
Experience: first voyage
Next of kin: Elden and Lois Awes,
  parents

Paul Northcutt, deckhand
Age: 24
Experience: 4 years, 2 months
Next of kin: Eve Northcutt, mother

THE *ALTAIR*
Crew List, February 1983

Ronald Beirnes, Captain
Age: 47
Experience: 24 years
Next of kin: Nancy Beirnes, wife

Jeff Martin, engineer
Age: 23
Experience: 2 years
Next of kin: Don and Roberta
  Martin, parents

Randy Harvey, deckhand
Age: 23
Experience: first voyage
Next of kin: Richard and Marguerite
  Harvey, parents

Lark Breckenridge, deckhand
Age: 24
Experience: 5 months
Next of kin: Kelly Breckenridge,
  wife

Brad Melvin, deckhand
Age: 26
Experience: 3 years, 3 months
Next of kin: Wayne Melvin, father

Troy Gudbranson, deckhand
Age: 21
Experience: first voyage
Next of kin: Jody Gudbranson, wife

Tony Vienhage, deckhand
Age: 27
Experience: 3 years
Next of kin: Mary Vienhage, wife

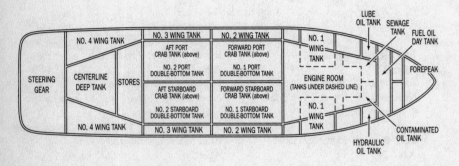

Tank arrangement for the *Americus*

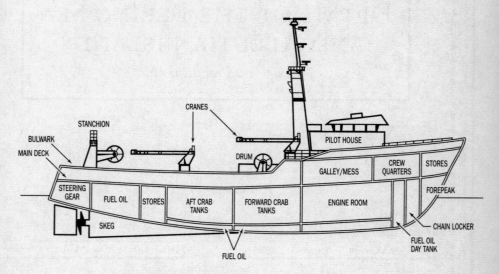

Profile view of *Americus* with trawling gear

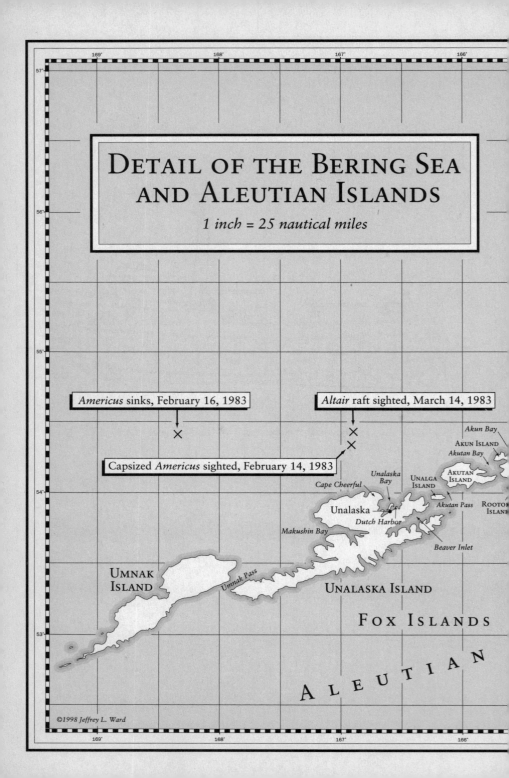

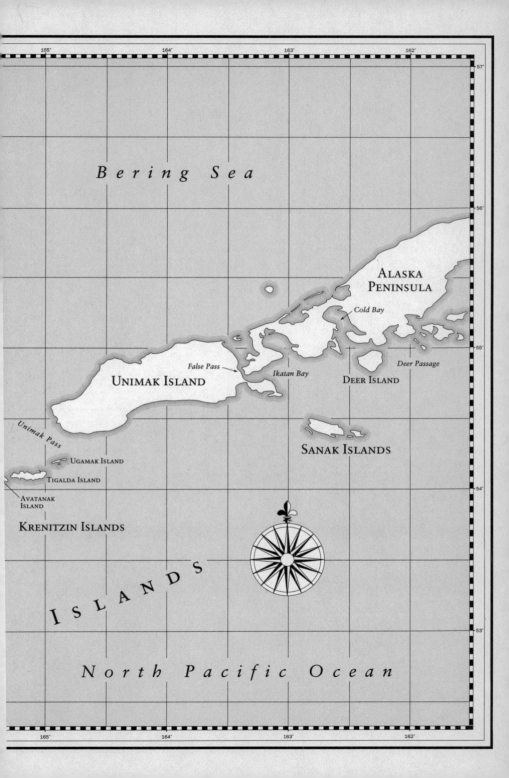

CONTENTS

PROLOGUE

THE OLD FISHERMAN BACKED HIS BOAT FROM ITS BERTH WITH EASE. When his bow was clear of the vessels moored on either side of him, he feathered the throttle and turned the wheel, making an unhurried pivot to starboard, and headed toward the channel that led to open water. Francis Barcott, seventy-five years old, had been working the water for sixty-one years; his place at the helm of the *Veteran* was the most familiar in his life. Fishermen darning clean meshes in their nets on the docks called him "the Old Man" and deferred to him. Years of deliberation were etched on his face, and some sentimentality, too, shaded his eyes. He looked as though he might have aged quickly as a young man and then stopped altogether as the graying years passed by. His hands, though, were thick, hardened—the hands of a fisherman. Even when relaxed, a fisherman's fingers cup rigidly toward the palm in a palsy caused by years of holding tight to gear and pulling lines in the cold and wet.

The *Veteran* was a stately wooden sixty-eight-foot purse seiner, painted black with a white wheelhouse and a rakish, cleaver-sharp prow. She was built in 1926, when fishing was an alloy of aesthetics and utility, when the way a boat presented herself to the water and how precisely the net was set commanded nearly equal respect with how much salmon a fisherman caught.

Everything Francis knew about fishing he had learned decades earlier from his father. In the summer of 1913, in an open skiff, Anton Barcott had first set his own net on the ebb tide along the Rosario Bluffs near Deception Pass in the northwest corner of the state of Washington. Like thousands of other young farmers and fishermen from the islands of the Adriatic, Anton Barcott had heard of the legendary Pacific Northwest salmon runs. Believing himself to be as good a netman as any, he set out to make his fortune there and was not disappointed.

In the late summer or early fall, when the moon and the tide and currents were right, millions of sockeye salmon would pour from the Pacific Ocean through the Strait of Juan de Fuca into Puget Sound and then race east directly toward the bluffs where the netmen would be waiting. Within yards of land, where the graveled bottom rose sharply, the salmon would instinctively turn left to make their final migratory run northward toward British Columbia and the spawning tributaries of the Fraser River. But the fishermen's nets would intervene, their orange corks marking half-mile perimeters, stretching like enormous open arms along the surface, their weighted webs extending downward a hundred feet. Near the nets' edge the boats were lined thirty or forty abreast, with thirty or forty more idling, awaiting their turn in line. In peak season fishermen would routinely haul five thousand pounds of salmon over the bulwarks from a single net.

The letters Anton Barcott wrote home to his native Vela Luka, an island village off the Dalmatian Coast of Croatia, were filled with wondrous details of his newfound home on the western edge of America. The fish were even more plentiful than he could have imagined. Some farmers used pitchforks in the local rivers, heaving salmon as they would hay, some used traps hung from wood pilings to intercept the fish in the narrows between islands, and others used horses to haul their nets in the shallow water along the beaches. In every direction the rocky, steep-banked, tree-studded islands with deep, protective harbors reminded Anton and his fellow Croatians that they were as close to home here as anywhere on earth.

The first wave of immigrants had begun to settle in small villages along the coast of Puget Sound at the turn of the century. When he arrived, Anton Barcott chose to live in Anacortes, which had been bustling with industry since the Alaskan Gold Rush of 1889. Located on the north shore of Fidalgo Island—actually a fist-shaped peninsula thrusting westward into Puget Sound and separated from the mainland by the ribbon-thin Swinomish Channel—Anacortes was the closest port to Alaska and the Orient except for Bellingham, fifteen miles to the north. The town's founder, Amos Bowman, a civil engineer and landowner, had heard the rumors about the coming of the transcontinental railway and bet that with its deep water, natural harbor, and easy connection to the mainland, Anacortes could outrival Seattle and Bellingham and even San Francisco as the West's primary port. He bought hundreds of acres, named the village after his wife, Anna Curtis Bowman, and quickly persuaded lenders and buyers to rally around his plan.

In just one month, between December 1889 and the end of January 1890, the land rush caused the population of Anacortes to rise from five hundred to ten thousand. Wood-frame houses and brick buildings sprang up as trees were cut and milled and salmon-red clay was excavated and molded into blocks. Suddenly, there were sawmills, boatyards, fruit canneries, fish canneries, and general stores, a necklace of commerce and industry strung along the waterfront that lured Welsh, Irish, Greeks, Germans, Icelanders, Swedes, Norwegians, and Croatians across oceans. Charles Quincy

Adams, a wayward great-grandson of John Quincy Adams, was sent to the new town to make something of himself by running the mill his grandfather owned there. Soon there was a school, a district courthouse, churches, boardinghouses, cottages, and a red-light district too. Anacortes had become a boomtown.

Just as the boom was in full swing, as Bowman and his colleagues were framing in their city, the railroad companies decided that the railroad terminus would be located in Seattle. Like Anton Barcott, those who could not afford to leave Anacortes stayed. The population stalled at nearly ten thousand for almost the next hundred years.

Still, Bowman was not wrong about Anacortes's promising natural attributes. Because of its unique location, because it faced west toward the Strait of Juan de Fuca and northward toward the narrow lee of Vancouver Island, both of which funneled salmon from the Pacific to their spawning rivers, Anacortes fishermen had easy access to the largest runs of salmon in the world.

The native tribes offered evidence of this well before the city's population was swelling on the if-come. The British explorer George Vancouver noted in his logs in 1792 that the tribes—the Samish, Tulalip, Lummi, Salish, Swinomish—seemed to be prospering from local waters. He and others had witnessed their methods: pulling long-handled, fish-laden dripnets from shallow rivers they had staked with lattices of cedar lashed with bark, rigging traps across coves that would fill with schools of fish teeming in on the flood tide, or baiting lines woven from strands of women's hair.

For the immigrants who arrived in Anacortes at the turn of the century, salmon fishing would become a mainstay, too, and would help lead the town's recovery from the diversion of the transcontinental railway. Using modern means—hemp nets pulled by horses, or fish traps strung across narrow channels—Anacortes fishermen could haul thousands of salmon on a single tide. By rowing less than half a day, these fishermen could intercept the chinook, sockeye, pink, and silver salmon that ran in separate seasons from the middle of spring to the middle of fall. Although other coastal cities sent forth larger fleets, by 1911 Anacortes proclaimed itself "the Salmon Capital of the World." A dozen fish canneries flourished along the waterfront. Two years later the town boasted the greatest run of sockeye salmon ever recorded on Puget Sound—more than 39 million fish caught, more than $3 million earned. The Anacortes canneries could not keep up with the catch. Tons of fish were rotting on the docks, and tons more were being dumped within sight of the docks every day, the only lament being over lost dollars. Otherwise, the city was feverish from its own good fortune.

Anton Barcott had caught this boom tide, and when his son Francis was old enough, he passed on what he had learned. He taught Francis to read the tides and anticipate the mood swings of the weather, to hold still in heavy fog and listen for the tonal variations of the foghorns warning him away from reefs, or even to listen for the break of waves on the reefs themselves. He taught him how to splice rope and coil it tightly so there would be no loops to snare a man's feet on deck, where the slightest slip could be lethal. Francis learned to lead fish to the big net with the skiff, to set the nets gingerly enough to avoid snags from kelp or shredding boulders. He learned to sight from miles away the landmarks and buoy markers that affirmed a course or called for a correction. He learned to watch for specks falling on the water like pepper on a plate, recognizing the specks to be frenzied gulls diving onto herring just below the surface. Where herring rose, salmon were likely in pursuit.

Listening to the salty stories of the older fishermen, Francis learned to discern fact from fiction without dismissing the metaphysics of even the wildest tales. He heard from his father and uncles that Puget Sound could not possibly hold enough fish for all the fishermen forever. No waters could. But there were waters up north, they said, where the salmon came from, that contained more fish than anyone could imagine. And when he was seventeen, with his father and uncle, Francis Barcott sailed north to Alaska in his father's wooden purse seiner, the *Cleveland*.

Along the way, during that first three-month voyage, he learned new lessons. The weather, currents, and tides were more contentious and confusing than anything he'd ever encountered in Puget Sound. He learned to use the tools of the navigator—his eyes and his memory for dead reckoning, the compass and charts for plotting his position—and to consult the *Captain Hansen Handbook,* the tabular Bible of navigational aids, for noting the distances between landmarks all the way from Seattle to Bristol Bay. After just a few trips he could navigate without help from his father, from Anacortes up the Inside Passage to Ketchikan, through the Wrangell Narrows to Kodiak Island, through the labyrinthine shoals around the Shumigan Islands. When the weather permitted, he rode the ten-knot current of False Pass on the flood tide into Bristol Bay, weaving the boat through a maze of ghostly abandoned vessels whose navigators had committed the slightest error, but paid the fullest price.

In time Francis Barcott could pretty well steer from memory, consulting only the charts. He could run his vessel at night and in fog and in snowstorms, cleaving through any uncertainty. Along the way he learned how to anticipate the limits of his boat, his crew, and himself. Above all, he learned that a good fisherman didn't measure the danger of his occupation by how big or cruel the sea was, but by the potential margin for error. He learned to respect the smallest of margins.

Francis Barcott would pass these lessons on to a succeeding generation of Anacortes fishermen, including his sons, Lynn and Larry, and other young men he hired or recommended for jobs on other boats headed for Alaska. Some went on to become highliners, consistently productive captains, and prosperous boat owners themselves. Some would not be so lucky. They would drift from season to season, dock to dock. And the names of some others would be inscribed on a memorial by the Anacortes marina, dedicated to the town's fishermen who died at sea.

By the mid-1960s those young men who did prosper rode a new fishing boom that was greater in profit and in danger than anything

Francis Barcott had ever experienced. The boom was in crab, not salmon.

In the early 1930s, as Francis was making his first trips to Alaska, these crab began turning up in the nets of cod and salmon fishermen off Cook Inlet and Kodiak Island. King crab, so-called for their size, weighed up to twenty pounds and had ten legs that yielded incredibly succulent flesh. As best as anyone could tell, king crab ranged widely, starting at the northern end of Vancouver Island and the fjords of Southeast Alaska, following the flanks of the land bridge from the Alaskan Peninsula to Kodiak Island and the Aleutian chain all the way to Siberia's Kamchatka Peninsula. In fact, the Russians and Japanese had been landing the crab off Siberia for years. Cans of king crab labeled under the "Geisha" brand had been distributed worldwide as early as 1939, until Pearl Harbor and the declaration of war thwarted any further importing by the United States.

By the mid-1960s, 190 vessels from the U.S., Norway, Japan, and Russia had converted the crabbing grounds around Kodiak into a $15 million business. By the 1965–66 season the harvest, centered around Kodiak, had increased to 94.4 million pounds that yielded $22 million. Crabbing was gaining fast on salmon as Alaska's richest catch. On the retail end, frozen king crab commanded $4 a pound. A whole one, if you could obtain it in New York or Kansas City, cost $30. It was said that every day at least thirty-five thousand plates held some form of king crab. And the demand was increasing. Some boats unloaded more than a million pounds per season. Crew members returned home with over $50,000 for a few months' work, while their skippers averaged $150,000.

"It was like a fever sweeping the docks," remembered Bud Ryan, then a young Anacortes crabber. Like him, thousands of young, tough kids came from all over America looking for adventure and quick fortune and ways to express their toughness. For the next two decades crabbing would carry an increasingly greater share of the nearly one hundred thousand people employed in the Alaskan commercial fishing industry.

Nonetheless, Francis Barcott and his father continued fishing solely for salmon, reasoning that they would be better off doing what they did best in waters they knew rather than risking the expense of a new vessel to join a far-flung chase on the high seas. "I am a salmon fisherman," Francis said. "It's what I love."

Barcott witnessed the incredible changes the crab boom caused in the fishing industry. As the seasons progressed, federal legislation pushed foreign fleets two hundred miles off U.S. shores and provided low-interest loans to encourage the buildup of a larger U.S. fishing fleet. As a result, opportunists came to Alaskan waters on the decks of big new vessels equipped with sophisticated depth finders, interlocking radar, automatic pilots, hydraulic lifts, saltwater circulation tanks to keep the crab alive, and powerful halogen iodide lights that allowed the crews to work around the clock. A new boat cost a million dollars before it hit the water, and an annual overhaul and repair of any vessel would cost at least $30,000, about what a salmon skipper like Francis Barcott might make in the best of seasons back down in Puget Sound.

There were more-subtle changes too. Vessels now took on crew members who had never met until they stepped on deck. Skippers were itinerant, owing their allegiances to no small towns or family bonds but only to the chance to make big money. Owners who had traditionally captained their vessels became absentee operators. The independent subsistence fishermen, the captains who fished to uphold family tradition, found no place in the king-crab fleet.

Francis Barcott had witnessed this evolution with growing unease. Commercial fishing was already dangerous enough. By the mid-1970s the mortality rate among commercial fishermen approached seventy-five times the national average for on-the-job deaths. But by 1982 crabbing, because it occurred in treacherous seas off Kodiak Island and along the Aleutian chain during Alaska's stormiest months, had a mortality rate twenty-five times higher than the rest of commercial fishing and nine times that of mining and logging. Crabbing, then, carried a dubious cachet. It had become the nation's deadliest occupation and would become deadlier year by year for nearly the next decade.

"When I quit fishing in Alaska was when I realized I could no longer watch out for the others. That's when you no longer belong in the wheelhouse," Francis Barcott remembered, when he sailed home from Alaska for the final time. "I didn't want to be the one to make the mistake to cost people their lives."

PART ONE

"There are things about the sea which man can never know and can never change. Those who describe the sea as 'angry' or 'gentle' or 'ferocious' do not know the sea. The sea just doesn't know you're there—you take it as you find it, or it takes you."

—R. M. Snyder, early oceanographer

CHAPTER 1

On a clear March day in 1982, just off False Pass three hundred miles west of the Alaskan Peninsula, an alarm sounded in the engine room of the fishing vessel *Antares*. She was out of Anacortes, Washington, two thousand miles to the south. Steve Carr, the twenty-five-year-old engineer, climbed down the stairs to investigate. When he reached the engine room it was filled with smoke. He could tell by the thick, oily smell that the fire was coming from the hydraulic system that supplied power to run the winches on deck. He called the wheelhouse on the vessel's intercom and reported this to Kevin Kirkpatrick, also twenty-five, the captain and a lifelong friend. Kirkpatrick immediately throttled back and then shut down the work on deck, directing the crew of five to go to their fire-fighting stations. Carr donned a mask and an oxygen tank, armed himself with a carbon dioxide extinguisher, and plunged back into the engine room. Gradually, on the wheelhouse monitor of the engine room, Kirkpatrick could see the smoke clearing. Within minutes Carr called again over the intercom and said it appeared the fire was out.

Kirkpatrick gave the crew a break. They gathered around the galley table and ate a meal, each of them worn out by the rush of adrenaline but still tensed for the sound of another fire alarm. None came.

Before getting under way, though, Kirkpatrick and Carr headed back down to the engine room to assess the damage the fire had caused. When they opened the hatch, the innards of the *Antares* erupted. The rush of fresh oxygen had acted as a bomb for the still-smoldering fire.

Kirkpatrick scrambled up the stairs to the wheelhouse and sent out a distress call on his VHF radio. He stayed calm and went by the book: "MAYDAY, MAYDAY, MAYDAY," he repeated, before giving the vessel's name and call sign three times. He reported his latitude and longitude and that there was a fire on board. He reported the number of crew and gave a description of the 123-foot *Antares*. He waited for a response. In the meantime, several crew members climbed up the stairs into the wheelhouse. The fire was completely out of control, they told him. He repeated the distress call, and when a German fish-processing vessel just ten miles away picked it up and said it was heading in his direction, Kirkpatrick radioed back that he and his crew were abandoning ship.

As they had been trained, the six-member crew lay on the floor of the ten-foot-wide wheelhouse and wriggled into their thick neoprene survival suits. None took more than two minutes. They lowered the two life rafts into the water, making certain the rafts were still tethered to the burning vessel. Then, one by one, each of them plunged into the thirty-two-degree sea and paddled awkwardly toward the rafts, helping each other aboard. They could see the hull of the *Antares* glowing like a dull red coal at the waterline. When the heat became too intense, they cut the rafts loose. The German vessel arrived within an hour and the exhausted crew was helped on deck. All survived. But the *Antares* was destroyed, burned from the inside out as if by an enormous oven fire.

Weeks later, back in Anacortes, the *Antares*'s owner, Jeff Hendricks, negotiated to sell her for pennies on the dollar for scrap. Less than five years old, the *Antares* was one of the first of a generation of sophisticated new American fishing vessels. She had cost nearly $3 million and had taken a year to build. In a good season Hendricks could count on the boat to earn as much as $2.5 million. Now he was lucky to see $25,000 from the scrapyard, plus an insurance settlement. But under tow, on the way to port, the burned-out husk of the *Antares* sank in two thousand feet of water two thousand miles from home. With it, Hendricks's fledgling four-vessel fleet suffered a serious blow.

Named after the brightest star in the constellation Scorpio, the *Antares* had been born out of Hendricks's optimism and exhaustless ambition. When she was completed in 1977, the *Antares* secured his standing as the top vessel owner in Anacortes and one of the top fleet owners in the Pacific Northwest. During the previous three years Hendricks had proven himself with his first two boats, the *Sea Star* and *Alyeska,* built by Fairhaven Industries up in Bellingham. He had taken advantage of low-interest loans the government was offering prospective fishing-vessel owners to build them, and they had done so well in the Bering Sea that he was able to use them as collateral for financing the next venture.

In the mid 1970s, optimism was running so high about the newly discovered crabbing grounds near the Pribilof Islands, in fact, that Hendricks persuaded Dick Nelson and Bob Gudmundson, two Fairhaven managers who had overseen the birth of his first two boats, to break away from the company and start their own.

"Anacortes was ideal," Nelson said. "It had deep water and a low bank. There was already a shipyard facility there on property owned by the port."

There was also a three-hundred-foot dock, seventy-five feet wide, and a track for drawing vessels out of the water for repairs or sending a new hull down the ways. It didn't take much convincing for a new partnership to be born, and it didn't take much persuading for the town to make a sweet lease deal, especially since Hendricks had already commissioned the building of three big boats. In Anacortes, new jobs were a rare and welcome opportunity.

Nelson and Gudmundson opened shop on January 2, 1977, and within two weeks, two dozen locals were at work on Hendricks's first order. On spring nights that year, the Dakota Creek Industries shipyard at the foot of Commercial Street in Anacortes was ablaze like a giant fireworks display. With their soldering guns and oxyacetylene torches, welders fused metal to metal, sending millions of sparks skyward, announcing the birth of Hendricks's newest and first homegrown fishing vessel.

Hendricks had big plans for his new boat. He wanted the *Antares* to be just a little bigger, deeper, and longer than the *Sea Star* and *Alyeska* and other Pacific Northwest boats that had been patterned after the deep-sea tuna seiners that plied the Pacific from San Pedro to Hawaii. He wanted this new boat specifically designed and equipped to challenge the Bering Sea. The *Antares* would be all steel, with a square bottom and square stern, a stiff-ribbed, stiff-backboned vessel of a hard chine designed to snap back fast on keel with every roll. At 123.5 feet long and 32 feet wide, with a depth amidships of 14 feet, and 32 feet from the main deck to the top of the mast, she would be subtly larger than the previous boats. Like the others, her wheelhouse would sit forward and her bow would be slightly rounded, flaring upward from the bulwarks. The lightship hull, or shell, would weigh 195 tons with just over a 10-foot draft. Like her sister vessels, her hull would be sky blue, flaunting a distinctive white-winged emblem.

In the Dakota Creek shipyard, the *Antares* began as a sketch hand-drawn by Jeff Hendricks. The sketch was translated into blueprints by the Seattle-area designer Jacob Fisker-Andersen, a Danish immigrant with a respectable pedigree as a vessel architect. The blueprints were then projected and drafted to full-scale drawings in a barnlike drafting room at Dakota Creek. Every component of the hull—the keel, the ribs, the scantlings (cross sections), bulkheads, fuel tanks, and fish tanks—had a matching life-sized drawing that could be laid out on the floor of the drafting room.

The paper pieces were then translated into steel. At this stage the 123-foot fishing boat was no different from a child's model. Every component was prefabricated, a puzzle with all the pieces ready to be pressed into place. They had only to be matched against the drawings.

The keel was laid first. The backbone and balancing point of the boat, it looked like a big steel box—six feet long, four feet wide, thirty inches deep. Once the box was lifted onto stilts the ribs and cross sections were synthesized onto it by the crane operators and welders, the master craftsmen. The ribs were attached, seeming to spring from the keel as one organic sculpture; then the cross sections were lifted into place for welding. It took an entire month for this skeleton to take shape.

The bulkheads followed, section by section, giving the hull its outward physique. When all but the last piece of steel skin was in place, the workers would gather by the boat. The last piece was called the "whiskey plank," referring to the keg of whiskey that was traditionally opened once a vessel was finally complete. At Dakota Creek a keg of beer substituted for whiskey, and a company softball game usually followed, with the community invited to join.

"The boat went from being a thing to something real. It developed, blossomed, and grew," Brad Breckenridge, a crane operator, recalled with pride. "I had been fishing on boats in Southeast Alaska. But now I was building boats twice as big. It was just amazing. And the people would come down and watch it all happening. It was wonderful when you saw people you knew, people you went to school with, members of your own family, coming by to check things out."

Jeff Hendricks's boats were built for one thing—efficiency. Most of the space was either for storage or for work, but Hendricks had an eye for detail, too. He picked out the black-walnut trim for the *Antares*'s wheelhouse and three crew staterooms, each of which had built-in clothing drawers, a desk, and high wooden bunk railings to hold a sleeping crewman in during even the worst storms. He chose the color of the interior walls and the Formica counter and galley table himself. He ordered a microwave oven and a VCR and made a note to include all the latest available movie videotapes. The wheelhouse contained all the latest electronic gear—a magnetic compass, a gyrocompass, two automatic pilots, a new sonar system—to give whoever was handling the *Antares* the best possible chance to navigate, find the crab, and bring them to the dock.

"Up until that time there was a tradition that you don't build something to experiment with," Gudmundson, a former boatyard welder himself, recalled. "But Jeff Hendricks was different. He was an innovator. At the time of the launch it was a tremendous feeling."

It took nearly a year from the time Hendricks sketched the *Antares* until her hull hit the water. Once she was afloat, the crane operators lifted the fourteen-thousand-gallon-deep centerline fuel tanks, the four double-bottom fuel tanks, and six wing tanks—as well as four big crab tanks—into the bowels and set them in place. Before the big Caterpillar diesel engine was installed and workers moved in with miles of electric cable and pipe, she would be measured from various points along the waterline to the deck, accounting for the square mass of hull that lay under the water. This would determine her displacement, or actual weight in the water. It was the first of many baseline measurements that would key the estimates of her inherent stability and dictate where to configure her fuel tanks and holds and how to balance her loads.

Once the displacement was figured, a series of critical stability tests would be conducted to determine the material strength of the hull and its inherent equilibrium—in other words, the vessel's sea-worthiness.

To underscore the significance of these tests, the Coast Guard had determined that when severe weather or human error was ruled out, material failure, or the lack of a vessel's innate stability, ac-counted for eighty-five percent of the *known* reasons vessels were lost at sea. In the 1970s, the losses had been staggering—$60 mil-lion annually. An average of one hundred fatalities had been reported every year for the five years preceding the birth of the *Antares*, and the numbers would climb in the five years following her launch. One out of every two fatalities was linked to capsizing or material failure. And yet for every death whose cause was known, another of unknown causes was categorized by the Coast Guard as *vanished*.

The first stability test took a full day. Since there was no nautical equivalent of the wind-tunnel test aeronautical engineers use to mea-sure stress resistance on new aircraft fuselages, boatbuilders relied on a simple test. The technique was ancient and crude, but no one had determined a way to improve it. After a plumb bob was hung on deck, a crane operator loaded thousands of pounds of concrete weights in various locations, moving them farther and farther out on deck. Each time the load landed on deck, the hull would roll with the impact and return to a level position, and an engineer would record the time the vessel took to right itself. Each time the vessel rolled, the lead weight on the plumb would swing in an arc, which measured the angle of the roll.

This process was called "inclining," and it established a ves-sel's baseline stability. In other words, it pinpointed where the ves-sel's true center of gravity lay, its inclination to right itself from a roll, and how severe a heeling the vessel might withstand and still sail on. Everything else about the vessel—the number of crew mem-bers and crab pots carried, the amount of fuel and how it was distributed among a dozen tanks of various dimensions, the amount of equipment, supplies, and spare parts—would be determined relative to this measure.

Once a vessel was inclined, its designer would calculate the guidelines that would make up its "stability letter." This letter, kept on board, recommended how a skipper should load and balance his vessel to avoid a danger point, usually a roll in the vicinity of thirty to thirty-five degrees. Anything beyond that angle might cause a large vessel, particularly a tall one or one with equipment or cargo stacked high on its decks, to act like a building in an earthquake. The more the building sways, the more the center of gravity is raised and the heavier the top becomes, until it reaches a point of toppling under its own weight. The common nautical expression for this phenomenon is *capsizing.*

Every stability consideration had an effect on another. With a modern stability report prepared by an expert, a captain with a handheld calculator had merely to plug in the variables—including numerical values for weather and possible icing conditions—to determine how much he could carry on or below deck. The nautical term for this balancing act was *trimming,* and few captains trimmed exactly from the book or exactly alike. Captains often relied on their experience and instincts as well as how a vessel felt beneath their feet. No stability booklet could account for all the variables. Trimming, then, was about individual seamanship and therefore a great source of pride.

Even though the safety of a vessel and the lives of its crew rested on stability, a stability letter was not mandatory in 1977, when the *Antares* was built. In fact, the only mandatory precaution the Coast Guard required of commercial fishermen at that time was that all vessels carry life preservers. Still, the insurance companies preferred stability letters, deeming them cautionary notes from which to assess whether a captain was in compliance when claims of damage or losses were made. Jeff Hendricks had insisted on them, not only because they satisfied the insurance companies, which had far greater influence over his operation than the Coast Guard, but because they satisfied his natural curiosity, too.

"He spared no forethought," Gudmundson said. "He insisted on safe, secure vessels. And once you were safe and secure in the Bering Sea, you could take that vessel anywhere. Jeff was a highliner."

When she was finally outfitted and launched, nearly a thousand people turned out to see the *Antares* take a turn around the harbor. Each speaker that day agreed: A new era in U.S. commercial fishing was being launched. The Hendricks boats were thoroughly modern, the very best examples of what technology and wherewithal could do to make America competitive on the high seas.

"There was community pride in the air," said Gudmundson, the shipyard owner. Even the traditional purse seiners and gill netters, Francis Barcott among them, tipped their caps as the boat pulled away from the Dakota Creek dock. "It looked like a floating city," one fisherman remembered.

Even before the newest Hendricks vessel headed north to Alaska, another was being planned. Jeff Hendricks's goal was to have a small but state-of-the-art fleet. Six months after the *Antares* was launched, the Dakota Creek shipyard began work on a sister vessel.

The *Americus* would be cut from the same design and the same steel as the *Antares*. Duplicating the *Antares* pattern would allow the *Americus* to be built in nearly half the time, and, Hendricks reasoned, since her hull would be virtually identical, the costly and time-consuming stability tests would be unnecessary. The *Americus* would simply use the same stability report that had been calculated for the *Antares*. There was beauty in efficiency. Efficiency provided competitive advantages in technical ways traditional fishermen had never dreamed of.

If anyone had any doubts about using one stability report for more than one vessel, the *Americus*'s performance on her maiden voyage in 1978 would have erased them. She filled her crab tanks within the first twenty-eight hours of arriving on the crabbing grounds in the Bering Sea. Each deckhand made $14,000 in just over one day. When the *Americus* arrived back in Anacortes weeks later, the young men on board had more than $50,000 each and they paid cash for new cars and trucks. Hendricks's next duplicate vessel, the *Altair,* was all but paid for and nearly completed in the boatyard.

Ironically, Hendricks had not wanted to be a career fisherman, at least not when he was growing up in Ballard, a Scandinavian enclave of Seattle. Never a particularly good athlete or standout scholar, he had hoped be a commercial-airline pilot, but a heart murmur prevented this. In truth, he had already learned about the hard side of fishing from his father, who had come from a small farming–fishing village in Norway and had sailed to the North Pacific in primitive open-deck schooners in pursuit of halibut and scallops. "Hard? You want to know how hard it was?" his father, Sig, had often asked when young Jeff started to complain. "We had to pee on our hands to keep them warm."

When he was five years old, Hendricks witnessed the harshest consequence of the fishing life. His brother, who was seven, had been playing on the wharf at Fishermen's Terminal in Seattle while their father worked on his fishing vessel. A heavy mast under repair had rolled off a pair of sawhorses and struck his brother a fatal blow to the head. That memory, indelible, would govern every fishing safety consideration in Hendricks's career.

By the time he had graduated from high school, Jeff had fished in Alaskan waters often enough with his father and his uncle Olie to know what life as a fisherman entailed. Instead, he opted for a local community college and perhaps a career in real estate. He also met and married a classmate, a young woman from Anacortes. Her name was Linda Atterberry, one of three sisters from a well-connected Anacortes family.

Hendricks did go into the real-estate business but at exactly the wrong time. The aerospace industry had taken a downturn, hitting hard the giant Boeing airplane-manufacturing company, the largest employer in the state of Washington. With Boeing hurting, the economy of the entire Puget Sound region suffered, and residential and commercial real estate collapsed. In 1972, when he was twenty-seven, Jeff Hendricks decided to return to commercial fishing.

The great salmon catches had long since passed when Jeff and Linda Hendricks arrived in Anacortes that year. The smells of brine, creosote, pitch, and sawdust and the high-pitched whine of the mills' saws and the canneries' steam thrusters had all but disappeared as well. There were only two canneries left. There was only one mill. The local salmon-fishing fleet had dwindled, as had the fish in Puget Sound.

There were many reasons for the decline of the local fishing industry, but most could be linked to the swift advance of technology and the drive for greater profits in a booming market. For example, nearly twenty years earlier, Mario Puretic, an Anacortes fisherman of Dalmatian descent, quit complaining about the endless days of hauling nets by hand in the cold waters of Puget Sound and fashioned a piece of gear that could do it for him. Puretic designed a power-driven pulley, a simple-looking aluminum shell containing a series of grooved, hard-rubber rotating wheels. These sheaves would receive the lead or messenger line of the seine net and, when power from a diesel engine was applied, move the line up and over and down, pulling everything—cork, rings, web, weights—along.

The device was called the "Power Block," and a Seattle boat designer immediately snapped up the prototype and put it into production. Not only did it mean that fewer men were needed on the boats, but that they would be doing relatively lighter lifting, too. Moreover, it meant that nets could be dropped deeper and hauled farther than anyone had ever imagined. The results were threefold: The local fleet, armed with greater technology, descended on Puget Sound and nearly fished its waters out within a decade. Concurrently, the device helped open the world's deep waters to fishermen from Alaska to the North Sea. It was easy, then, for the ambitious boat owners to turn their backs on Anacortes and the depleted Puget Sound fishery. Hundreds of local fishermen, who had been hired simply to haul lines by hand, were let go.

"With the Power Block, guys started taking more chances. You figure you could set and haul quicker," remembered Ivan Suryan, a retired Anacortes fisherman and Francis Barcott's cousin. "In the old days you hired Croatians, even the young boys. They all had worked for their fathers and relatives. They already had experience and knew their jobs and knew how to work. Even with the Power Block, you had to be very tough. But those guys began disappearing in the 1960s and 1970s. You saw a new breed. . . ."

Still, in its heart Anacortes remained a fishing town when Jeff Hendricks arrived in 1972. A handful of fishermen, those lucky enough to land jobs on the big boats bound for Alaska and the Bering Sea, could still make big money—as much as $100,000 during the three-month crabbing season. The others fished local waters or did what they could to mask their disappointments.

As the economy of most of the state of Washington was falling in on itself, the king crab around the Kodiak Basin had also all but disappeared. Desperate, the Alaska Department of Fish and Game began listening to prospectors who were discovering abundant catches farther out to sea. Jeff Hendricks's uncle, John Jorgensen, a second-generation Norwegian from Seattle, was one of the more successful and enlightened among them. While fishing near the Pribilof Islands in the spring of 1972, Jorgensen made a huge catch of blue king crab. The more-common red king crab were also plentiful. At the end of that prospecting season, more than one million pounds of king crab had been landed in those newly tested waters. Jeff's father, Sig, and his uncle Olie went to the banks and secured the seed money for a new crabbing vessel for Jeff.

The new crab boom also marked a turning point for U.S. fishermen. The stakes had risen along with the financial risks, and only those willing to up the ante could compete. Private business syndicates formed with the help of banks and corporations. The federal Production Credit Association, modeled after farm-subsidy programs, was soon offering $80 million in low-interest loans to prospective boat owners who might revitalize America's commercial fishing industry.

The Hendricks family's timing was near perfect, even as other local fishermen were facing economic disasters. For years, native tribes had argued that commercial fishermen had used modern technology to deprive them of salmon and steelhead destined for their fishing grounds—the spawning rivers flowing into Puget Sound where their ancestors had woven nets from dried stalks of stinging nettles, fashioned hooks from hemlock branches, and harvested fish from dugout canoes more than nine thousand years earlier. Tribal lawyers cited a 120-year-old treaty guaranteeing the tribes their fair share of the harvest, and George Boldt, a federal district judge, was sympathetic. In 1974, Judge Boldt reaffirmed the treaty and defined "equal share" as fifty percent of a yearly quota of salmon destined to pass through traditional native fishing grounds. The most important provision stated that the tribes were to be allowed to take the first fifty percent of the total salmon catch. Local gill netters and purse seiners such as Francis Barcott would be forced to sit on the beach until government regulators declared that the native tribes had harvested their quota. The Boldt decision is cursed by local fishermen even today as it undeniably drove thousands of them off Puget Sound, into heavier seas and heavier weather in Alaska.

The Boldt decision confirmed what Jeff Hendricks had already speculated—that fleet owners who hoped for success would have to fish further out in the Bering Sea, where competition among foreign fleets was already fierce. Hendricks understood the risks and knew success would come not so much through risk-taking as through a shrewdly conceived, disciplined business approach. Fortunately for Hendricks and other U.S. owners, Senator Warren Magnuson, a powerful Democrat from the state of Washington, had been taking seriously complaints from his constituents that foreign fishing fleets backed by their governments had for years been robbing an under-capitalized U.S. industry right at its own shoreline.

Finally, Magnuson sponsored a law that would prohibit foreign vessels from fishing within two hundred miles of the U.S. coast. This, in effect, would make coveted fishing grounds the exclusive province of the U.S. fleet and would also raise the enforcement responsibilities of the Coast Guard. In addition, the law provided for big loans with little interest to vessel builders, the only collateral being the very vessel the loan financed. The Magnuson Act, signed by President Gerald Ford in 1976, was heralded as the next best thing to rearming America. In fact, the law served a narrow special interest, a group of fishermen–entrepreneurs who would quickly amass the capital to launch bigger and more technically advanced vessels capable of virtually clear-cutting the fishing zones near America's shores. The new law did nothing to lessen the competition for limited fish but only shifted the competition, favoring wealthier boat owners over smaller, subsistence fishermen.

The very next year, the year the *Antares* was built, the catch of king crab by American fleets within the two-hundred-mile limit nearly doubled from just two years earlier, for a total value of nearly $86 million. In a very short time Jeff Hendricks would evolve from a reluctant fisherman into a risk-taker, a hybrid hunter-entrepreneur. He would put others—including his own brothers-in-law and neighbors—through the same risks. And together, they would prosper.

When the *Antares* burned in the spring of 1982, Jeff Hendricks was well on his way to becoming a top fleet owner. During his ten years in the business he had also realized that to succeed, he would still have to sail beyond the two-hundred-mile protected zone and compete with foreign fleets. In order to compete he also would have to adapt.

For the past six years, he had heard of the success the Russian, Japanese, Norwegian, and even German vessels had achieved in converting from crab catchers to fishing trawlers when the crabbing season was over. These vessels, some as long as two football fields, were dragging trawl nets for pollock, which ran in huge schools near the bottom of the Bering Sea. These fish were not delicacies brought fresh to the docks for restaurants and dining rooms but were processed at sea into frozen fillets for fast-food restaurants or pressed into fish paste for surimi, a Japanese product used to make imitation fish or crabmeat.

Hendricks realized the potential for profit: A huge biomass of protein, worth more perhaps than salmon and crab combined both in tonnage and dollars, was swimming around in schools in the Bering Sea. He was also aware that foreign fishing vessels had a head start in capitalizing on the emerging global demand. As early as 1979, Hendricks was sketching out conversion plans to give his vessels added value as both crabbers and trawlers capable of fishing nearly year-round. By the time his newest boat, the *Altair,* went after her first crab early in 1980, he had already committed to becoming one of the nation's first fleet owners to undertake a nearly year-round fishing season.

"Things would never be the same. . . ." Hendricks would recall. "The old romantic days of the subsistence fishermen who would go up there from Newport, Oregon, or Seattle or even Anacortes were over. You had to diversify."

Determined to surpass traditional commercial crabbing operators, he dispatched a few promising crew members to Nova Scotia to observe Canadian trawling techniques in the North Atlantic. He negotiated with a Japanese company to receive and process his catch in a joint venture, something the Magnuson Act did not discourage. He ordered new winches and net reels and stern ramps for his vessels. In early 1981 the first trawl-gear fittings were done at Dakota Creek. More than five tons of additional equipment was added to four of his five vessels: the *Alyeska, Antares, Americus,* and *Altair.* (Hendricks also owned the *Alliance,* a 103-foot vessel built solely for crabbing, and, because of its smaller size, did not convert it.) In December of the same year the vessels underwent a second conversion for more trawling gear, adding heavier winches and drive motors, cranes and cables totaling 21.92 tons for each vessel. The vessels were now committed to double duty. Again, Hendricks was in the right place at the right time, and his business instincts were about to pay off.

By 1982 the king-crab catch around Kodiak Island had fallen to just over one million pounds, and boat owners who were not equipped to fish farther out were put out of business. By 1983, the Kodiak king-crabbing grounds would be closed altogether.

Hendricks's vessels had already bypassed the Kodiak crabbing grounds. In the spring of 1982, his fleet enjoyed a successful crab season farther out in the Bering Sea. Each vessel had to trim far differently because of the added weight of the trawling gear, but each captain had adjusted well, eliminating a number of crab pots to compensate for the loss of deck space, resorting to new fuel-carrying configurations, and even experimenting with flooding the crab tanks to give their vessels more gentle rides. The nearly thirty tons of added gear had forced the captains to experiment with their own seamanship, and each had come through the season not only without hazard but with a plentiful catch, too.

The trawling season had been another story, however. Hendricks's crews were inexperienced, the weather had turned bad, and the catch was disappointing, especially compared to the tons the foreign fleets were dragging in. Hendricks knew he and his crews needed more experience, and his vessels needed to add even more equipment.

There would be another inducement for expanding the capabilities of each vessel by the spring of 1982. For the foreseeable future his organization would be crippled by the loss of the *Antares.* Hendricks had been counting on her to pull in between $2.5 million and $4 million worth of crab and bottom fish that year. His remaining vessels—the *Alyeska, Alliance, Americus,* and *Altair*—would have to take up the slack.

CHAPTER 2

THE ANCHOR INN WAS ABOUT AS FAR FROM THE ANACORTES waterfront as any fisherman cared to roam and still be among kindred spirits. Located twenty blocks up Commercial Avenue from the city wharf, it was one of the town's most popular taverns, where fishermen, refinery workers, construction workers, loggers, and laborers gathered to either celebrate or curse their jobs. In the mid-1940s the site had housed a garage; twenty years later, the grease pits had been filled in and paved over, a new floor added, the wooden walls polished up. A bar was installed, along with beer taps, two pool tables, some booths, a wall designated for darts, a television screen, and a jukebox. It didn't take long for a crowd of dedicated drinkers to convene.

Among them, George Nations and Glenn Treadwell, two of the captains in Jeff Hendricks's fleet, would earn respected titles as "regulars" and all the privileges that went with their status—pre-emptive selections of the television channel, tunes on the jukebox or turns at the pool table, a preferred booth or place at the bar, and most important, without a word spoken to the bartender, fresh bottles of beer to replace the empties.

Nations, whose sharp, dark features advertised his Cherokee blood, had grown up in Lyman, a little town along the Skagit River in the forested foothills of the Cascade Mountains. His family had come from the hills of North Carolina, as had many, to find work in the logging camps and timber mills along the flanks of the Cascades. He had joined the Army at seventeen, before finishing high school. When he got out he tried a number of occupations—logging, long-shoring, window-washing, even working on crews that cleaned up local oil refineries or fertilizer plants or salvaged the interiors of burned-out buildings.

Treadwell had moved to Anacortes from Seattle with his family when he was twelve. He and his brother, Dwayne, quickly adjusted to their more countrified surroundings. They picked strawberries in the summer, rode their bicycles to Hart Lake, and hitched cheese balls or earthworms to their hooks to catch bass, trout, and catfish. Treadwell worked part-time at Larry's Mobil service station during high school and wrestled for the high-school team, although it would have been hard to picture him as combative. At 5 feet, 11 inches, he had a fit but unimposing build, kindly blue eyes and a voice that sometimes wavered and thinned.

Treadwell met Nations after a two-year stint in the National Guard, when he returned to Anacortes and began working for a local disposal company. He and Nations had been assigned to the same cleanup crew. Treadwell admired Nations's irrepressibility and sardonic sense of humor, and they had a few things in common too—Indian blood, a thirst for beer, and a penchant for hard work. The two became fast friends.

In the fall of 1967, Nations, who was twenty-seven, was working two jobs and piecing together only a modest living. Although he had quit the disposal company, he complained to Treadwell about having to get up at 4:00 A.M. to drive two hours to Seattle to park cars for his brother, who owned an auto-sales lot. He complained about having to return to Anacortes by 10:00 A.M. to work ten- and sometimes twelve-hour days longshoring. All those miles, all those hours, and less than $25,000 a year to show for it.

The more he drank, the more Nations growled and complained, and Treadwell, then twenty-five, had the good sense to appear sympathetic. He, too, had quit the disposal company but was perfectly content to run small cranes and winches and skiploaders on the docks scattered from Bellingham to Everett. He never considered the possibility that he could earn twice, maybe three times as much money fishing in Alaska.

As the evenings wore on and the empty beer bottles stacked up, Nations focused on the fact that Linda, his youngest sister-in-law, was going to marry a college kid from Seattle by the name of Jeff Hendricks. Word was that Hendricks's father was a businessman with banking connections and that his uncle was a big-time fisherman with a couple of boats. Even though Hendricks had fished in the summers for his uncle, apparently his father was going to set Jeff up in the Seattle real-estate business. If that didn't pan out, they had offered to buy Linda's prospective husband a fishing boat.

Over many beers, Treadwell often heard how Nations had believed he was marrying into a wealthy family when he married Janice Atterberry, the middle of three sisters. Each of the Atterberry girls—Linda, Janice, and Nancy—had been among the brightest, prettiest, and most successful in their Anacortes highschool classes. They were cheerleaders and homecoming princesses, they dressed sharply, and held key positions in student government and on student publications. Though Nations was correct in assuming that the Atterberrys were one of the most prominent, politically connected families in town, he did not know that Janice's father, Maurice, an itinerant entrepreneur, had spent money as fast as he had made it and finally all but abandoned the family to wander through British Columbia looking for business opportunities in mines and logging camps. To support the family, Janice's mother, Elsa, took a job in a fish cannery. She taught her girls to make their own clothes, which they continued to do all through high school, although no one, including George Nations, would have ever guessed it. Now he and Janice had a four-year-old son, Jeff, and were expecting another.

Hendricks was not a welcome addition to the family, at least as far as Nations was concerned. He clanked Treadwell's beer bottle with his own and the two cursed privileged kids, their own jobs, and anything else their minds latched onto until, just before closing hour, Janice Nations came through the door to retrieve her husband.

That was the first Treadwell had heard of the not-yet-emerging entrepreneur from Seattle.

"The next time I heard Jeff Hendricks's name, it was at the Anchor Inn again," recalled Treadwell.

Nearly five years had passed. Nations had been best man at Treadwell's wedding, and Janice had been Evelyn Treadwell's bridesmaid. As couples they rented motor homes together and traveled to Canada and eastern Washington. Every fall George and Glenn took two weeks off and hunted elk together in southeastern Washington.

Nations was still pulling down two jobs, and Treadwell continued to work on the docks. They were drinking beer and shooting pool after work one night in 1972 when Nations told Treadwell how the Seattle real-estate market had gone flat and that Jeff Hendricks, now his brother-in-law, had gotten clobbered. Jeff and Linda had moved back to Anacortes.

Then, Treadwell remembered: "George said that his brother-in-law's father or uncle or whoever had popped for a $2 million fishing boat." He remembered seeing the indignation welling in Nations's face as he swigged a beer and chalked his pool cue. "It wasn't what he said. It was how he said it. I could hear the resentment."

Treadwell asked Nations if he was thinking about helping Hendricks on the boat. Nations answered with a look of disdain, saying he wasn't particularly interested in working like a dog so his brother-in-law could get richer. Treadwell asked him if he had been offered a job. Nations said he hadn't. And there was resentment in that answer as well.

In the fall of 1972 Hendricks piloted his first boat, the *Sea Star,* with Ron Beirnes, his brother-in-law and second-in-command, into the Bering Sea. On that trip they and their crew landed enough crab to net out the costs for fuel and supplies and even pay the crew shares of the catch. Prosperity was within Hendricks's sights when he returned home to Anacortes. He was also feeling some sense of family obligation. He asked George Nations if he'd like to take a break from his two jobs and join him and Ron for the next trip north.

At the Anchor Inn late one winter night in early 1973, Nations reported to Treadwell that while "he wasn't all that enthused about going to Alaska and freezing his ass off," he was considering the offer. Indeed, a few weeks later Nations did go to the Bering Sea on the *Sea Star.* Hendricks was at the helm. Ron Beirnes was the engineer and second-in-command. Nations worked as an ordinary deckhand.

When Nations returned, he described the punishing, tedious work and the equally harsh weather to Treadwell. Winds reached seventy miles an hour, he told him, the waves twenty-five feet, temperatures twenty degrees below zero. When the vessel lay over the crabbing grounds, work was not through until the last seven-hundred-pound pot had been baited and set, the decks washed down, and the vessel was making a run to the next crabbing grounds or to port to pick up more pots. Cigarette breaks, showers, meals, and sleep were all snatched in the few spare minutes they had. Sometimes, he said, day and night blurred together as all sense of time disappeared.

"Right away, George said he was going back," Treadwell said.

"The work was long and physical and the weather was shittier than he could imagine. He loved it, he said. You could do anything you wanted to. You could make the money that would allow it. It seemed like a real opportunity."

That fall another spot opened on the *Sea Star,* and Nations called Treadwell to ask if he wanted to give crabbing a try. Within an hour he'd made reservations to fly to Dutch Harbor, Alaska, more than two thousand miles away, to rendezvous with Nations and the *Sea Star.*

"Dutch Harbor was definitely the last frontier," Treadwell remembered. "Guys were sleeping in bunkers and Quonset huts. There were only three phones on the whole island. And two of them were on one fish processor owned by the Japanese. You'd stand in line for five hours waiting to call home. I didn't mind. It was such an adventure just to be up there. I knew when I got home I would have so much to tell."

On his first trip aboard the *Sea Star,* Treadwell pushed crab pots around and learned to stay out of the way when the boat rolled and the huge pots pushed back. George Nations, too, was still learning. So was Hendricks, who was back home managing the business, which included supervising the building of the next boat in his fleet. Ron Beirnes was running the *Sea Star* in his stead. A round-faced, full-bodied, affable man of Irish stock, he enjoyed listening to a good story and telling one in turn. As captain he preferred to delegate responsibilities, not so much to preside over the ship's democracy but to lighten his own load. He grew up in Anacortes and started as a deckhand when he was twenty-three, apprenticing, along with his brother, Vern, with some old masters of the Anacortes salmon fleet including Delmar Cole and Francis Barcott. When Hendricks's father had bankrolled the first vessel of what would become a fleet, Ron Beirnes leapt at the chance to become not only a skipper but a business partner with his brother-in-law.

Around Anacortes, Beirnes was known as a family man. He was devoted to his wife, Nancy, the oldest of the three Atterberry sisters. His two daughters were married to Kevin Kirkpatrick and Doug Knutson, two star high-school athletes who had broken into the Hendricks organization because of their family ties to Ron. They were working on deck and apprenticing to become captains themselves, as Nations was. Beirnes's fourteen-year-old son, Tony, had already announced his own intention to become a fishing-boat captain as well, and Ron encouraged him.

Beirnes had already accumulated hundreds of days in the Bering Sea by the time Treadwell climbed on board his vessel. The *Sea Star* skipper had become known for his safety standards on board and for encouraging a certain level of comfort as well. His crews enjoyed working for him. He never drove them beyond their limits or lost his temper. At age thirty-seven he was earning a reputation as one of the most reliable and compassionate captains in Anacortes, and Treadwell would soon find out why.

"On the very first run we were just setting the last of the crab pots—they were brand-new, so we had to cut the twine that held the doors shut," Treadwell recalled. "I was cutting and I must have looked up for a second, because the next thing I know I put a huge cut across my hand. The next day was supposed to be the money day when we pulled the pots and took the crab into port. But Ron insisted in heading back right away—that's just how he was.

"With George it would have been different. He treated his crews differently. Anyway, Ron brought the boat all the way back to Dutch Harbor. It took almost forty hours. By the time we got there the cut had pretty much closed and there was no need for stitches. There was no doctor on the island anyway. The nurse gave me a tetanus shot and told me to go home to Anacortes. I said no. I had just started. I didn't want to go. So she made Ron promise I wouldn't handle crab or get my hand wet because of the possibilities of infection. Now, this was a crab boat; no one, even the nurse, expected me to stay dry. But Ron stuck by his promise and kept me away from the crab and anything that would have made me wet. Again, that's how different he and George were."

As he climbed the ranks of the fleet, George Nations could not escape the fact that he had landed the opportunity only because he was related by marriage to Jeff Hendricks. Nor could he escape the fact that he had been raised poor. This wore on him from the day he first stepped on the deck of his brother-in-law's boat. The only way for him to gain high ground, he figured, would be with hard work. What he lacked—Jeff Hendricks's education and financial backing, Ron Beirnes's easygoing self-possession—he would overcome by outworking them. That was all he knew, and he would, indeed, quickly earn a reputation as a "grinder."

By the time Nations and Treadwell returned home from Treadwell's first trip north in the fall of 1973, a new Hendricks vessel was close to completion. She was being built in the same yard that produced the *Sea Star* up in Bellingham, a much larger and more prosperous town north of Anacortes. The new vessel would be christened the *Alyeska,* the Aleut name for one of Alaska's most prominent volcanic peaks.

In the off season, Nations continued to work two jobs: as a longshoreman with Treadwell and delivering autos for his brother's car dealership. But he now told Treadwell that he hoped to become skipper of the *Alyeska.* Every day after work, through the winter of 1973–74, Nations would drive north to check on her progress in the boatyard. Treadwell would join him when he could.

Hendricks had insisted that the *Alyeska* would be the most advanced fishing vessel for its size afloat. There were two giant cranes for lifting and moving crab pots on deck. There was an electric bait chopper to replace a man with a twelve-pound sledgehammer, and a crab-sorting table with a conveyor belt that made the work twice as fast—Hendricks's innovations. But it wasn't only the engineering that impressed both Nations and Treadwell. With its microwave, VCR, and solid-wood paneling, the *Alyeska*'s galley rivaled that of any café in Anacortes.

Even though he desperately hoped to become a captain in Hendricks's fleet, and it looked as though he would, George Nations still could not disguise his contempt for his brother-in-law, his boss. It was not in his nature. In the fall of 1974, aboard the *Alyeska,* Nations's resentment boiled over in a scene that Doug Knutson, the cook at the time, recalled.

"Jeff was in the wheelhouse and George was the relief captain. He and the others were sitting around while I was cooking. I was making tacos because Jeff had ordered them. Anyway, George came over and said something like, 'Tacos? Jesus Christ, we had tacos the other goddamn night!' I said, 'They must have been pretty good, because Jeff asked for them again.' And with that, he stepped up to the stove and pissed all over everything. He said: 'See how he likes 'em now.' "

On Christmas day of that year, the *Alyeska* made its first trip north, with a crew of six. Jeff Hendricks was the skipper, and George Nations, after less than two seasons at sea, was his relief and engineer. They took the scenic Inside Passage up, passing along the lee of Vancouver Island and through the island maze that tourists pay thousands of dollars each year to experience. "I had never seen anything so remote and so beautiful," recalled Treadwell, on board as a full-time crew member. "The islands that were total forests, the pure white mountains, the narrow passages, tiny village settlements, the little independent sawmills, the glacier-filled bays."

He saw the aurora borealis draping the night sky with dancing light and remembered feeling humbled. "It was like looking at the beginnings of our solar system," he said. "And there were so many killer whales, we all quit counting. Dolphins just tagged along for hours."

Where the Seymour Narrows opened, more than a thousand miles from Anacortes, the *Alyeska* ran an obstacle course of small icebergs, each one bluer than any sky. All along the way, watching steam rising from snow-covered volcanoes, Treadwell sensed that this part of the earth was still beginning.

They ran past Cape Decision and were a day into the open water of the Gulf of Alaska when the weather turned on them. Huge ocean swells—the size of mountains, it seemed—carried the boat high in the air. Suspended at the peak of each wave, with both the bow and the stern out of the water and the propeller churning nothing but air, the entire boat vibrated violently until it crashed down the slope of the wave and buried its bow in the roiling green seas. Once the bow smashed down so hard, it jarred a radiator hose loose in the engine room. An alarm went off, a piercing and terrifying sound at sea. Treadwell and Nations tumbled into the engine room and clamped the hose. When they came up they clung to the galley table and shouted up to Jeff in the wheelhouse that they had fixed the problem, at least temporarily. Treadwell felt as if he was losing a wrestling match with gravity. For the first time in his life he felt nausea from fear alone. He meekly suggested that they might all be better served if the skipper backed off the speed and allowed the boat to ride out the storm. But this was Jeff Hendricks's chance to be a pilot. "Jeff made the statement, and I'll never forget this," Treadwell remembered—" 'Let's see what this boat is made of.'

"Guys were being lifted out of their bunks. Rick Chiabai, one of the deckhands, spent the whole time sick in his bunk. We were sitting around the galley table and George asked me what I thought and I said, 'This is my first storm, you guys tell me.'

"Sometime in the night we began to ice up. This was the first time I'd seen it. The weather was real sloppy and we were taking a lot of spray and it would freeze to the boat. Things were getting worse and worse. What happens is that ice plugs up the scuppers so there is no way for water to run off the deck. And the water on the deck freezes. Everything freezes—crab pots, railings. The next morning we were covered with ice, three inches thick. I couldn't believe it. It looked like another planet. We went out on deck and spent the next thirty-six hours straight using baseball bats and metal pipes to chip the ice. Guys looked like ghosts in space suits on the moon."

Time would not dull the memory of that first trip aboard the *Alyeska*. Treadwell made $57,000. And while he would acquire the knowledge and skills to be promoted to a skipper within just a few years and would consistently earn in excess of $100,000 per season, his fear of the dangers was unshakable. While earning a reputation for company loyalty and fairness, Treadwell would also develop a reputation for being unable to push hard enough in an industry that offered its biggest rewards only to those willing to go right to the brink of disaster.

Nations, meanwhile, went to the bank and applied for a $100,000 loan to buy a house overlooking the Guemes Channel and the boat traffic between Anacortes and Puget Sound. It wasn't much of a house, the banker pointed out, and probably not worth what Nations wanted to put into it. But Nations persisted. As a maintenance man, he had once cleaned it. Owning it now meant everything, even a measure of revenge on his own past.

At the close of 1982, after nearly a decade with the Hendricks fleet, Nations and Treadwell had spent more than their share of nights celebrating their good fortunes. They had highly coveted commands in the most advanced commercial fishing fleet afloat; they had six-figure incomes, and new trucks. Nations now had three children and was building a new home. Treadwell had upgraded his home and had two kids of his own. Together they shared the worry about the upcoming crab season in the Bering Sea. The loss of the *Antares* meant the loss of several million pounds of crab and potentially even more bottom fish they would have trawled for. Subtracting one vessel's contribution to the company meant that each of the vessel skippers—Beirnes, Nations, Treadwell, and the others—would stand to lose big money out of their own paychecks, money they'd been banking on to pay their mortgages and other bills during the off-season. Compensating for the loss would mean catching more crab and later netting more bottom fish than any of the skippers—or Hendricks himself, for that matter—had ever imagined.

CHAPTER 3

ON THURSDAY MORNING, FEBRUARY 3, 1983, AFTER NEARLY four months of preparation, the twin three-hundred-ton crabbing vessels *Americus* and *Altair* and each of their seven-member crews were ready to sail from Anacortes. The weather was unusually clear and warm for winter on Puget Sound. The consensus on the city dock at the foot of Commercial Street, where the vessels were moored in tandem, was that this was a good omen. The 1,120-horsepower turbocharged diesel engines idled evenly. In the boat-yard by the dock, just the month before, each vessel had undergone its third and final retrofit. A trawling crane atop a twenty-foot-tall stanchion and supporting gantry had been added to the *Alyeska,* *Americus,* and *Altair,* along with a new steel deck plate. All in all, each boat had added nearly eight tons of equipment during the last month. To compensate, Hendricks ordered his captains to subtract an equivalent tonnage of crab pots, just as they had done the previous season.

The 123-foot steel-hull vessels had each been sanded and repainted a deep sky blue with red trim and red boot stripes to mark their depth in the water. Belowdecks, each carried more than seventy thousand gallons of fuel. Each held five tons of frozen and refrigerated goods in storage and another two tons of dry goods in the ships' stores, enough to last the separate crews through April. The rest of their supplies and equipment—including more than two hundred crab pots weighing approximately six hundred ninety pounds each, ten thousand pounds of frozen herring bait, and fresh water—would be loaded in Dutch Harbor.

Within the hour, the vessels would be nudged away from the town dock by their captains for the ten-day, two-thousand-mile trip to rendezvous in Dutch Harbor with the *Alyeska* and *Alliance,* their sister vessels that had departed three days earlier. The four vessels would spend the next three months on the crabbing grounds in the Bering Sea. When that season ended, the *Alyeska, Americus,* and *Altair* would then convert to dragging trawl nets for bottom fish and the *Alliance,* strictly a crabbing vessel, would return to Anacortes.

Some crew members would return home at the end of the crabbing season; others who had remained in Anacortes would fly to Dutch Harbor to relieve them. But the ritual taking place on the dock this day would not be rushed, no matter how eager the crews were to get under way. As with Friday night high-school football and basketball games, church services, and Eagles Club barbecues, these annual leave-takings were major events. Of the two hundred townspeople gathered at the dock, most were parents, aunts, uncles, siblings, or friends of the crew members, whose average age was just over twenty-three.

For years young men clamored to get jobs on the new Anacortes vessels—"A-boats," they came to be called—and bragged when they did. The vessels' nickname identified the town they came from, but more important it was a recognition of what had become one of the most profitable and respected fleets in the Pacific Northwest. Among the onlookers—some curious, some envious—one thing was understood on the dock that day: Once the young crew members stepped aboard the Hendricks vessels, they would be getting a crack at big money. With luck, in a matter of months they could earn four times what they might make in an entire year at the refineries or as laborers or carpenters in town. Ever since the *Antares* fished its first full season in 1977 in the Bering Sea, the A-boat crews could expect to earn between $50,000 and $100,000 every three-month season, easily three or four times what their teachers—their fathers too— earned in an entire year. Other fleets could post such numbers, but not as consistently, and few came close to the reputation of the Hendricks vessels for efficiency, innovation, and impeccable maintenance.

To be chosen from dozens of young men who aspired to become Hendricks crew members was both an honor and an opportunity. Word of a rare crew vacancy passed quickly along the docks throughout Puget Sound. But Hendricks favored young men from Anacortes, partly because, as an outsider, he felt he owed the town something. When new crew members brought home the good news, their families afforded Hendricks as much honor as if he had been born and raised in Anacortes, like them.

Hendricks, however, was not on the dock on the morning of February 3. He was in Nova Scotia studying a new technique for dragging huge nets for bottom fish which would help him to maximize his investment in his vessels and crews. Such was the exigency of a new era that required fishing vessels to fish a long way from land and often in weather so severe it threatened human and mechanical endurance.

On the deck of the *Americus,* George Nations, its captain, was barking orders to Brent Boles, his twenty-four-year-old relief skipper. He was about to turn the vessel over to Boles for the trip to Dutch Harbor so that he could stay behind to oversee construction of a new house he and Janice were building not far from Ron and

Nancy Beirnes's down at the beach. When the *Americus* was a day out of Dutch Harbor, Boles was to radio him and Nations would then fly north to take command.

Other skippers, Francis Barcott among them, noted this with derision. It was traditional for a captain to make the trip north with his crew. But then, Nations had always scoffed at tradition. The only conventions he accepted were the hard work and danger. All else, he repeated often, was nothing but "sentimental bullshit." Besides, Nations was convinced Boles was up to the job. Although this would be the first time he had sole responsibility for the crew, Boles had made the trip to Dutch Harbor more than ten times before. As deck boss and then relief skipper, Boles had more than proven himself during the nearly five years he and Nations had sailed together. Nations ascertained in Boles the ingredients he possessed himself—courage, instincts, and toughness.

Nineteen years Nations's junior, Boles emulated the *Americus* skipper. He swaggered like Nations, growled like him, and drove the crew just as hard. He also knew, as well as anyone, the resentment Nations felt toward Jeff Hendricks. Nations made no attempt to hide it, especially when he drank, which was often enough that Hendricks had suspended him for one season just a couple of years earlier. Still, when Nations returned to the wheelhouse the next season, it was to the acclaim of his crew.

As recently as six or seven years earlier Boles had not imagined his future would be on the deck of a crab boat in the Bering Sea. He had been impressed when his classmates went to Alaska to fish in the summers, returning with $30,000 and dropping cash for new cars, but not enough to seriously consider fishing for a living, even as a way to earn extra money. A high-school track star and running back, he wanted to play college football, and everyone who saw him play acknowledged that he possessed the physique and heart for the game. The town postman's son and youngest of five, he was already riding a football scholarship to nearby Everett Community College when the *Antares* was being built in the Anacortes boatyard.

LOST AT SEA

Like just about everyone in town, Boles could not help being awed by the spectacle. He had stood with his buddies watching the *Antares* take shape. His high-school football teammates Kevin Kirkpatrick and Doug Knutson had already been out on the *Alyeska,* the *Antares*'s predecessor, and had returned with hefty paychecks and heroic stories. Boles had also heard the local fishermen sizing up the new vessel, discerning the lay of her keel, the cut of her bow, and giving her their grudging approval.

He and his buddies had been eighteen or nineteen then, and none was above having his ambitions redirected. They were impressed enough to apply for part-time jobs in the boatyard to help shape up the next vessel due, the *Americus.* By the time she was ready for launch, Boles knew he wanted a place on her deck. So did his friend and football teammate Brian Melvin, who worked with him in the boatyard. And they both got lucky. That year, 1978, they were among only a few chosen as deckhands for the new boat.

Five years later Melvin was getting his first crack in the wheelhouse as skipper of the *Alyeska.* And Boles, thanks to George Nations, was getting a shot at showing that he could run one of the Hendricks vessels too. Boles knew that becoming a captain meant tripling his take-home pay—and he was already making more than $50,000 a season. Following Nations's lead, he had worked hard and had money in the bank. He had a girlfriend. There were prospects of marriage, and they were strong enough to compel him to buy a new house and talk seriously about spending less time in the taverns when he was home from the Bering Sea.

In temporarily taking command of the *Americus,* Boles had also become responsible for two unseasoned young men who might present some problems. Victor Bass, just nineteen, was a self-proclaimed Casanova who had already stated that his primary motivation for fishing in the Bering Sea was to make enough money to start a modeling business. Richie Awes, twenty, was a golden-boy basketball star for the Anacortes High Seahawks who had warned everyone that his greatest fear was seasickness. That would sort itself out in time, Boles thought. What he held against both of them was that they were greenhorns. This would be the first fishing voyage for either of them.

Boles knew that George Nations was asking a lot of him in breaking in these new crew members. But he delighted in the prospects even as he cursed them. As temporary skipper he'd been given license to kick some of the bullshit out of his young crew before the Bering Sea did. At least he could ask for help from Larry Littlefield, the twenty-nine-year-old engineer who'd fished with the Hendricks crews for nearly three years, and also from his friend and high-school football teammate Paul Northcutt, twenty-four, who'd started fishing when Boles did. It would be their responsibility to drive home what they'd learned from at least four seasons in the waters up north. Timing was everything, he would tell his younger shipmates. You had to learn when to push and when to pull and when to stay the hell out of the way. You had to learn to tie the knots and make them secure, otherwise you could lose a crab pot or worse. Just trying to close a hatch cover could cost you an arm. One roll of the boat changed gravity, adding probably a thousand pounds of torque to a two-hundred-pound swinging steel hatch. Try to close it at the wrong time, when the boat was rolling with you, and you were inviting the door to slam the life out of you.

Boles knew he couldn't teach it all. The greenhorns would have to learn by getting their knees and knuckles busted up, just as he had done, just as Paul and Larry had. The most important lesson to teach them was to respect the fact that they were a danger to everybody else unless they kept their heads up.

But Boles knew that his greatest challenge on this trip was to drive Jeff Nations into proving himself to his father. An introverted, bespectacled, bookish kid, Jeff had already fished the Bering Sea with George one full season, long enough to get a taste of something he did not want to do. This infuriated his father, but Boles knew that Jeff, now nineteen, wasn't cut out for crabbing. He wanted to be a journalist, and although he had divulged this to everyone except his father, George Nations had his suspicions. Boles had often listened to him scoff at his son's private ambitions as he held court at the Anchor Inn. His kid had been handed a treasure map to the pots of gold, more than George had ever dreamed of when he was that age.

The irony of his task was not lost on Brent Boles. If he succeeded, Jeff might be handed the wheel of his own big fishing boat in a couple of years. Boles could be working against his own best interests. After all, despite Jeff Hendricks's wherewithal, there weren't a lot of captains' slots to be handed out. They were down one as it was with the loss of the *Antares*.

Jeff Martin, the 23-year-old relief skipper of the *Altair,* moored just behind the *Americus* at the dock, stood on the forecastle deck outside the wheelhouse beside Ron Beirnes, his captain. Classically handsome, with dark sandy hair, a finely featured face and a physique to match, Martin was a head-turner. He had been a star middle linebacker at Anacortes High and a good student. He liked to read, could play classical piano, wrote romantic poems, and was considerate and quick-witted. He didn't even mind being called "Jeffrey" by the girls. He had started college in eastern Washington, but like many of his hometown friends, Jeff was not immune to the lure of big money. Returning home on holidays, he'd meet his high-school buddies on the dock as their boats came in. It was only a short trip up Commercial Avenue to the car dealerships that posted WELCOME HOME SALE flags like Independence Day banners whenever the fleet came back from Alaska.

When an opening had come up on one of the A-boats in 1981, Jeff Martin seized it. Ron Beirnes, having had half his stomach removed to treat ulcers, tired easily now and was in need of a good relief skipper for the *Altair;* Martin, already pronounced a natural fisherman by the local veterans he sailed with over the summers, was an obvious choice.

Jeff Martin learned quickly, worked hard and efficiently, and endeared himself to everyone. With just two years' experience in the Bering Sea, he was already being groomed to run one of Hendricks's vessels, and he knew it. He told this to his parents and his fiancée on the eve of his departure for Dutch Harbor in 1983 and had even talked about earning some equity in Hendricks's company. A big crab season could speed things along. Next year he might even get to take the *Altair* north as the skipper. In a sense, he was Brent Boles's rival.

Together, Beirnes and Martin watched as George Nations jumped from the rail of the *Americus* and shouted his final commands to Boles. The rest of his crew broke off their good-byes and snapped to, including Nations's son, Jeff, who hugged his mother, Jan, and new baby sister, Kristin, and jumped on deck.

Boles handled the throttle and steering controls gingerly, moving forward then aft and forward again, swinging the *Americus* away from the dock as though coaxing a willful horse from a corral. When the vessel had cleared the dock and the *Altair,* Boles eased her into a wide arc, the American flag emblem flaring like a comet across the flank of her bow. Then he headed slowly into the channel, sounded the horn for the whole town to hear, and nosed her westward for the run through Rosario Strait toward Cape Flattery, the tip of the Olympic Peninsula. There he would turn north-northwest. If the weather held, that would be the last big turn either the *Americus* or *Altair* would have to make until they rounded Unalaska Island in the Aleutians and reached the entrance to Dutch Harbor, two thousand miles away.

Jeff Martin watched Boles maneuver the *Americus* and knew the *Altair* would be following in a matter of minutes. He was glad he'd drawn Beirnes as his skipper; the older captain was a lot easier to work for than the combustible Nations. Ron still enjoyed a beer or two with the crew, who were always as welcome in the wheelhouse as he was in the galley, where he preferred to spend his time. He was never sullen, even after the long working days were getting to everybody else, even when the pots came up half empty. He was never remote and never played favorites. Jeff Martin admired his skipper and vowed to emulate him, just as Brent Boles modeled himself after George Nations. Strong relationships like these were considered essential because at sea, as in military operations, there was no democracy, no time for consensus.

Jeff Martin, the most intellectually complex of all the crew members, would seem the least likely to have tolerated the absoluteness of a ship's hierarchy. But, in fact, he loved its symmetry. He often mentioned this to his parents, Don and Roberta Martin, and to his longtime girlfriend, Cheryl Sandvik, who was studying to be a teacher at Western Washington University in Bellingham. Over Christmas Jeff and Cheryl had gotten engaged but agreed not to tell their parents until Jeff returned home from the winter crabbing season. Now, Cheryl stood with her future in-laws on the dock as Martin called down his good-byes, casting Cheryl one last loving, conspiratorial glance, which she acknowledged with a secret smile.

Tony Vienhage, the *Altair*'s tall, laconic cook, stood near Beirnes and Martin and tipped his baseball cap to his wife, Mary, and his sister, Maxine Larson, who had taken the morning off from her job at the local cannery to be there for the send-off.

Nearby, nineteen-year-old Jody Gudbranson clung tightly to her baby girl as she gazed up at the *Altair*, now on the brink of carrying away Troy, her husband. She and Troy had gotten married in 1981 and when Jody graduated from high school the following year, she was holding their daughter, Rochelle.

Troy, at twenty-one, was the youngest on the *Altair*. With Randy Harvey, twenty-three, who had taken his brother's spot, he was the least experienced. But Troy told Jody that he was the most determined to prove himself.

Jody had begged Troy to hold her the night before this departure. "What would you do if something happened to me?" she asked. It was her way of measuring her husband's sense of peril and expressing her own.

That night she clung to him as long as possible. He did not

answer her question directly, but he tried to reassure her that he'd be fine.

As she watched him waving confidently from the *Altair* that morning—so conspicuous because he was taller than the rest and was wearing the bright red flannel shirt she had bought him for Christmas—she thought, What did he know? He'd never been fishing far out in the Bering Sea.

Jody saw no evidence of the fear she felt in the face of Nancy Beirnes. As Nancy glided from family to family that day, there was no way of telling that the wife of the *Altair*'s captain was in many ways just as anxious about this trip as was Jody. She had been all the way to Dutch Harbor several times as a passenger on the boat with her husband. She knew what he was getting into. She also knew the intense pressure her husband and her brothers-in-law, George Nations and Jeff Hendricks, were under to make up for the loss of the *Antares*. The banks were riding on a big season, like every year. But this year—heading north with one less vessel—was worse. Ron and George and Jeff needed a big payload before they could afford to expand the fleet.

Along the dock similar good-byes were shared. Any signs of dread were held in check. Fatalism had become a simple fact of life in Anacortes. Reminder enough stood by the town marina, around a crook in the harbor, a half mile away. There on the dock, a twelve-foot-tall obelisk was inscribed with ninety-six names, those of the fishermen the town had lost over the past fifty years. There were more than three times the number of names on this monument as there were on the memorial in the middle of town to those lost to World War II, the Korean War, and Vietnam combined.

Other fishermen on the dock that day handled the *Altair*'s lines as Ron Beirnes assembled his crew around him: Lark Breckenridge, twenty-four, with just five months' experience, whose older brother Brad, a crane operator, had helped build both the *Americus* and *Altair;* Randy Harvey, whose deckhand job had been handed down to him when his older brother, Rick, had signed on for a far less punishing job on a herring catcher, and Brad Melvin, twenty-six, whose brother, Brian, was skipper of the *Alyeska* running three days ahead. Pride and confidence radiated from their faces as they posed for group photos just before casting off. They tried to look casual and jaunty as Beirnes pulled the boat away from the dock, under a fine blue sky accented by the snow-covered peak of Mount Baker, looking down on them from the east.

The *Americus* was now a speck out in the channel as Ron set the *Altair*'s bow in the same direction. Jody waved; the crew waved back. Tony Vienhage's sister, Maxine, snapped one last shot of the big boat for the family scrapbook. A young girl moved out of the crowd and tossed a bouquet into the water.

The crowd dispersed, many among them driving to the bluffs overlooking the straits for a final glimpse of their sons and husbands and boyfriends. Nancy Beirnes had only to pause at the top of the hill leading to her new house to see the *Altair* heading into Puget Sound.

Before the day was through, she would go upstairs to the side-band radio Ron had installed. By bouncing radio signals off the ionosphere it was capable of reaching anyone anywhere in the world unless bad weather interfered. She would double-check the call frequency she and her husband had agreed on. As they had for nearly twenty years, Ron and Nancy would try to talk to each other on the radio every night.

Meanwhile, at the dock, a fisherman threw a line and retrieved the child's bouquet from the water. Flowers on the water were unlucky. Flowers, for fishermen, were used only as funeral wreaths.

CHAPTER 4

AT THE FOOT OF CAPE KALETA ON THE STARK NORTHEAST headlands of Unalaska Bay stands a 204-foot granite pillar known as Priest Rock. Mounted on a steel stand forty feet above its rock base, a light beams every twelve seconds. Every captain of the more than five thousand vessels that annually enter and exit Unalaska Island's Dutch Harbor, the chief port of the Aleutians and the gateway to the Bering Sea, notes the sighting of Priest Rock in the ship's log. Its domed head resembles a clerical hood, and its light gives one last benediction for mariners passing into the open sea, just as it welcomes their return.

Priest Rock presides over twelve-knot currents, twenty-foot tides and tidal rips and bears witness to some of the most violent atmospheric and oceanographic riots occurring on earth. The waves roiling at its feet may have originated from the Aleutian Basin, the

Pribilof Canyon, the Seward Peninsula, Siberia, the Arctic Ocean—any or sometimes all of these places at once. They may have been born of Arctic winds or a seismic disruption in the Bering Canyon forty miles away, or they may have traveled nine hundred miles south from the polar ice pack. They may have pushed along a great circle route from the Alaska mainland west toward the Siberian Peninsula and then ridden cold currents south and east as forerunners of a storm.

The Bering Sea Priest Rock oversees is young and tantrum-prone, shaped only in the last million years. The basin occupies a small elliptical area extending 930 miles from the Bering Straits in the Arctic north to the 1,200-mile-long Aleutian chain in the south. At its widest, the sea stretches for 1,240 miles and drops 2.5 miles to its deepest trench. But for the most part the Bering Sea is shallow, less than a hundred fathoms, which explains its unruly behavior.

Much of its bottom, known as the Pacific Plate, is an evolving shelf, plastic and mobile, like the coastal mountain ranges of the western United States from the same geologic generation. As the Pacific Plate moves west and northwest, it collides with the North American Plate, an older, more trenchant formation. Where they meet, the leading edges of the Pacific Plate dip deferentially and descend toward the earth's core, where the rock melts, loses density, and is forced upward again under incredible pressure. As a result, more seismic activity is recorded in the basin of the Bering Sea than anywhere else on earth. Earthquakes are born. Volcanoes erupt. Islands appear overnight, are spotted, charted, reported, and sometimes vanish or recede to pinnacles just beneath the surface within a month's time.

In winter, during the crabbing season, a collaboration of cosmic forces adds to the havoc of the Bering Sea. The spin of the earth and the loosening pull of the sun allow the wide, warm Japanese Current and the dense, high-velocity air masses of the jet stream to run clockwise along the continental shelf of east Asia. At the same time a frigid mass of water descends from the Arctic, where it joins with the Bering Current, a contentious band of extremely cold water moving counterclockwise. Where these opposing forces of warm and cold collide, terrible weather is born.

Beginning in the Arctic, strong winds gain power in their passage over the ice pack. Diving down the twelve-thousand-foot mountains of Siberia or the Alaska mainland, they are funneled and compacted into intensifying energy for the drive across the open sea. During the seven-month winter crabbing season—beginning in late September—gales reaching sixty miles per hour occur as part of the normal daily weather pattern. Unpredictably, however, gale force can alchemize into hurricane force. And because the Bering Sea is narrow and shallow, its shoal-like bottom drags at the passing, wind-pushed waves, slowing them down, reshaping them into a retinue of confused, sharply rising peaks that overtake each other like interlocking saw blades. These waves can climb as high as five or six stories, completely overwhelming fifty-foot-high vessels.

During certain weeks of every month, the pull of the moon prevails on the Bering Sea, creating thirty-foot tides that send billions of tons of water rushing as swiftly as river torrents through the narrows between the basin's islands. At times, when the earth, sun, and moon are aligned, water running south on the ebb or north on the flood tide is pressurized at four thousand pounds per cubic foot. The stupendous upwellings that result make it look as though the sea is boiling, filling to the brim, and spilling over the horizon.

At other times, seemingly bottomless whirlpools form, appearing to drain the sea of its surplus by directing it to the center of the earth. Norwegian seamen claim to have seen them before in their own part of the world, where they called them "maelstroms." Once witnessed, they swirled forever inside a fisherman's head.

As they move northward from the Aleutian Islands, fishermen measure their approach to the Bering Sea by many factors: the drop in the barometer, the roll of the boat, the inability to see the bow because of the fog or freezing rain or snow, or the inability to distinguish 1:00 A.M. from 1:00 P.M. due to the lack of light. Ice adheres to the hull, the rails, the rigging. Freezing spray builds more ice, threatening to entomb the entire vessel in a thick, granite-hard white blanket. Under the added tonnage, vessels capsize and often sink. Routinely, crew members must arm themselves with ax handles, baseball bats, and sledgehammers, to pound the ice off the decks and railings for hours on end in order to stay afloat.

Beneath the Bering Sea's tumultuous surface, however, is the richest fishery left on earth. The very forces of competition between wind, temperature, currents, tides, and variable density which cause havoc on the surface, cycle and recycle the water from top to bottom underneath. As a result no part of the sea is deprived of the oxygen, light, and essential nutrients that attract and sustain the immense population of shrimp, crab, halibut, hake, herring, cod, pollock, and salmon that keeps a billion-dollar local industry alive.

In the morning darkness of February 8, 1983, Brian Melvin, the twenty-five-year-old skipper of the *Alyeska*, maneuvered his vessel past Priest Rock into Unalaska Bay and headed for the port of Dutch Harbor. The four Hendricks vessels had set out from Anacortes in two shifts three days apart in order to stagger the loading of crab pots and unloading of fuel in Dutch Harbor. The *Alyeska* and *Alliance* were dispatched first because their skippers, Melvin and Glenn Treadwell, were less experienced than George Nations and Ron Beirnes, and their crews would presumably need more time to load and transfer fuel. The *Alyeska*, a faster vessel than the *Alliance*, arrived first.

"As far west as you can go without being east": The local motto aptly described Unalaska Island, a barren, windswept piece of loose change midway between the tip of the Alaskan peninsula and the far end of the Aleutian chain. In winter, completely draped in snow and ice, with a seventy-mile-an-hour wind blowing under a black sky that spit snow and hail like artillery fire, Dutch Harbor seemed to hang on the edge of the universe. "If this isn't hell, then it gives you a pretty good glimpse," fishermen often said to each other as they entered the port.

As the gateway to the world's richest fishing grounds and within fifty miles of the great circle route to the Orient, the town was teeming with fishing trawlers, crab boats, and floating processors the size of sports stadiums. Tin-roofed canneries lined the crescent-shaped harbor, where shoreline processors were producing two million pounds of fish products a day. Tramp steamers and container cargo ships bound for ports anywhere in the Pacific Rim were moored randomly. The stench of the place was unmistakable, a moist, mossy mixture of fish guts and diesel fuel—"the odor of money," the fishermen liked to say.

At the height of the winter fishing season in 1983, five thousand new people came through Dutch Harbor every day. To serve them were twenty-one cab companies sharing the frozen or muddy roads with tractors and backhoes, dozens of boardinghouses, and ten establishments calling themselves hotels, not to mention an equal number of whorehouses. There were two grocery stores, six stores selling guns and ammunition, and twice the number of places with liquor licenses as there were churches. The only noticeable decline was in the resident fur seal and eagle population, prompting one local to quip, "We're more interested in the job pool than we are in the gene pool." The airport had begun a connecting service to Anchorage, and its two telephones recorded more long-distance phone calls than any similar utility anywhere in the state. And the voices might have been in a dozen languages.

As many as fifty vessels could arrive in a single day, and yet the Coast Guard decided against establishing a Coast Guard station, to the relief of most fishermen. But there was not even a rescue boat or helicopter port within easy reach. A new clinic built in the late 1970s handled fourteen hundred injuries a year, but no permanent physician was on-site. As far as law enforcement went, the only authorities were two police officers and a courthouse in a single-story building next to the Russian Orthodox church—left over from the time the town was an outpost for Russian fur traders. Built in 1826, complete with two blue onion-shaped domes, it was the oldest Russian Orthodox church in the western hemisphere.

Brian Melvin steered the *Alyeska* past the harbor docks, stacked to the sky with crab pots, and through the maze of processors and other boats at anchor, awaiting their turn at the loading docks. When he spotted the big *Sea Alaska* floating processor, he checked in by radio and headed for it. The vessel, a converted freighter, would act as a host for the Anacortes boats, storing and allocating fuel, supplies, and equipment as well as off-loading and processing their catch.

The trip north from Anacortes had been uneventful, and Melvin was grateful. This was his first trip as a full-fledged captain, and he knew plenty of tests awaited him from now until he got his crew home safely. The first test, he knew, would be to make certain that during their stay, none of his crew succumbed to the temptations of Dutch Harbor. Melvin had spent enough time there himself to know the consequences of lingering on shore. The term "being in Dutch" spoke for itself.

Next to the Russian Orthodox church sat one of the town's most dubious attractions—a squat little building that looked like a bread box. Inside, a stained Formica counter, a popcorn machine, a tired-looking jukebox, and a bandstand were the main accommodations. An indifferent nude hung on one wall, a Marilyn Monroe poster on another. A hodgepodge of tables and chairs with bent and broken legs made the place look pretty well broken in, or just broken, as if the proprietors had given up trying to repair things. But this ambience somehow added to the allure of the Elbow Room, the grungy little watering hole *Playboy* magazine had crowned "the raunchiest bar in America."

Before there was a bridge connecting the village to the harbor, fishermen had rowed anything that would float or had donned their own survival suits and swum across the channel to reach the bar. The Elbow Room was a place of solace or swagger, depending upon the size of the catch or the amount of tequila downed and coke snorted. Gossip and gripes were exchanged. Tips on crew vacancies aboard the best boats or the hottest talent at the whorehouses floated along with the currents of boozy companionship. Small and cramped, with a critical mass of boozed-up seagoing cowboys, the Elbow Room could quickly become a combustion chamber.

Brian Melvin had drunk his fair share at its bar, alongside George Nations and Glenn Treadwell, Doug Knutson, Larry Littlefield, Brent Boles, and the other guys from Anacortes. He'd yelled encouragement when some crewman fresh off a crab boat had publicly counted his newly earned share and rung the big ship's bell at the bar, announcing drinks for everyone—which might mean a shoulder-to-shoulder crowd.

"I saw eighteen-year-olds peeling off hundred-dollar bills to pay two-thousand-dollar bar tabs and leaving hundred-dollar tips," Melvin recalled. Like most fishermen who'd stopped by, he'd seen the coke and smoke dealers cleaning up in the bar's notorious Blue Room, without bothering to conceal their transactions. He had judged arm-wrestling grudge matches, ducked left hooks and flying shot glasses. He had lugged his buddies back to the boat, past fishermen passed out in the snow, and he'd nursed his own hangovers and cursed the place all the way into tomorrow. And come back the next time around.

One Anacortes fisherman, however, did not survive the revelry. Mike Leiske, a deckhand, died on the way home from the Elbow Room on Christmas night, 1976. One minute he was lining his empty tequila shot glasses up at the table. The next he was staggering out the door as if bracing into a hundred-mile-an-hour wind. In the morning someone on the dock spotted him floating between two hundred-ton boats. Leiske's name had gone up on the memorial along with the other Anacortes fishermen who had died at sea. No one had seen fit to split hairs. He was, after all, a fisherman. But there had been a rule imposed after that on all the Anacortes-based boats. A buddy system was mandatory anytime and anywhere in Dutch Harbor.

The morning they arrived, Melvin and his crew had too much work ahead of them to be distracted by the Elbow Room. Two hundred and eight crab pots—each weighing 690 pounds and roughly twice the size of a refrigerator—had to be lifted by crane and stacked on the *Alyeska*'s deck. This was twenty fewer pots than she carried the previous season, before the final retrofit for trawling gear added an estimated thirteen tons above deck. Melvin and Hendricks agreed that eliminating twenty pots, or about seven tons, would offset the weight gain from the big new stanchion and other trawling equipment. Still, stacked six rows high, the crab-pot load would be twenty feet tall and add seventy-two tons to the deck. And the loading would take nearly twenty-four hours to complete. The crew also loaded two hundred fifty cases of frozen herring, each weighing thirty pounds, to bait the pots.

Six hours after Melvin and his crew began loading the *Alyeska*, Glenn Treadwell guided the *Alliance* into Dutch Harbor. Smaller, at 103 feet, with the wheelhouse aft, she ran two knots slower and looked like a distant cousin to the other Hendricks boats. She had been built strictly for crabbing and so could not take on additional trawling gear. Hendricks, in partnership with Dakota Creek, the Anacortes shipyard, had taken over the boat from its previous owner before the bank did. With less deck space, the *Alliance* took on 90 crab pots and 120 cases of frozen herring, its normal load.

Melvin and Treadwell, and the other Anacortes skippers as well, would be going after tanner crab, a member of the spider-crab family and no relation at all to the much more glamorous king crab that had caused the boom in the Bering Sea. Tanner crab were smaller, with pear-shaped bodies, beady red eyes, and long, spindly legs. Nothing about them suggested any culinary attributes. When they invaded king-crab pots in the 1960s and '70s, crabbers would crush them, hoping to rid the ocean of these scourges. But when the bottom fell out of the king-crab fishery, the highly leveraged canneries and fleets of Kodiak Island were forced to look for alternatives. Out of desperation, industry marketers came up with the name "snow crab" for the lowly tanner crab. All it took was a name change. Suddenly, snow crab became de rigueur on menus in all-you-can-eat restaurants, especially in the Midwest. Some simple conversions were made: King-crab pots were fashioned with smaller doors so the tanner crab could not escape, and the machinery for cleaning and canning king crab was adjusted so that tanners could be easily processed. A whole new fishery was born. The price of tanner crab had risen from a nickel a pound in 1978 to two dollars at the dock in 1983. The year before, 70.6 million pounds of tanner crab yielded $82 million in sales.

Melvin and Treadwell had ample financial incentive to move quickly on the following day. The trip north to the crabbing grounds in the Bering Sea would take a full twenty-four hours, and dropping the crab pots would take more than forty-eight hours. To ensure the largest possible catch, they planned to bracket the seabed with clusters of pots instead of dropping them all in a single location, and each cluster could be as much as thirty miles apart. When the last pot was dropped, they would return to Dutch Harbor for a second load, which they would drop again in the Bering Sea. This way, one week after they had first arrived in Dutch Harbor, they would be ready to pull their first pots the minute the season opened. There was another incentive too: competition. At least five hundred other vessels would be after the same prizes.

As a way of conserving the resource, the Alaska Department of Fish and Game and federal regulators had imposed what was called the "Olympic method" of determining the length of the crabbing season. The Olympic method followed the calendar—allocating only so many days to fish each fishery, but not limiting the number of vessels allowed access to the fishing grounds. It did not put a cap on how much fish or crab could be harvested in the number of days it determined for a particular season. In turn, the Olympic method put smaller, fly-by-night fishermen on the same footing as larger, more-capable, and more-efficient vessels and sent every boat pell-mell after the fish regardless of the weather conditions. It wasn't a season these vessels were participating in, it was a short-term frenzy. And when fishermen hurried, when they worked continuously to catch all they could as quickly as they could, they often put their boats and crews at risk.

The crews of the *Alyeska* and *Alliance* loaded crab pots for eighteen hours, snatching meals in quick shifts. Sleep would come during the run north to the Pribilof Islands. When they reached the crabbing grounds, the real work—the baiting and dropping of the pots—would start. When the work ended would not be determined by a clock.

Throughout the night, as their crews loaded pots and bait and the vessels took on fresh water and supplies, Treadwell and Melvin conferred over the weather reports conveyed by satellite and listened for more specific reports relayed from other vessels heading to and from the Pribilofs through a radio station in Kodiak. What they heard suggested they should head for the southeast side of St. George Island, the southernmost of the Pribilofs. There, where a shelf ran shallow, they would drop the first load of pots, not all at once, but enough to prospect for a jackpot mountain of tanner crab. Working more than twenty-four hours, they would set pots in three locations, never more than half a day's run from each other, before returning to Dutch Harbor for more.

On the morning of February 9, the *Alyeska* and *Alliance* left the docks in Dutch Harbor and rode out past Priest Rock. Melvin and Treadwell set their courses north-northwest for the two-hundred-mile trip into the Bering Sea. The seas were relatively calm, a light snow was falling, and the wind was light, with an occasional squall. On deck, the crews mended mesh on the crab pots, ground hundreds of pounds of frozen herring, and stuffed the mush into the two-quart plastic containers punched with tiny holes that would be placed in each pot to lure the crab. The routine was cold, wet, monotonous. The only incentive any man had was to finish their job and get off the rolling deck and out of the wind and spray—"the Maytag effect," Treadwell and other fishermen called it, "because you felt like you were being tossed around like a damp rag."

In order to break the monotony, crew members had to devise their own entertainment. "One of the guys working the bow of the *Alliance* tried to outsmart gravity. Because the vessel's wheelhouse was in the stern, the bow was light. When the bow was bucking waves, riding upward on a crest, one of the crew would crouch, tense, ready . . . and someone cranked on 'Jumpin' Jack Flash' on the boom box . . . and when the bow fell, the crewman leapt, launching himself and screaming like hell," Treadwell remembered, describing how the young men could fly ten or twelve feet off the deck before gravity and the bow caught up.

"That was about as much fun as anyone could have out there," he added.

Within hours, once the real work began and their beards and sweat iced up, once snot froze in their noses, the laughter would give way to curses, and the curses, too, would become more occasional as the wind-whipped sea closed in around them.

In the middle of the night on February 10, they reached the crabbing grounds in the southern lee of the Pribilofs, two hundred miles from Dutch Harbor. When the fathometer showed the depth they were looking for, Melvin and Treadwell set the bows of the *Alyeska* and *Alliance* into the thirty-knot wind and proceeded against the line of the tide. One by one the giant crab pots were dragged off the stack by a crane and across the icy, pitching deck. In succession each was rigged, baited, its doors tied shut. Another crane lifted them, one at a time, onto a hydraulic launcher, a wide metal ramp where each sat poised, ready to be catapulted on signal from the skipper in the wheelhouse.

Their goal was to bait and launch one pot every five minutes, or about eight pots for every mile. A three-quarter-inch-thick polypropylene line was tied to each pot, spliced by a figure-eight car-rick-bend knot every 150 feet. These sections, called "shots," were added or subtracted depending upon the desired depth. A three-shot line, for example, was for a maximum depth of 450 feet. The line was carefully coiled atop the crab pot ready to be launched and a six-inch cork float was attached near the end of the line. Farther up was tied an inflatable rubber balloon known as a "trailer bag." Each was numbered and its location noted by the captain. Farther still was tied a larger inflatable rubber buoy known as the "diver" or "marker bag." The number stenciled on it, assigned by the Alaska Department of Fish and Game, identified the vessel respon-sible for the buoy and the pot below.

As each pot was launched, the crewmen heaved the twenty-pound trailing buoy behind it. The plan was to let each pot soak and attract crab for three or four days until the season began. By that time they would have returned to Dutch Harbor to load more pots. When Melvin and Treadwell returned to retrieve their first load of pots, they would refer to the chart, the locations noted, and to the radar and electronic plotter. If all agreed, they should be able to swing their vessel parallel to the marker bag and find the yellow line attached to the trailer bag without even looking out the wheelhouse window. A crewman would then throw a gaff hook to snare the line between the trailer and the cork, reel it in, and run the end of the line through a series of hydraulic-powered pulleys until the crab pot was barely beneath the water's surface. Then the yellow polypropylene bridle atop the pot could be easily snagged by a steel hook at the end of the lifting crane. One or two deckhands would swing the crab pot back onto the launcher until it locked into place; another would swing the door open and retrieve the empty bait can. The crane operator would then tilt the pot opening over the alumi-num sorting bin—a large rectangular table with raised six-inch sides—and the crew, with the aid of the crane, would shake the crabs out.

A good pot would yield three hundred crabs. They would be

sorted by size and tossed into thirty-thousand-gallon tanks of circulating seawater to keep them alive for delivery less than a week later. Females and juveniles would be discarded out the "shit chute," a shallow, eighteen-inch-wide, open aqueduct sunk across the width of the deck, used for flushing the rejects and other detritus back into the sea. These chutes were built-in hazards. On a rolling deck in icy weather, more than one deckhand on many fishing vessels had taken a painful misstep into the chute and turned or broken an ankle.

Launching and retrieving pots was hard work and relentlessly routine. If any breaks were taken over a twenty-hour period, they were snatched in two or three minutes. "Thank God you don't have long enough to piss. Because if you did, you'd freeze it off out there," Jeff Hendricks remembered someone telling him before he left on his first voyage to the Bering Sea.

The deck of a crab boat contained an infinite amount of dangers, and the monotony of the work only dulled a fisherman's sense of potential disaster. A line trailing a sinking crab pot was as lethal as a high-voltage wire. Wrapped around an ankle, it could launch a crewman over the side in seconds; all crewmen carried knives on their belts for just this reason. When suspended, the pots themselves swung from the end of the crane and gathered momentum with every roll of the deck. Sometimes they broke loose. "Anyone in the way might as well be standing in the path of an oncoming train," Treadwell observed. And just when it was least expected, the Bering Sea could send a murderous wave over the bulkhead, knocking anyone unprepared and unbraced off his feet. The key to staying alive was keeping both soles of their soft-rubber boots on deck. Someone, too, would always have to be on the lookout, prepared to shout any number of warnings: "Peeler!" when a potentially lethal wave was about to wash over the deck; "Line!" when a coil had come unleashed and was lashing; "Hook!" when the big steel gaff at the end of the crane cable was swinging wildly with the force of a wrecking ball.

During the long voyage to Dutch Harbor, Melvin and Treadwell had already conducted fire drills and man-overboard drills and assigned every man his position in case of emergencies. They had rehearsed putting on their cumbersome survival suits, each crew member on the floor, shimmying the rubbery material over his body. The goal was to get the hood almost completely over his head, right down to his eyebrows, and have the front zipped up over his chin in under a minute. That might be all the time anyone had. Any longer could mean trying to put the suit on underwater, which would be like wrestling with a sea lion. But without a survival suit, layered with special insulation to protect against hypothermia, falling into the Bering Sea, a veteran oceanographer said, "would be like skydiving in outer space."

Deep-sea fishermen are all too aware of the details of hypothermia. Cold water drags heat from the body at twenty-five times the rate cold air does. First, the body temperature rises; then crashes. Violent shaking racks the body. Blood recedes first from the hands and feet and then retreats from the arms and legs to insulate the vital organs. Consciousness and coordination start to wane. The body's core temperature drops below ninety degrees. Shivering gives way to stiffness. The skin starts to turn blue, respiration grows shallow, and the pulse plunges. Within minutes, depending upon the person's fat content and clothing, survival instincts give way. The body temperature drops below eighty degrees, and the person loses the ability to tread water. He becomes physically and mentally inert. Coast Guard rescuers recalled victims, still conscious but unable to move, literally disappearing as a rescue ring was tossed within reach or as a rescuer reached out a hand. The crewmen of the *Alyeska* and *Alliance* all had heard these stories.

"The joke at the docks was that we Norwegians had figured out a way around this," Doug Knutson, now a fishing vessel captain, recalled sardonically. "They carried rocks in their boots. That way, if they fell overboard they'd sink quickly and avoid all the misery."

Swimming skills were not considered necessary for jobs on the Bering Sea. But if a man was wearing protection, even a simple life preserver to help keep him afloat, drowning might be averted. A life preserver could buy as much as half an hour. A full survival immersion suit could buy several hours, and an up-to-date life raft with a canopy could buy days for crew members, if the seas obliged. Although none was required by law, all the Hendricks boats were carrying the latest survival equipment. It was one reason Hendricks had a reputation for thoroughness.

When the *Alyeska* and *Alliance* returned to Dutch Harbor early Sunday morning, February 13, the *Americus* and *Altair* were tied up at the *Sea Alaska* dock, their crews loading pots and taking on supplies. A short, impromptu reunion was held among the crews of the four A-boats. They exchanged jokes and boasts of standing up to rough seas and cold weather and working superhuman hours on deck. But there was still plenty of work, and it would go on nearly nonstop between now and the next day, when all four vessels would move out. Brent Boles knew that George Nations would be flying in from Seattle that afternoon and would be anxious to put to sea. Ron Beirnes was equally anxious to get to the crabbing grounds.

The reunion lasted less than an hour. Still, some of the crew mailed valentines home. Jeff Martin snapped some photos of the other crewmen positioning crab pots on the snowy deck of the *Altair* and sent them off with a note to his fiancée, Cheryl Sandvik. Rich Awes called home to announce they'd made it to Dutch safely and he hadn't been seasick for even a minute. Vic Bass called his grandmother and confided that he might postpone his plans to go to California to become a model, depending, of course, on how much money he earned on this trip. His grandmother relayed this to his parents, who were greatly relieved at the prospects of saving their son from a modeling career. Troy Gudbranson called his wife, Jody; they had a minor skirmish. She wanted to go to a rock concert. He wanted her to stay home with their baby. She remained resolute, and when they hung up he was angry.

Steve Carr, previously the engineer of the lost *Antares* and now engineer of the *Alyeska,* climbed aboard the *Americus* to visit with his friend Larry Littlefield. But Littlefield was having a problem. A valve had frozen on a fuel-transfer line and he needed to replace it. On orders, he was to begin transferring approximately twenty-eight thousand gallons of diesel fuel—about thirty percent of the *Americus*'s total fuel capacity—from his vessel to the *Sea Alaska* processor. Fuel was fifteen cents cheaper a gallon in Anacortes than in Alaska, and since Sea Alaska Products, Inc., was a partner with Hendricks, they would be saving about $40,000 in fuel costs if all four boats carried fuel north, transferred it to a holding reservoir on the *Sea Alaska,* and then replenished themselves as the seasons wore on. They had done this routinely, and sometimes, depending on the rise in fuel prices, they had saved even more. This transfer was yet another of Hendricks's shrewd business decisions.

Transferring fuel, however, was a delicate process, since when fuel was eliminated, a vessel's ballast shifted and became lighter, making the boat potentially less seaworthy. Littlefield knew that in this particular fuel transfer the *Americus* would be losing approximately one hundred tons of fuel* from the holding tanks beneath the decks and that the vessel's weight would need to be carefully watched for balance as the transfer was taking place. The vessel's big double-bottom tank held more fuel and therefore provided the best ballast, so Littlefield would more likely have opted to pull fuel from the smaller wing tanks located along the vessel's inner flanks. This took more time but was safer. He had told Dean Brenengen, the dock fuel supervisor, to begin this transfer when the fuel-line valve froze, stopping the process. When a replacement valve was located and installed, Littlefield, according to Brenengen, ordered him to begin transferring from one of the "front" fuel tanks.

---

* A gallon of diesel fuel weighs 7.2 pounds.

Carr noticed that Littlefield had also filled two of the four thirty-thousand-gallon crab tanks with seawater. The two full tanks were diagonally across from each other. Carr recognized this to be a technique called "cross-tanking," a method of adding ballast—in this case more than 130 tons—just below the deck to compensate further for the fuel transfer. Nations had begun experimenting with cross-tanking the year before. He saw this as a way of trimming to make up for the loss of fuel the *Americus* burned while trawling far out at sea. Flooding the crab tanks was more efficient than stopping the vessel to shift the remaining fuel from tank to tank to rebalance the vessel.

Jeff Hendricks was aware of Nations's experiments. He also recognized that Nations had become a competent seaman, so he allowed cross-tanking at his brother-in-law's discretion, even though it was not addressed in the stability booklet. It was a minor concession for Hendricks but a major point Nations had scored in his own favor.

According to the loading plan, the *Americus* and *Altair* would carry no more than 228 pots each, thirty less than their original calculated capacity. This plan took into consideration the added weight of the trawling gear, the loss of deck space it caused, and the transfer of fuel. Pots were stacked six rows high, and when the stacking was complete a crew member would climb up and secure the top pots tightly to each other with double chains. This was crucial to the stability of each boat. Once under way in rolling seas, the strain would be considerable. If pots came loose, the vessel's topside weight would be dangerously—perhaps fatally—redistributed. As the loose pots slid from side to side, the vessel could literally rock uncontrollably, the way someone might stand up and rock a dinghy.

The crew of the *Americus* had taken on 280 cases of frozen herring and was adding the last of the crab pots when Glenn Treadwell returned from the airport with George Nations. The two friends climbed on board.

"George asked Brent Boles how much fuel had been consumed," Treadwell remembered. "Brent started to tell him about the fuel transfer and George cut him off. 'Beer. I'm talking beer, not diesel fuel,' he said."

Even though it was stated company policy that no drugs or drunkenness would be tolerated aboard, it was customary for each of the A-boats to carry a hundred cases of beer. Beer was their only indulgence. "It was up to each of us captains to define what drunkenness meant," Treadwell remembered.

George Nations, the only Hendricks skipper ever suspended for drunkenness, popped open a can and offered one to Treadwell. The two climbed the stairs to the *Americus* wheelhouse, where Nations could scan the deck. He eyed the new trawl gear, counted the number of pots on board—twenty-eight fewer than last season—and cursed. If each pot turned up three hundred or so that were keepers, at two dollars apiece, you were already throwing away around $17,000, which could multiply to $100,000 or more depending on how many runs the *Americus* made from the crabbing grounds to the processor.

Nations then went to the chart table and pulled out the *Americus*'s stability booklet. He and Treadwell had done stability calculations dozens of times. Still, Nations insisted, calculations based on a vessel's blueprints were not as true as the feel of the boat or how she sat in the water under various loads and conditions. Nothing on paper could take into consideration the variables the Bering Sea might throw at a captain.

Nations cursed the weather, and the fact that he was back in Dutch Harbor. But he saved his most sincere curse for the loss of the *Antares*. By all rights she should be alongside them. The company had lost a $3 million boat and the capacity for laying the equivalent of six hundred crab pots this season. The Antares might have returned a catch worth between $1.5 and $2.5 million over the crabbing season. That was a conservative estimate and didn't even begin to account for the lost revenue from missing the trawling season.

"We talked about Brian's and my run up to the Pribilofs and where we unloaded our strings of pots," Treadwell recalled. "We also talked about the *Antares,* the loss. And George said we'd all have to work our crews' asses off."

Nations finished his beer and, with Treadwell in tow, went off to find Ron Beirnes. It was late in the afternoon on February 13 and already dark.

Beirnes and Melvin were sipping beers in the living room of a *Sea Alaska* house trailer with Ken Griffin, the Alaska Fish and Game biologist based in Dutch Harbor, when Nations and Treadwell found them. They were discussing the crabbing prospects south of the Pribilofs where the *Alyeska* and *Alliance* had already set their first load of pots. Beirnes was inclined to head there too, he said. Nations grabbed a beer from the refrigerator and asked Griffin to volunteer alternative positions, particularly down around Sand Point, 260 miles to the southeast in the lee of the Aleutians, back the way they had come. Suspecting that most of the fleet would be headed for the Pribilofs, Nations reasoned that the *Americus* might have better results on a less-crowded crabbing ground.

Griffin had taken a particular interest in the Anacortes boats, partly as a measure of respect. He admired Jeff Hendricks's exacting standards. He liked Ron Beirnes. He even liked George Nations. He understood the economic pressure the A-boat skippers were under after losing the *Antares.* He also appreciated that the Anacortes crews brought supplies for his family—small appliances, dog food, milk (it was $4.25 a gallon in Dutch Harbor), diapers, etc.—and he would supply them with up-to-date information about the size and movement of a potential catch and throw in valuable opinions of his own. Which wasn't to say that Griffin was favoring one captain or one fleet over another for the sake of some small gifts.

"Most never asked us," the biologist recalled.

Directing fishermen to the catch was a convenient way for the Alaska Department of Fish and Game to maintain some control. Control was something new to Alaska, ever since the king-crab boom of the early 1970s had turned into a calamity by the beginning of the next decade. No one could estimate the potential harvest of tanner crab, just as no one had been able to guess at the tremendous rise and fall, within five years, of the king crab. The biologists could only base their guesses for the tanner crab on the hard lessons of experience. One year, 132 million pounds of king crab were harvested; a year later the harvest fell to 28 million, a year after that there were no king crab. Yet there were no quotas limiting the take of tanner crab, still a relatively new fishery. The best Griffin could do was keep track of where the crabbers dropped their pots and how many pounds they brought to the docks.

The problem, one that had been evolving with dwindling catches, was that the crabbing seasons were becoming shorter. The day the A-boats and their five hundred competitors, many smaller and slower, would leave Dutch Harbor to retrieve their pots would mark the beginning of a make-or-break race. According to the Olympic method, a captain could leave Dutch and the crew could set the pots early, but they could not pull them until the state of Alaska said it was time. Before each vessel left the dock, it would be inspected and certified—not for safety, but to ensure that it sailed without any previously caught crab in its tanks. The system allowed each vessel to catch as much as possible and return to the processors, but in a limited time—less than three months in the winter season of 1983. But the overriding fact was that nearly eighty percent of the overall catch was made in the first two weeks. So, in an indirect attempt to impose quotas, the season was really a race against the clock, regardless of weather conditions and the hazards of such a breakneck pace.

Ron Beirnes was very much aware of these competing factors, which hastened him to delegate the *Altair*'s fuel transfer to Jeff

Martin while he visited the Fish and Game expert. His single over-riding goal was to maximize every hour in the Bering Sea.

Griffin pulled a chart of the Sand Point area out of his briefcase. It showed several dark clusters signifying where Fish and Game crab prospectors reported that they had located schools of tanner crab in fishable depths. Then he showed them a chart of the Pribilof area. There were considerably more clusters representing crabbing beds, and they were spread over a greater area. The captains also acknowledged that the round trip to Sand Point was twenty-four hours longer than the round trip to the Pribilofs. If they were to make it in time for the opening of the crab season, just four days away, the *Americus* and *Altair* could carry only one load of pots each to Sand Point. There would be no time to return for a second load, which seemed crucial. The choice seemed obvious: The Pribilofs offered their best opportunity.

If they went to the Pribilofs, they had time to make two trips and possibly double their money. The imperative, because of the loss of the *Antares,* was almost overwhelming. But Nations, exercising his contrary streak, was still debating taking a chance on Sand Point when Griffin excused himself to go home for dinner. Melvin left a short time later to return to the *Alyeska.*

It was getting late, and Beirnes and Nations were still debating and drinking when Treadwell returned to the *Alliance*. The boats were tied four abreast by now: the *Americus* closest to the dock and still taking on pots, followed by the *Alliance, Altair,* and *Alyeska.* The flotilla looked invincible and ghostly, lit up by blazing halogen lights under a lightly falling snow.

Brian Melvin boarded the *Altair* around midnight and made himself comfortable in the galley, joshing with his brother, Brad, his friend Randy Harvey, and the rest of the crew. He was impressed by how Jeff Martin, Ron Beirnes's backup, seemed to be taking charge. Tony Vienhage, the cook, set another place at the table and Melvin lingered for a final meal before the *Altair* cast off.

Knowing this would be their last opportunity for some time, Brad Melvin, Randy Harvey, and their other buddies aligned themselves in mock challenges to the captain of the *Alyeska*. They boasted that the *Altair*'s four thirty-thousand-gallon seawater circulation tanks would be plugged with crab and that they would be on their way back to Dutch Harbor and counting their money before the *Alyeska* pulled its first pots. Who knew? This could be the last time for a long time they could get away with razzing Brian Melvin as a friendly competitor. Next year they might be on his boat or asking him for a job.

After he cleared his dishes from the galley table, Troy Gudbranson climbed over the rail of the *Altair* and trudged through the knee-deep snow to a telephone booth and called his wife, Jody, one last time.

The phone rang once and he heard Jody's voice at the other end. Quickly, he offered an apology for the argument they'd had the morning before. It was 1:49 A.M. on February 14, Valentine's Day. "It's cold up here," Troy said, sounding as if he needed reassurance. "I miss you."

Glenn Treadwell was startled out of his sleep by the sound of someone crossing the deck of the *Alliance*. He rose from his bunk and climbed into the wheelhouse to see Ron Beirnes picking his way along the deck to get to the *Altair,* which was tied, flank-to-flank, between the *Alliance* and the *Alyeska*. Treadwell climbed back into his own bunk to get more sleep but minutes later was roused again by Ron's voice and the sound of the *Altair*'s diesel engine. Treadwell looked at his watch. It was 2:00 A.M. *Ron is really motivated,* he thought, noting that it was usually Nations who liked to be the lead boat away from the dock. Treadwell made his way to the forecastle deck to help Beirnes cast off. He could see Jeff Martin and Lark Breckenridge already casting off the mooring lines and Brian Melvin helping them disengage from the *Alyeska*. Treadwell did the same, loosening a line from the *Alliance* and signaling Beirnes that he was clear to back the *Altair* away.

Treadwell looked at his watch again: 2:30 A.M. There was no moon. The air was filled with snow. Even the flood of yellow halogen mast lights could not quite penetrate the darkness.

"See you guys later," Brian Melvin shouted from the forecastle of the *Alyeska*. "Just keep your asses out of our way when we get there."

One by one the *Altair*'s crew taunted him as the vessel pulled out into the harbor. In the darkness, Melvin recognized each voice.

Brad and Brian Melvin, Rick and Randy Harvey, Lark Breckenridge, Jeff Martin, Tony Vienhage, Brent Boles, Larry Littlefield, and Paul Northcutt had all hung together in Anacortes, even after high school. As boys they had sat together for hours at the city dock, waiting patiently for the tips of their fishing rods to bend to the pull of a salmon or rock cod. They plucked butter clams from the sand flats and mussels from the rocky coves of Dewey Beach. They stirred the water on moonless nights off March Point and marveled at the white phosphorescence their hands could create. They built bonfires on the beach at Deception Pass, gigantic ones, and watched the sparks fly skyward so high that they seemed to merge with the stars. They drank and smoked and lay in their sleeping bags, sighting the constellations; they debated the intelligence and ferocity of the killer whales that chased seals nearly right into town, and who'd seen the most, or who'd come the closest to one; they talked about real love and death and God and their common aspirations in proper order: to make good money, drive a respectable vehicle, have a good wife, a good home, and to have a good time.

Fear was never discussed. The majority had survived the Bering Sea, and the others hadn't yet experienced it. In their own minds they were invincible and their boats indestructible. Each offered the other living proof.

———

Ron Beirnes swung the *Altair* to starboard for the cruise out of the harbor. Melvin on the *Alyeska* and Treadwell on the *Alliance* could see the length of her as she passed by. They could see the distinctive white wing on the side of her bow and her red boot stripe riding just above the waterline. They could see water spilling off the deck and over the sides, and they knew where the water was likely coming from. Ron Beirnes, as was his custom, had probably ordered all four of the *Altair*'s crab tanks flooded with continuously circulating seawater, adding around 260 tons to the vessel's load belowdecks. The extra weight would not only cause the vessel to ride lower in the water, it would provide a slower, cushier roll. Better for sleeping, more like a cradle. That was Ron's style.

Treadwell could see the new trawling stanchions—more than thirty-five tons of gear—fighting for deck space with the crab pots still stacked as high as normal. He focused again on the boot stripe, distinguishable in the harbor lights—and lower to the water than before the *Altair* had taken on its crab pots. Still, its position seemed to be normal considering the load. Besides, Treadwell trusted Ron to know the feel of his own boat.

Both Melvin and Treadwell had fished with Beirnes so long, they knew his embarkation routine by heart. It would be their routine too. As he took the *Altair* out of the harbor, he would make some last checks in the wheelhouse: both radar screens, both depth finders, and all three LORAN-C receivers, the devices that used satellites for position fixes and directions, just as airplanes did. He would make certain both single-sideband radios were tuned to the frequencies he had been given by a terminal manager at the dock and that the code they had agreed on to announce the size and location of their catch was posted within view. He would check both VHF-FM radio telephones, one outfitted with a scrambler for secure conversations with the *Americus* and the other Anacortes boats. He would check the closed-circuit television system that monitored the main deck and engine room. He would make certain the panel lights were set for the alarms installed to warn of rising water in the lower compartments, lowering water levels in the crab tanks or fuel tanks, or problems in the engine room. Beirnes would also check to see that the battery-operated emergency position-indicating radio (EPIRB) was in its bracket outside the wheelhouse. If the unthinkable happened—if the *Altair* capsized and sank—the device, about the size of a transistor radio, would break loose and float freely, broadcasting its position for forty-eight hours on frequencies monitored by satellites and military and commercial aircraft.

"The point was, you had a good feeling," Melvin said. "You never felt alone out there."

No government inspector dockside in Dutch Harbor had to remind Ron Beirnes or George Nations or any of the other skippers to do these things. Like most fishermen they believed government should stay out of the commercial fishing business. Government was already setting quotas and taking fishing days away.

Beirnes would likely have made one last check. He would open the settee in the wheelhouse and count ten survival suits. They were heavy and hard to get on, but they were life insurance.

When Beirnes was satisfied that everything was in order, he would probably turn the boat over to Jeff Martin, give him the course for the Pribilofs and the watch schedule for the crew members. Then he would go to his stateroom and sleep.

Brian Melvin was lingering on the deck of the *Alyeska* just before 3:00 A.M., watching the *Altair* clear the spit and head toward the red buoy marking the exit from Dutch Harbor when George Nations arrived at the dock. Nations began shouting questions to his crew. Had the fuel finally been transferred? Were the last of the crab pots on board? Were they chained down? He planned to cast off around 8:00 A.M., he announced. The forecast for the lower Bering Sea called for a break in the weather, followed by increasing winds and building seas, a typical winter pattern. By late the next day, big weather from the Alaskan mainland would be moving southwest.

When Nations pulled out the next morning, Melvin and Treadwell would be able to pull the *Alyeska* and *Alliance* into position, finish transferring fuel and loading the last of their pots, and try to move out ahead of the storm too. Even then, Melvin knew their chances of making it all the way to the Pribilofs before the wind made the seas big were unlikely.

"The weather won't stay calm up there for more than a few hours," he told his crew.

Although at twenty-five he was relatively young for a captain, Melvin had fought the Bering Sea enough to shed any pretense of his own invincibility. He knew that when the waves rose up, a fishing boat, no matter how well equipped, was no more significant on those waters than a moth.

Melvin could still see the *Altair*'s running lights as the vessel headed into the portside turn at Priest Rock. For now the weather was tame, the water calm, the winds light and from the north-northeast. What waves there were kissed the boat gently on the starboard beam.

Half an hour later, at 3:30 A.M., the fishing vessel *Silver Wave* was returning from the Pribilofs to Dutch Harbor when it passed within 150 feet of the outbound *Altair*. Dagfin Halvorsen, at the helm of the *Silver Wave,* could make out the *Altair*'s profile as the two vessels passed, port to port. *Looks normal,* he noted to himself, *on a course for the Pribilofs*. He later remembered that "the winds were silent, the weather clear, and the seas only about two feet."

CHAPTER 5

A BLIP APPEARED ON THE GREEN RADAR SCREEN IN THE WHEELHOUSE of the *Neptune Jade*, a 750-foot Singapore-registered freighter en route to the Orient. It was 12:15 P.M. on Monday, February 14, and the radar indicated the source to be located about twenty-five nautical miles northwest of Priest Rock and Dutch Harbor. Normal enough in this sea-lane, the vessel's captain noted. Except that the blip was not moving. The *Neptune Jade* was closing on the position, 24 nautical miles away.

The helmsman switched to a general radio frequency to call the vessel. If assistance was needed, they'd relay a call back to Dutch Harbor. There was no answer. The helmsman set his course directly toward the position of what might be a ship in distress. Since weather reports indicated a storm descending on the area, any broken-down vessel caught in open water would be in peril.

Three hours later, a crew member in the wheelhouse spotted an overturned vessel. The *Neptune Jade*'s skipper took charge, guiding the cumbersome merchant ship within thirty yards—as close as he dared in a sea building with increasing winds—then circling. The hull appeared to be about eighty feet long. A red stripe ran horizontally along the bottom. The rest of the hull was blue. Curiously, there was no indication that the hull itself had been damaged. Aware that the *Neptune Jade* was too large to safely maneuver alongside, the captain circled again, widening the arc, and ordered his crew to look for survivors, or bodies, or debris. None was spotted.

The captain circled a third time, making an even wider arc. Finding nothing, he grabbed the radio and dialed the Coast Guard emergency channel and described what he and his crew were seeing. There was no reply. He switched radio frequencies, sending out a widespread alert to anyone within range. The captain was following an unwritten "good Samaritan" code at sea, which, because of distances and slow travel time, asked as many vessels within range of a distress signal to converge on the position to look for survivors.

The freighter *Aleutian Developer* was the first vessel to pick up the call, but it was running six hundred miles to the southwest. Over his own radio, the ship's captain relayed the *Neptune Jade*'s alarm and the reported position of the overturned hull to the U.S. Coast Guard Communication Station in Kodiak: *latitude 54 degrees 19.6 minutes north, longitude 166 degrees 54 minutes west*. The time was 2:40 P.M.

The Kodiak "Comstay," the oldest facility of its kind in the U.S., was responsible for tracking the comings and goings of hundreds of vessels a week along six thousand miles of crescent coastline from the Canadian border in the southeast to Attu Island at the far western tip of the Aleutians and the Russian border. Seventy officers and enlisted personnel were stationed there in 1983, at least twelve on watch at all times, monitoring dozens of radio channels in soundproof cubicles. They listened for suspicious radio traffic that might expose the positions of possible drug traffickers; they listened for trespassing foreign fishing vessels; they listened for weather reports and bits of marine information they might pass along; they listened for calls for assistance, often dispensing advice, and they acted as 911 operators when situations arose. Nearly nine hundred thousand square miles of open water fell within the station's watch, nearly twice as much as the entire land mass of the continental U.S. Add in tens of thousands of islands within the two-hundred-mile U.S. coastal boundary, and the Coast Guard station's responsibility compared to watching over a small galaxy.

Gary Howell, the skipper of the fishing vessel *Alaska Invader,* overheard the *Aleutian Developer*'s radio relay. He checked his position: about fifty miles to the southwest of the overturned hull, or more than four hours away. But there was no other radio traffic from vessels small and maneuverable enough to come alongside for a possible rescue. Howell swung the *Alaska Invader* north, then radioed a sister vessel, the *Pacific Invader,* which he could see on the horizon. Together, they headed full speed for the location.

Hearing that the Coast Guard Comstay had received his relayed message and that the *Alaska Invader* and *Pacific Invader* were on the way, the captain of the *Neptune Jade* circled one last time, still finding nothing in the water. Then he made a decision that could later be open to question. After reporting once again the position of the hull and that it appeared to be drifting slowly south-southwest, he resumed his route to the Orient, leaving the overturned hull behind. He had been on the scene for just over thirty minutes.

About forty-five minutes later the merchant vessel *Ocean Brother,* en route to Japan, called the Coast Guard Communication Station in Honolulu. It, too, reported an overturned hull: *latitude 54 degrees 17 minutes north, longitude 166 degrees 58 minutes west.* That position was about 3.5 nautical miles southwest of the first sighting. It would have been unlikely for a large hull to have drifted that far in forty-five minutes, but not impossible. The variables would include the current, the direction and velocity of the wind, how much of the vessel was riding out of the water. The latest sighting was relayed to Kodiak Comstay, which sent the message along simultaneously to the U.S. Coast Guard Air Station just down the road on Kodiak Island and to the Coast Guard North Pacific Search and Rescue Coordinator in Juneau.

At 3:45 P.M., almost two hours after the first reported sighting by the *Neptune Jade,* the Coast Guard rescue coordinator in Juneau transmitted an urgent priority call on the marine weather-advisory station:

A fishing vessel has been reported overturned in position 54-19.6 N, 166-54 W. Vessel description: eighty feet, with blue hull, red below waterline. The vessel Neptune Jade *is on scene. It is unknown the name of the fishing vessel or persons on board. Vessels with any additional information and any vessels in vicinity are requested to keep a sharp lookout, assist if possible, and advise Coast Guard Juneau or the nearest Coast Guard station.*

This report was one of several mistakes the Coast Guard made that morning. The first was not verifying the initial position that had been relayed from the *Neptune Jade* to a vessel six hundred miles away. The second was not considering the more-than-3.5-mile discrepancy between the two sightings forty-five minutes apart. The third was in transmitting a priority call giving the position of the first sighting, not the latest, by the *Ocean Brother,* which still had the hull in sight. Finally, no consideration was given to the possibility that the sightings might be of two separate hulls. Meanwhile, the *Ocean Brother* circled about half a mile from the overturned vessel and, finding no survivors or bodies, resumed its course eastward. Contrary to the Coast Guard advisory, there were now no vessels tracking the overturned hull.

There were also no Coast Guard cutters within five hundred miles of the position. Around 4:00 P.M., the Coast Guard launched a C-130 four-engine search plane from Kodiak. Flying west into the approaching darkness, the propeller-driven C-130 Hercules was designed for stability in foul weather, not speed. It would take the plane nearly three hours to reach the latest location given for the overturned hull.

At 6:00 P.M. on the same day, the crews of the *Alyeska* and *Alliance* had just finished transferring fuel to the *Sea Alaska* processor and had loaded all but the last few pots. Brian Melvin and Glenn Treadwell were standing together in the wheelhouse of the *Alliance* drinking coffee when suddenly the Coast Guard's "Urgent Marine Information Broadcast" interrupted the normal hourly weather report over the radio receiver.

The word around the dock was that the hull in question was probably one that had burned a week before out near Akutan Island, seventy-five miles to the northeast. There had been several sightings, and the charred hull had been reported drifting south-southwest toward Unalaska Island, the home of Dutch Harbor. Melvin and Treadwell reminded themselves of this and noted that the bulletin they had just heard reported the overturned hull to be about eighty feet—much smaller than any of the A-boats.

Around 7:00 P.M. Gary Howell checked in with the Coast Guard over the radio. The *Alaska Invader* had reached the Coast Guard's reported position of the overturned hull and found nothing in the dark. Two three-hundred-foot Soviet fish-processing vessels, the *Svetlaya* and the *Turkul,* were about thirty miles north of Dutch Harbor when they overheard Howell's radio call. Both Soviet ships headed for the reported position of the wreckage.

At 8:00 P.M. Melvin gave orders for the *Alyeska* to cast off from Dutch Harbor. Treadwell cast off ten minutes behind him. When the *Alliance* cleared Priest Rock and made the turn north, Treadwell called Melvin on the radio. They agreed, as a matter of professional seamanship, to alter their courses slightly to the north-northwest and run near the position the Coast Guard had given for the overturned hull.

The *Svetlaya* arrived at the given coordinates around 8:30 P.M. and the *Turkul* about ninety minutes later. Both Russian ships began circling, probing the dark with their searchlights, but they reflected only chromium-colored foam off empty waves.

The *Alyeska* and *Alliance* arrived at the position nearly two hours later and sighted the two Russian vessels—huge, government-backed, highly efficient floating factories despised by most of the American fleet. Without contacting them, Treadwell and Melvin decided to run north-northwest on parallel courses, five miles apart, relying on their radar to do the searching. For two hours, in worsening weather, they combed the sea; between the two boats they covered approximately twenty square miles. Still, they found nothing. They called the *Sea Alaska* dock in Dutch Harbor to report that they were resuming their courses to the Pribilofs before the storm overtook them, in order to keep their rendezvous with the *Americus* and *Altair*.

Loni Sullivan, the acting chief of police in Dutch Harbor, heard the urgent Coast Guard broadcast at home Monday night. Despite the port's strategic and economic importance to the entire North Pacific, the Coast Guard budget did not allow for a permanent presence. So Sullivan acted in loco parentis. He called the Coast Guard Rescue Coordination Center in Juneau. Since the position of the overturned hull was reported as only twenty-five miles from Dutch Harbor, he would organize a rescue operation, just in case this was not the same vessel that had burned near Akutan Island. If it was yet another capsized vessel, the crew could possibly be trapped inside, perhaps sustained by an air pocket. More than once, survivors had been pulled from overturned vessels hours after they'd capsized.

Sullivan spotted the hundred-foot crabber *Golden Pisces* still at its dock. Buster McNabb, the owner and an old friend of Sullivan's, agreed to lend his red-hulled boat for a rescue operation and set about gathering his crew. In the meantime, Sullivan called Bill Evans, a commercial diver. If this was a newly capsized boat, Sullivan would send the diver under the hull to rap on the wheelhouse where survivors were most likely to be trapped. If there was a reply, they'd use an oxyacetylene torch to cut an escape hole in the hull. If not, they'd cut a hole to retrieve what bodies they could.

At 4:25 A.M. on Tuesday, February 15, the processor *Svetlaya,* still searching for victims, nearly collided with the overturned hull. The captain conferred on the radio with the captain of the *Turkul,* and it was agreed that the *Svetlaya* would lay alongside while the *Turkul* kept circling, looking for survivors. One of the *Turkul*'s crew thought he glimpsed a body. But he lost sight of it.

Four hours later, at 8:25 A.M., Loni Sullivan and Buster Mc-Nabb on the *Golden Pisces* reached the location radioed by the *Svetlaya.* The Coast Guard C-130 four-engine search plane that had been dispatched from Kodiak flew overhead. The wind was picking up out of the northeast. The seas were showing frothy peaks.

The new location was marked: *latitude 54 degrees 17 minutes north, longitude 167 degrees 22 minutes west.* The hull was now drifting west-northwest, just a few miles from the position the *Ocean Brother* had given.

The *Golden Pisces* circled, and as it did, Buster McNabb stared in disbelief at the hull. It looked much longer than eighty feet. It had new rubber bumpers. The hull was blue with a red boot stripe. There was a crab-pot float drifting nearby, and it bore the Alaska Department of Fish and Game registration No. 33598. He seized the radio and gave the numbers. "Call Fish and Game, and ID the boat they come from."

The wind had picked up velocity out of the north-northeast. The waves were consistently reaching twelve to fifteen feet now and pummeling the hull. One of the divers volunteered to go over the side, but both Sullivan and McNabb said it was too dangerous. Half an hour went by. They could only keep circling, watching help-lessly while the seas continued to build.

"Suddenly, it just started getting rougher and rougher. People were laying in the wheelhouse puking," recalled Steve Beard, a deckhand making his first voyage on the *Golden Pisces.* "I remember seeing the hull and then you didn't because the swells were so high.''

The men watched as one large wave rose higher than the others and slammed into the hull, dumping hundreds of tons of water on the stern and causing it to drop under the impact. The bow rose above the water, and as it did, McNabb saw an American flag flashing across the side. There was only one boat with that distinctive insignia. Loni Sullivan recognized it too. They radioed the terminal in Dutch Harbor to relay what they had seen.

Ten hours after Brian Melvin had abandoned his search for the overturned vessel, he was halfway to the Pribilofs, relaxing in the wheelhouse of the *Alyeska,* drinking coffee, listening to radio chatter among boats just to pass the time. Every boat had a time to check in with the cannery shift foreman in Dutch Harbor to exchange and update information. Melvin's schedule called for him to check in at noon, in two more hours. But as he listened, the familiar voice of Chuck Beach, the superintendent of the *Sea Alaska* processor, broke in over the radio: "Which one of the A-boats is out?" he asked.

"They are all out," Melvin heard another voice answer, one he didn't recognize. Maybe it was a skipper of one of the boats back in Dutch Harbor. He felt a rush in his guts.

Beach came back on the radio: "There's a hull upside down, and it could be one of theirs."

Melvin punched the button on the radio microphone. "This is the *Alyeska,*" he said, his throat dry.

Beach relayed what he had been told: The vessel had new rubber bumpers, a blue hull, a red stripe, a flamboyant American flag emblem on the bow. Another boat standing by had said the hull was definitely longer than eighty feet.

"Jesus Christ, George," Melvin said out loud to himself. "The fucking *Americus*?"

Melvin felt suddenly weak. He tried to imagine what it would be like—the water rushing in through the hatches and vents, the blackness, the cold.

He could not let himself believe this. He tried to raise both the *Americus* and the *Altair* on the sideband. Neither George nor Ron came back over the radio.

He called Chuck Beach again on the radio and double-checked the position. Then he called Treadwell. The *Alliance* was running an hour behind. The vessels were now more than one hundred miles from the position. The two captains conferred while looking at their charts, searching for shallow water back in the direction of Dutch Harbor where they could drop thirty pots, each lightening their loads by ten tons. Once they informed their crews, Melvin and Treadwell headed their vessels back the way they had come, dropped their pots, and ran full-speed toward what a voice over the radio had described as the capsized *Americus*.

"I just had this piss-poor feeling," Melvin recalled. "We dropped pots to clear the decks and because I didn't know what was going on. We might be sitting on a time bomb ourselves."

More than reflex prompted Melvin's reaction. As far as he could tell, his vessel, the *Alyeska,* was loaded and trimmed more or less exactly as both the *Americus* and *Altair*. He had unloaded the same amount of fuel. He had even flooded all four crab tanks as Ron Beirnes had. But the voice on the radio advised that George Nations and the *Americus* were down. Where was the *Altair*? Melvin's own survival impulse, bordering on panic, overrode any disbelief that this could be happening.

Brian Melvin knew he had to collect himself. He estimated that he and Treadwell were at least a half day's sail from the emergency site. Because the *Alyeska* had a top-end speed of twelve knots, two knots faster than the *Alliance,* Melvin calculated that his vessel would arrive at least two hours ahead.

The next time he asked for the hull's position, another radio voice he did not recognize told him that the hull was no longer afloat. Still, he headed the *Alyeska* full speed for the last reported location. Later in the night he heard a garbled radio message that a Russian vessel had reported spotting a body floating near the position of the overturned vessel. Melvin stared out into the darkness. Then he got on the vessel's intercom, called the crew into the wheelhouse, and solemnly told them what they would be looking for: possible survivors, but bodies more likely.

The Coast Guard C-130 is capable of staying aloft for twelve hours, although constant banking and turning sucks fuel and shortens time in the sky to approximately eight hours. There are human limitations too. Tests show that mental fatigue sets in within two hours, especially in bad weather at night or in open water, where there is no visual variance to relieve an observer's eyes.

Coast Guard Lieutenant Larry Hazel guided his C-130 over Unalaska Island and Dutch Harbor at approximately 10:30 P.M. on February 15. From there he took a heading of 50 degrees, bearing to the northwest, a thousand feet over the water. Normally the C-130 would carry a crew of seven: a pilot, a copilot, a radioman, and four crew members, two on each side of the aircraft, who relieved each other every hour. But on this night there was a personnel shortage. This aircraft was the second to be dispatched to search for the overturned hull, and they were allowed only two crewmen on watch for the entire eight hours. Worse, the weather was working against them. Out of the blackness, snowflakes exploded only a few feet from the windshield in a mesmerizing blizzard that made it difficult, at best, to see.

To compensate for poor visibility and a crew shortage, Hazel set up for a relatively narrow ladder pattern, the standard grid search technique the Coast Guard uses to comb the sea with either aircraft or vessels. He flew five miles in one direction, completed a slow 180-degree turn, and then picked up the pattern in the opposite direction. The grid covered about 250 square miles. The technique is said to be ninety percent effective; the remaining ten percent, however, could mean as much as twenty-five square miles.

The night Lieutenant Hazel flew the C-130 back and forth above the Bering Sea, the potential for intercepting a drifting, overturned hull or spotting a life raft would be far from ninety percent effective. The weather was worsening and the cloud ceiling dropping. He descended to under five hundred feet, low enough for the aircraft's belly searchlights to illuminate the waves, but only in small swaths. Their best chance, Hazel knew, was to pick up an emergency flare or a signal from the emergency position-indicating beacon. He called Kodiak and asked the communications station to contact Dutch Harbor to find out if the A-boats were carrying EPIRBs. Hazel knew merchant vessels were required by law to carry EPIRBs, but fishing boats were not.

"Affirmative," was the answer.

In any given year the Coast Guard Comstay picked up more than three hundred signals from EPIRBs, more than two-thirds of which proved false. Nonetheless, the C-130s were dispatched in response to nearly every signal, burning up thousands of gallons of fuel on unnecessary search-and-rescue missions. Still, no warbling signal from any locating device was received over the special rescue radio frequency that night. So the search was left up to the eyes of the aircraft's crew. And as the men scanned and the hours passed, their senses began turning against them.

"You find yourself daydreaming and slapping yourself in the face. You start talking to yourself," Coast Guard airman Pete Degalu, a veteran of hundreds of searches, told a reporter.

"I punched smoke* for the top of a Styrofoam cooler; thought it was a life raft," said airman Dave Braum, one of two men on watch that night. "After a while everything you see looks like a life raft."

"I saw a couple of pieces of Styrofoam, seaweed, various small chunks of wood—punched out smoke on everything I saw. Mostly

---

* Smoke flares are launched to mark and illuminate objects for closer search and possible rescues.

there was nothing to see, just water, clouds, snow, rain," crew mate Monte Barnett would add.

The false sightings became more frequent. Each time Hazel circled, spiraling lower, yet each circle disclosed nothing. After nearly eight hours in the air Hazel turned the C-130 back before light, even as another Coast Guard search aircraft was en route from Kodiak.

Loni Sullivan finally radioed his decision to abort the dive for survivors back to Dutch Harbor five hours after they arrived at the overturned hull. He and the crew then turned their attention to searching for life rafts or crew members who might have made it into survival suits. After six more hours of searching, they turned for home, eleven hours after they'd arrived. Close enough for one final glance, the crew of the *Golden Pisces* noted that the hull seemed to be settling lower in the water.

Brian Melvin and the crew of the *Alyeska* arrived at approximately 10:15 P.M. on February 15, the same time as the advancing edge of the storm. "All our eyes were out there," Melvin said. "We turned on a track going very slowly with the whole crew in the pilothouse. Our quartz vapor lights were going, but it was still real dark. The waves made things dark. There was nothing out there. Our radar wasn't picking up a thing. We changed course for another position."

It was now 11:45 P.M., nearly thirty-six hours after the freighter *Neptune Jade* had first sighted the capsized hull and abandoned it. Treadwell and the *Alliance* crew were at least three hours behind.

"I was in a chair on the starboard side of the wheelhouse, at the chart table, plotting another course to run west," Melvin recalled. Wieslaw Krawczyk, a former Polish seaman nicknamed "V," was standing by him, handling the wheel. "V spotted it first," Melvin recalled. "All of a sudden he hollers, 'Shit! There it is!' It was looming right in front of us. It looked like a huge rock, low in the water, too low to pick up on the radar. But there it was. We were on a collision course!"

As the *Alyeska* tacked, Melvin remembered, an indelible image appeared, illuminated by his mast lights and as familiar as his own house.

"You could see the copper bottom paint. It was there, plain as day. A swell went down and you could see the flag on the bow. You could see. It was definitely the *Americus*.

"I felt sick. The hull was floating. There was enough air left in it to float. The weather was too bad to get somebody over. The wind was blowing probably thirty to thirty-five knots. There were guys on my boat who would have gone over if I'd asked them to. Those guys on the *Americus* were their friends too. But I was responsible. I was in shock. It was real quiet except for the wind in the rigging and the waves. I'm just there looking, not going very far, feeling totally helpless. Then I called Glenn and told him. I told him I would hold by the hull until I saw his lights on the horizon. When we saw his lights we would start circling, looking for survivors. And then I called the Coast Guard and told them it was the *Americus*.

"I had been calling the *Altair,* trying to raise them. I thought they must have no idea. But there was no answer back," Melvin said, remembering the feeling of panic approaching. He called Hendricks at home in Anacortes and relayed what he knew, trying hard to disguise his fear.

Treadwell, too, recalled feeling only panic and the frustration of running too slowly, even though he was being pushed by a sea trailing from the north. "I felt so far away, like we'd never get there. Hell, I felt far away from everything at that time."

The *Alliance* rendezvoused with the *Alyeska* at approximately 2:30 A.M. on February 16, four hours after Melvin had arrived. Glenn Treadwell brought his vessel alongside the hull. Staying close, he began to circle while Melvin guided the *Alyeska* into lengthening grids, running east then west in five-mile stretches, searching for survivors. After an hour the *Alliance* joined the search, and together the two boats ran in parallel grids, plotting courses the wind, tide, and currents might have taken a life raft or survival suit. They had covered an area approximately thirty-five miles wide by twenty miles long by the time the Coast Guard cutter *Sherman* arrived at approximately 6:30 A.M. Melvin described over the radio the search the two fishing vessels had made.

At first light the *Sherman* launched a helicopter to search the north side of Unalaska Island, west of Cape Cheerful, following a course southwesterly for nearly a hundred miles along the north side of neighboring Umnak Island. No sightings were reported, and it returned late in the morning. Meanwhile, two C-130s and an additional helicopter churned overhead, flying parallel grids, to no avail. The Coast Guard icebreaker *Polar Sea* was en route with divers aboard. A P-3 Orion subchaser aircraft with high-tech radar dispatched from the Naval Air Station in Adak spotted no rafts or bodies. Several other helicopters also circled the overturned hull. Melvin guessed right that they held television camera crews.

"After four or five hours of doing this I had a real sick feeling," Melvin said. "I don't even know how I can describe it, what I was feeling. Larry, Brent, Paul were on that boat. George was a friend, a mentor. It was just sickening. I still had hope for them though. They were tough guys, fighters. Somehow I believed we were going to pick up a raft." Meanwhile, he had tried repeatedly to alert Ron Beirnes on the *Altair* but had made no contact.

At approximately 11:30 A.M., Melvin received a call from Treadwell: "Get back to the hull quick!" The *Alyeska* arrived within thirty minutes; Melvin throttled down alongside the *Alliance*. The crews of both boats lined the decks in silence as they watched the stern of the hull sink. Again, as it did, the bow rose, revealing the emblem of the American flag and the vessel's name: *Americus*. Then the Bering Sea engulfed the hull like a tide across a tiny spit of sand. In less than two minutes it was gone, silently. The charts indicated the location to be 54 degrees 24.5 minutes north latitude, 168 degrees 21.8 minutes west longitude. There the sea is more than 4,200 feet deep.

Minutes later, as the crews of the *Alyeska* and *Alliance* continued to watch in silence, two life rings and an inflated, six-person life raft, empty, popped to the surface. Melvin got back on the radio and reached the Coast Guard cutter directing the search operation. The cutter had tried to reach the *Altair* too. Still no contact.

"Maybe Ron is already up in the Pribilofs on a fantastic load of crab," Melvin told his crew, trying to read their faces and determine their fear.

The Coast Guard Comstay had been trying for hours with its most powerful transmitter to reach Beirnes too. Around 2:00 P.M. the Kodiak station contacted the *Alyeska* on the radio and advised Melvin that they were now including the *Altair* in their search for survivors as well. Melvin, in turn, called Anacortes and advised Jeff Hendricks.

"We got a new forecast. It was a storm warning," Melvin said. "We were only three hours out of Dutch Harbor; we could have gone back in. But we decided to keep searching. Finally, Glenn and I decided to run up to the Pribilofs. We were still trying to raise Ron on the radio, to let him know what was going on."

To this day Melvin cannot recall when he arrived at the point of no hope. Neither can Treadwell. But they both agreed that on the afternoon of February 16, the *Alyeska* and *Alliance* would push on together toward the Pribilofs. Whether it was for a rendezvous with the *Altair* or a rescue mission was now hardly debatable.

A few hours under way, Treadwell was resting in his berth on the *Alliance* when his relief skipper stopped the vessel. A crew member thought he smelled diesel fuel on the water. They shut down the engine, drifting, listening in the dark for a slap on the water or a call for help. They waited, hearing nothing but the sound of the sea and the wind.

An hour later they were moving again when a deckhand spotted a coil of yellow polypropylene rope. They threw the gaff and brought it in. It was new and in good condition, typical of the equipment found on any of the A-boats' decks. But it revealed nothing. The resin-coated rope was used by most crab boats as line for pots, and on any normal day it was not uncommon to come across dozens of coils, part of the trifles discarded by choice or accident around the crabbing grounds.

"We headed northwest sixty to seventy degrees and we started making ice," Melvin recalled. "It was downright shitty out, black. The storm hit and caught us out in the middle. The winds were blowing eighty–ninety miles per hour. The temperature dropped to twenty degrees below zero. The toilets froze, water froze everywhere in the boat. We were already two full nights without sleep. Before we got to the Pribilofs I laid down. Larry Lefave was on watch. When I got back to the wheelhouse, Larry had all the survival suits laid out. The guys were real concerned."

The lines between panic and precaution were suddenly converging. Melvin knew it was up to him to sort them back out.

The two old friends stood facing each other silently, their eyes wide and locked. Melvin saw that Lefave could no longer contain his fear and that he, as captain, had to summon all his reserves to keep his own fear in check. Melvin swallowed hard. They wouldn't need the suits, he said stiffly, as long as they kept their heads straight. He ordered them put away. Lefave started to rebut him. When Melvin moved forward, Lefave backed off. He would tell the others that the suits were being put away—for now.

Melvin retreated into the wheelhouse alone. He could see the heavy ice on both boats, and he could feel it building on the *Alyeska*. She felt tired. Melvin ordered the speed reduced to cut down on the freezing sea spray cresting the bow, but the maneuver had no effect. Whipped by the wind, foamy combs from cresting waves transformed into ice crystals the moment they cleared the railings and exploded like breaking glass onto the decks. He considered dumping more crab pots and running downwind with the storm instead of bucking into the waves that were spraying ice on his boat, but they were closing on St. George Island, the southern extreme of the Pribilofs. To turn now would mean running away from possible protection. He could feel the *Alyeska* begin to roll lazily, uncertain of herself, the rudder growing sluggish. He made a mental note of how long it would take to break the survival suits out again.

Melvin lost track of how many hours he had been running into the storm. There was no reprieve, only the sensation of rising up wave after wave, followed by a plunge and a crash of freezing spray. "By the time we ducked in under the Pribilofs, we were in an ice fog," he remembered. "It was coming right up off the water. When we anchored, we were completely closed in. You couldn't see a thing." Bering Sea mariners fear this condition the most, when extreme cold and extremely dense moist air combine to form a slushy shroud that adheres to any surface and envelops anything in its path.

The crew was exhausted, but still Melvin established deck watches, rotating the men hourly, arming them with baseball bats and sledgehammers to knock ice from the life rafts, aerial wires, scuppers, railings, the deck, and the wheelhouse itself. If the hatch doors sealed over, the whole crew would be entombed. He checked with Treadwell, making certain neither of them had overlooked a single precaution—and to reassure each other that they would survive the storm.

Every hour Melvin called the *Altair* on the radio, but heard nothing from the void beyond his own wheelhouse. He sat alone, staring at the glowing green radar screen. He drank coffee nonstop and felt wracked with fear and exhaustion. His mind fought to stave off the conclusion he sensed was drawing near.

What if both boats had capsized? It could have happened only in the middle of the night, Melvin figured. The guys would have been thrown from their bunks into water so cold it would knock the breath out of them. Their world would suddenly be turned upside down. Their escape route would be the reverse of what they knew. The handles to their stateroom doors would not be where they had been. The stairs that led from their staterooms up to the wheelhouse, where Ron and George had stored the survival suits, would now lead down into the water. To escape, then, they would have had to jettison normal survival instincts. They would have had to plunge downward, away from light and air, to get to the escape hatches. It would be like heading straight for hell. Melvin's thoughts were making him crazy.

What if they had been trapped inside the hull? How long could they have lasted? Were the guys on the *Americus* still alive by the time he had gotten there on *Alyeska*? His own crew had volunteered to go over the side. And he'd held them back. With those waves and near-freezing water, it would have been suicide.

But what if someone was still alive? Brad, his brother, and the other guys on the *Altair*? Melvin got on the radio and called Jeff Hendricks again in Anacortes and, in despair, told him everything he knew, everything he didn't know, and everything he feared.

CHAPTER 6

J EFF HENDRICKS'S FIRST INSTINCT WAS TO GET TO THE AIRPORT AND
fly his own plane north to Dutch Harbor. He was a qualified diver.
Those were his people out there. But he also had responsibilities for
the families of his crew in Anacortes.

He fought for self-control as he dialed the Coast Guard on the
sideband radio he kept at home. What did they know? Did they have
planes in the air? Did they have divers? Had no other vessel heard
from the *Altair*? How much trouble were Brian and Glenn in too?
How long would it take him to reach Dutch Harbor? Was it better to
stay? What could he tell the families? What should he tell them? The
thought of breaking such terrible news paralyzed him.

Finally, Hendricks decided to call Doug Knutson, Ron Beirnes's
son-in-law. Knutson was one of Hendricks's veteran captains and,
ironically, would have been skipper of the *Alyeska* on this trip; he'd

been her captain for almost six years. Instead, Hendricks had persuaded Knutson to stay behind in Anacortes to oversee the building of the fleet's newest vessel, the *Arcturas*, which Knutson would later command. Feeling a loyalty to his crew on the *Alyeska*, Knutson had originally balked at the idea, but he also felt he should step aside for Brian Melvin, his friend and football teammate. The two had sailed together since graduating from high school. Knutson regarded Melvin as a superb fisherman and seaman and felt he deserved the chance to run his own boat. So he relinquished command of the *Alyeska* to him.

Now Hendricks, still reeling, relayed the news that the *Americus* was down and the *Altair* was missing. Brian Melvin and Glenn Treadwell and their crews might be in big trouble too. He asked Knutson to help him begin the long list of phone calls to the families of the *Americus*'s crew.

Francis Barcott was aboard his boat, long-lining for cod on Puget Sound's Olympic Peninsula, when the news came over the radio in the wheelhouse the afternoon of the sixteenth. It was spreading from boat to boat like a squall across the water: an Anacortes boat had capsized in the Bering Sea. Another was missing. Each carried a crew of seven. The entire crew, all fourteen, from Anacortes.

"One boat down, the other they can't find? The other is down too," he told his crew. Among them was Vern Beirnes, Ron's brother. Francis Barcott had watched the boats pass directly in front of his house less than two weeks earlier on the way from Anacortes to Dutch Harbor. He had recognized most of the crew, some of whom he had trained and recommended for jobs on the A-boats. He knew their families. "All those kids, good hard workers. What were they doing out there? Experimenting? It takes a lifetime to learn fishing. You learn little by little. You don't try to get away with murder."

———

Judy Littlefield remembered that it was 5:05 P.M. when Jeff Hendricks called. "You don't forget the second the world stops," she said. Her husband, Al, had been in the backyard with a local doctor showing off his Labrador retriever, a natural-born hunter, renowned for siring "birdy" offspring. They called George Boles, the postman, who had just gotten off the phone with Hendricks himself, and went to his house for what little consolation they could offer.

Just blocks away, Lloyd and Jean Bass, Victor Bass's parents, sat in their living room, he on a rocker, she on a sofa. They had closed the drapes after getting the call from Hendricks. Lloyd remembered the moment: "Jeff said, 'I think I have some bad news. I don't know for sure, but we think one of the boats is down. We can't get hold of the other.' "

Lloyd Bass recalled being terrified at the sound of his own question: "Which boat is down?"

"The *Americus*," Hendricks said hoarsely. Vic's boat.

"We just sat there, waiting and waiting," he continued, trying in vain years later to describe what it was like, to sit, staring at the telephone, waiting for it to ring, terrified that it would.

Reverend Hilary Bitz remembered getting the call from Jean Bass, Vic Bass's stepmother and a member of his Lutheran congregation. "It was around six P.M. and I was preparing for a seven P.M. Lenten service. In fact, this was Ash Wednesday. Jean called and told me what she had heard. It had almost Biblical proportions. She asked me to pray, to beseech the Almighty in any way I could. Not everyone had heard, of course, and an hour later I had to break the news to the congregation." Within a week he would lead three public prayer services for thousands of townsfolk. And privately, he says, even now he struggles with the concept of a God because of what had happened.

Early that evening the news came in like a draft under the door of the high-school gymnasium, where fans had packed the stands to watch the Seahawks basketball team take on archrival Bellingham.

When it reached the bleachers, each row stirred in succession, bending like grass. Certain people among the stands were being sought out and there was clearly nothing random about their selection. When the word found them, they stood, stunned, their faces frozen, and led each other through the crowd. Outside, relatives waited in cars, trying to conceal their terror.

Eve Northcutt had just flown home from Puerto Vallarta, from the trip her five kids had given their widowed mother for Christmas. "When I walked in, the kids were all there. I thought that was an amazing homecoming because it was about eleven o'clock at night. I said, 'It's too bad Paul's up fishing, because then you all would be here.' " Barry, her oldest son and a former Army medic who had served in Vietnam, embraced her as he broke the news. The words detonated in Eve Northcutt's ear. "I screamed and ran out of the house."

As the news spread, the *Altair* crew families, lacking concrete evidence that the vessel had vanished, held out hope in the face of the unknown. The *Americus* families, however, suffered with all the immediacy that technology could bring. Within hours after the *Americus* was identified, television crews from Anchorage and Seattle were en route to the Bering Sea. The image of the foundering Anacortes boat was broadcast on national television.

"It seemed like every fifteen minutes they'd break in with the news, with the shots of the boat," Lloyd Bass would recall. "It was like looking at a grave."

"You couldn't get away from it," recalled George Boles, Brent's father. Yet all he could do was sit with his wife, Frances, and stare numbly at the screen. "This is the fishing vessel *Americus*," they heard the leaden-voiced commentators say countless times before finally turning off the sound.

"It was so awful because you could only see the bottom and you knew those kids were still probably in there. . . . The TV reports said they figured they'd send in divers, but the seas were too high.

We could sit there and watch the seas . . . and the boat," he recalled.

Down the hill and across town, Bud and Lois Awes stared at the television screen too. Weeks before, the whole family—daughters, sons, and grandkids—had gathered in the living room to toast Richie Awes and wish him good luck on his first voyage north. "I remember going downtown and watching the boat my son ended up on being built and thinking, My God, there is no way those boats could sink . . . " Bud Awes remembered. "Those kids would be going up to Alaska and coming home all smiles and change jangling in their pockets. When Richie said he'd gotten a job on one of the boats, we still naturally had second thoughts. But he insisted how lucky he was. He was really excited to go."

Watching the overturned *Americus* on their TV, Bud Awes thought the hull seemed to be riding lower in the Bering Sea with each new broadcast.

A few blocks away, Al Littlefield, Larry's father, felt the same agony every time the images flashed across the TV screen. "It was worse than being shot over and over. There was the red bottom floating upside down. . . . I knew every one of those kids on that boat . . . their parents . . . I would just sit there watching Larry's boat floating, my only son. . . . I couldn't even talk."

The next day, Thursday, February 17, nearly three thousand people converged on the field down by the Cap Sante marina near the memorial for Anacortes's lost fishermen.

The opening words of Norm Young, the acting mayor, reminded everyone gathered that this was a prayer vigil, not yet a memorial: "I light this candle with the fervent hope that it will serve as a beacon to guide your young men home," he shouted above the wind.

During the candlelight vigil that followed, no one mentioned the word *loss*. *Missing* was the operative word at that hour. No bodies had been sighted, after all. But the faces of those gathered in the field conveyed that this was not a vigil of hope, but of neighbors knotted together in hopelessness and pain.

Early on Saturday, February 19, Glenn Treadwell and Brian Melvin, exhausted, maneuvered their vessels past Priest Rock and once again into Dutch Harbor. Two Coast Guard officers met them at the dock. They were sorry about the loss of the *Americus,* they said, and assured the two skippers the Coast Guard was doing everything it could to locate survivors and to make contact with the *Altair.* Still, they wanted to ask them some questions.

Had they watched the *Altair* and *Americus* being loaded? Had they watched the vessels leave Dutch Harbor? Did they notice anything about the way they rode in the water? What about the *Alyeska*? Had Brian loaded his vessel differently than Nations and Beirnes had loaded the *Americus* and *Altair*? How much fuel was he carrying? How much were the *Americus* and *Altair* carrying?

Treadwell answered guardedly, but his thoughts were still reeling with contradictions. "They must have gotten caught in a huge trough," Treadwell remembered thinking at the time. "But those boats could have taken a seventy-degree list and still rolled back. It had to be something else. Sure, it could have been the way they were loaded. Hell, it was overwhelming how much stuff they had stacked on board. But what was I supposed to do, tell them how to load their gear? Besides, Brian had loaded more or less the same way."

The officers pressed further. Had they seen no debris? Heard no distress signal on a separate radio frequency the Hendricks company might have set up between vessels? Had anyone been to the Elbow Room before leaving?

They wanted too many details. Melvin and Treadwell were drained, devastated; this was an unnecessary grilling. Melvin told the investigators he was through answering questions. He was speaking for both skippers.

On the plane home that afternoon, Glenn Treadwell downed

vodkas laced with orange juice as grief and anger washed over him.
He was still seething at the Coast Guard interrogation at the dock.
Every few minutes he dissolved in tears, then became angry again,
especially at his best friend, Nations. "If he wanted to take chances,
if he wanted to go the way he did, why, for Christ sakes, did he
have to drag his son along too?" he remembered thinking. He
thought about Jan Nations and her remaining son and daughter.
What was he to say to her? That he should have double-checked
George's calculations? Asked where the fuel was coming from?
Why they had to carry so many pots? Why he was cross-tanking?
That George was to blame?

That night Evelyn met him at the Seattle–Tacoma airport, and
they drove north back to Anacortes in silence. They stayed up late,
watching the tapes of the news broadcasts on the VCR. Treadwell
drank beer as he watched the *Americus* foundering, and choked on
his tears. The TV reporters and anchors, speculating wildly about
what had caused the accident, infuriated him, but he told Evelyn
what unsettled him most—that he figured he and Brian had possibly
come within a mile of the *Americus* the first time they searched,
before they turned north toward the Pribilofs.

"You can't blame yourself," Evelyn assured him. But Glenn
could not be consoled.

The next morning Jan Nations came by with Kristin, her four-
year-old daughter. Glenn rose, still exhausted from a fitful sleep,
and hugged them both. Jan pulled him aside, looking hard at her
husband's friend. "What happened? I want to know. I want to hear
it first from you," she said.

Treadwell looked away and said he didn't know.

She looked at him imploringly. Treadwell had seen that look
before, when Jan had burst into a tavern to retrieve her husband,
pleading with Treadwell to get Nations home. He had seen the look
when she begged him to persuade George to stop verbally abusing
their son Jeff. Now Jan was asking for much more than Treadwell
had in him to give. She was asking for his version of the truth.

He repeated what he said. He didn't know. And he saw disbelief in Jan's eyes.

Just then the phone rang. It was Jeff Hendricks, wanting to know if Treadwell was all right. He also wanted him to know that newspaper reporters were swarming all over Anacortes.

Jan had already found them at her front door the day the word came back from Dutch Harbor. One of the stories had described the Nationses' house in palatial terms, comparing it to a tiny bungalow one of George's crew members had been renting. She had been in her sister Nancy's house later when a television crew bullied its way inside and trained the cameras on the families, asking questions intended to force tears before a viewing audience. She told Glenn and Evelyn that she and Nancy would have nothing more to do with the press after that.

Janice's questions and the threat of the press were simply too much for Treadwell. He turned to his wife and urged her to pack some things. Within thirty minutes they were in the car and heading to the highway, trying to get as far away from town as they could. Treadwell couldn't talk to any reporters. He didn't want to talk to anyone until he sorted things out, including what he would say and to whom. But just before they reached the freeway, Treadwell pulled over. He looked at Evelyn and could see his own pain reflected in her face. "What the hell," he said. "I didn't do anything wrong. I'm not guilty of anything. I am not guilty."

He turned the car around.

After they'd reached the *Americus* families, Jeff Hendricks and Doug Knutson began calling the families of the *Altair* too. The Coast Guard still had not heard from Ron Beirnes, and Hendricks knew anyone with ties to the *Altair* would be fearing the worst. He wanted to offer what hope he could.

They reached Jody Gudbranson at her mother's house. "They were telling me that the *Americus* had been found capsized. I remember asking right away, 'What about the *Altair*?' And they said something like they couldn't get hold of Ron but not to worry, nothing ever happens to him and that he almost always had his radio off when he fished. I don't know what I was feeling. I was feeling scared for the guys on the *Americus*. I remember that. But I don't remember exactly what I was feeling with what I had been told about the *Altair*. It was something, though, and I couldn't make myself calm.''

With the sideband radio Ron had installed, Nancy Beirnes had been trying to reach her husband on the *Altair* from the moment her daughter Suzanne, Doug Knutson's wife, called to tell her the *Americus* was down. Almost always, Ron was there when Nancy called. Usually he called first, at a set time, around 6:00 P.M. For Ron Beirnes, family prevailed. So during those first days when the *Americus* was down, while the massive search for survivors continued, weather interference was cited as the probable cause for her husband's silence.

"Maybe Ron is onto a big load of crab and they're working nonstop," Knutson, her son-in-law, volunteered more than once. A solid, laconic man with iceberg-blue eyes, Knutson still could not be certain, more than a dozen years later, whether he had been outright lying to Nancy or simply rationalizing against what his experience and instincts had told him was the inescapable truth.

Nonetheless, Nancy Beirnes invited the families of the *Altair*'s crew to her home every evening for nearly a week, ostensibly for the radio call, hoping that they would hear that the weather had cleared or that Ron and the boys had pulled in that jackpot of crab. Nancy welcomed the company. Visitors required her to move, and movement, any movement at all, brought a reprieve from what was on her mind and the minds of those who came to her home. By moving she staved off the sense that she, too, was drowning. It was up to her to maintain her composure and to support the others—part of her responsibilities, she felt, as the captain's wife. When the doorbell rang, she appeared warm and natural, as if this were a dinner party thrown to break the monotony of another dull winter evening in the Pacific Northwest. She eased each neighbor into the living room of the two-story house she and Ron had just built, where others were already clustered in muted conversation.

Nancy knew nearly everyone who visited her home that week: Punky Harvey, a normally effervescent woman who worked at the Thrifty supermarket in town, was Randy's mother. Her other son, Rick, who had once dated Suzanne, had spent many evenings at the Beirneses' dinner table as well as many days at sea fishing with Ron. She and Ron were still fond of him. Wayne Melvin, Brian's father, dropped in regularly for the radio call, and when it yielded no answer, he was usually the first to leave. Jody Gudbranson came with her sister Kathy, who was married to Danny Knutson, Doug's younger brother, and a Hendricks crew member. Crystal Sadlowsky, Jody's mother, came too. Nancy had known her since high-school days. In this town it was impossible not to know someone your own age, and their kids too.

Facing Paul Northcutt's mother, Eve, however, was difficult. Her son Paul was not on the *Altair*. He was on the *Americus*. He was gone. Eve's presence offered circumstantial evidence of the worst fears circulating through Nancy's house.

By the end of the evening on Saturday, February 19, after another futile radio call, after Reverend Bitz said a prayer, the families drew closer in Nancy's living room.

"We all agreed, we couldn't sit like this," Crystal Sadlowsky remembered. "We talked to Doug Knutson and said we would be willing to pool our money to help look for the boys. I really didn't have any money to speak of then, but I told Doug I would contribute whatever I could to charter a plane or do whatever it took to find his father-in-law and my son-in-law."

Doug Knutson and Kevin Kirkpatrick were deputized to fly north to charter a private search plane, at the company's expense. Two days later, as they flew north from Seattle, the first official memorial service was held at Anacortes High School. The Reverend Gale O'Neill, pastor of the Anacortes First Baptist Church, dedicated the service to the family and crew of the lost *Americus*, with prayers added only for the safety of the missing *Altair* crew.

The two-engine Cessna writhed against the battering wind the morning of February 22. But the pilot, a former Coast Guard search-and-rescue aircraft operator, kept the throttle up and the nose pointing generally northwest. Occasionally, he would ease off, conceding, dropping westerly, the way the wind pushed the aircraft, the way the wind might have pushed a life raft, a survival suit, or a body.

Knutson and Kirkpatrick had chartered the Cessna in Anchorage the previous day, a day after the Coast Guard temporarily halted its own search due to bad weather. In Cold Bay, the former air base two hundred miles east of Dutch Harbor at the end of the Alaskan land bridge between the Aleutians and the mainland, they picked up Brian Melvin, who had stayed behind in Dutch Harbor to tend to the *Alyeska* and *Alliance,* and wanted to help in their search. Before boarding the Cessna, Knutson carefully questioned Melvin about the events surrounding the lost vessels: the trip north to Dutch Harbor, the loading of crab pots, the first run to the Pribilofs, and the return to Dutch Harbor on the thirteenth for more pots as their sister boats, the *Americus* and *Altair*, were getting ready to head out.

Was there anything unusual? This was the obvious question, and Knutson approached it from many angles. He wanted to know how the *Altair* and *Americus* had been trimmed. Melvin told him he was certain that Ron Beirnes had filled all four of the *Altair*'s crab tanks with water, as was his custom. As far as the *Americus* was concerned, Melvin didn't know for certain, but his own engineer, Steve Carr, had reported seeing two of its tanks, one fore and one aft, filled with seawater.

Now all three young Anacortes captains were staring out the windows of the chartered plane scanning the Bering Sea, looking hard where the currents created seams in the water. When the pilot dropped low, they focused on the places where the sea ran up on rocky beaches or small patches of terrain—barely enough to be called an island, but enough to snag a life raft or a body. They spotted the wreckage of the boat that had burned, the one Melvin had initially suspected to be the source of the Coast Guard bulletin. They spotted other hulks gone aground in years past. They spotted little else.

By the end of the second day they had tracked the Bering Sea's currents and prevailing winds far beyond the range of any drifting hull or life raft and had not found any evidence suggesting that the *Americus* and *Altair* and their Anacortes crews had ever sailed its waters.

That night the three captains stared silently into their drinks at the Flying Tigers, the tiny cafeteria and bar situated next to the airstrip in Cold Bay. For a long time no one wanted to say what was on his mind. Finally, someone did. Melvin doesn't remember who; neither does Knutson. It didn't matter.

"That's it."

Knutson called the charter office and canceled the flight for the next day. Kirkpatrick made reservations for their return flight to Seattle. "The hardest part was knowing that when we quit, that when we came home, my parents, friends, parents of our friends were going to know we had given up. They were going to know that if we had given up, there was nothing else to do," Melvin remembered.

"Okay," Melvin kept telling himself on the flight back to Seattle. "You did everything you could."

Still, his first words when he stepped into his father's house in Anacortes were "I'm sorry."

Painstakingly, he recounted everything he knew, sparing details of his own ordeal until his father asked. Was Brian certain his brother Brad and the rest of the crew of the *Altair* were gone for good? That's all Wayne Melvin really wanted to know.

"I'm certain," Brian heard himself say repeatedly until exhaustion caught up with him and he quit answering altogether.

Late that night Melvin met his best friend, Rick Harvey, at the Anchor Inn. Rick, too, had lost his own brother, Randy, who'd taken his place on the *Altair*. Together, they sat at the bar and spoke quietly. Rick had not asked for details, and Brian was relieved not to have to offer any. With their backs to the door, they drank beer and held their own private wake for their two brothers.

The next day, at Rick Harvey's urging, Melvin spoke to his neighbors and those who had either lost someone on the *Americus* or were still officially missing someone on the *Altair*. When asked how he was getting along and what he planned to do, he told them, "I'm going back up. I have to. It's what I do."

Meanwhile, Jeff Hendricks, acknowledging that the *Altair* was gone, faced another round of difficult telephone calls.

"Words are hard to come by," he repeated each time to a father, a mother, a brother, a sister, wife, girlfriend. "I'm trying to find words. I feel so helpless. . . . We don't know; we may never know."

The phone rang at Al Littlefield's. Al recognized Hendricks's voice immediately. "Al," he said, "they found no survivors."

Judy Littlefield took her husband by the arm and led him out of the house. They walked together silently, until they ran out of road, then turned around and walked some more. When they returned home Reverend Bitz was waiting on the porch. Al Littlefield embraced the pastor and then held his shoulders, looking directly at him. "Planes and boats can miss people," he said plaintively.

Later, long after Reverend Bitz had left, Al poured himself a nightcap. He sat alone, sipping his scotch, and then, looking north, said, "Larry, we're keeping you at your word. You told us you would survive."

The telephone rang at Jody Gudbranson's late on the evening of the twenty-fourth. Jeff Hendricks was sorry to be phoning so late. He apologized again and told her they were calling everything off. When Jody had composed herself somewhat, she called her sister, Maxine, and together they went to her mother's house. Through tears, all Jody could ask was, "Why did they lead me along? Why didn't anybody tell me how dangerous this was? Why did they say things would be fine?"

More than a week had passed since the overturned *Americus* had first been spotted, and only one incontrovertible fact remained: The Coast Guard, Navy, and even Hendricks's own skippers had searched a total of twenty-six thousand square miles of the Bering Sea and found no survivors of the two Anacortes boats. No matter who Jeff Hendricks spoke to—his boat designer, his boat builders, the insurance adjusters, reporters, his own family, the families of the victims, his surviving captains and crew, or his lawyers—the question they asked was the same: How could two of the most sophisticated boats in the entire fleet, with huge margins of safety built in, skippered by two men with nearly thirty years' combined fishing experience between them, disappear without even a call for help?

PART TWO

"We need to sit on the rim
of the well of darkness
and fish for fallen light
with patience."

—*Pablo Neruda*

CHAPTER 7

IN THE CONFERENCE ROOM OF THE THIRTEENTH COAST GUARD District headquarters at the top of the federal building in Seattle, Captain John De Carteret took his place at the table for the daily staff meeting. It was 8:30 A.M. on Thursday, February 17, and as usual, Admiral Howard Parker was presiding. De Carteret and Parker were both graduates with engineering degrees from the U.S. Coast Guard Academy in New London, Connecticut. They had been friends for years, having shared duty stations on both coasts. The Seattle assignment was considered a plum—high profile, and in a city renowned for its beauty and recreation—particularly for men who liked to sail, as both did, often together. For Parker, as a commanding officer nearing retirement, this would be a prime place to ease out of the service. For De Carteret it offered enough responsibility to keep his stock high back in Washington. At fifty-one, the chances for an admiral's stripe were growing slim but not beyond reach.

The order of business this morning, as usual, was to review all incidents that had occurred during the previous twenty-four hours; the district's territory covered approximately ninety-five thousand square miles of navigable U.S. waters between the California border and Canada. De Carteret, a tall, owlish-looking man with thick dark hair, opened the file folder and scanned the log. There had been three search-and-seizures of vessels suspected of running drugs from mother ships, something that was happening all too frequently. There had been two rescues at sea—one off the central Oregon coast and another a hundred miles farther north. A crewman with an apparent case of appendicitis had been airlifted from a merchant vessel off the northwest Washington coast and flown to a hospital in Port Angeles. An oil slick had been spotted off the bar at the mouth of the Columbia River, and a helicopter had been dispatched from Astoria to look for any vessel that might be leaking fuel. Half a dozen other merchant vessels in De Carteret's territory had been cited for safety hazards.

A final matter had been transmitted from Juneau, Alaska. This one grabbed Parker's and De Carteret's attention. A crabbing vessel had capsized and sunk in the Bering Sea approximately forty miles north of Dutch Harbor. There had been no distress call and no witnesses. Search-and-rescue aircraft reported that, as of midnight, no survivors had been spotted.

De Carteret was not the least surprised. A twenty-seven-year veteran and chief of the district's marine safety division, he had served nearly eight years as a deck officer and engineering watch officer on board Coast Guard weather patrol vessels in the Bering Sea. He knew what it was like up there this time of the year. Come hell or high water, these boats went out; to fishermen, seventy-mile-an-hour winds and thirty-foot seas were nothing more than a professional challenge, and the statistics that resulted from their heroics were devastating. De Carteret knew them by heart. More than a thousand life-threatening commercial fishing accidents had been reported just the year before along the Atlantic, Gulf, Pacific, and Alaskan coasts, and the Bering Sea. An average of 108 fishermen were dying annually, and one third of those casualties were occurring in the Bering Sea and Gulf of Alaska. The leading cause of death was from capsizing.

De Carteret had spent the past eight years as a marine-safety specialist. He'd investigated the aftermath of dozens of deadly fishing expeditions up north, and he knew any number of things could go wrong: Huge green seas could overwhelm any vessel, ripping off hatch covers and exposing the vessel's innards to thousands of tons of water, or a hatch could be left open inadvertently; an undetected leak, even a minor one, could be lethal in heavy seas, and the alarm systems installed to detect them often broke down and were not replaced; a hose could break, causing internal flooding that might spread to the engine room and storage lazarett; the steering could go awry, causing the vessel to careen wildly and heel beyond its ability to right itself, or the navigational and radar systems could blow out, blinding the vessel to navigational hazards, including other vessels.

There were just as many human risks, too.

De Carteret was acquainted with dozens of fishing families and knew that in the old days, fishing had been a father–son occupation, a family enterprise. From their fathers, uncles, and other relatives, young men learned respect for what the sea was capable of doing to even the best of boats. But the king-crab boom changed all that. Now kids were going to sea with little experience and returning with enough money to buy their own boats and call themselves captains. De Carteret and his fellow Coast Guardsmen had felt the brunt. Naïveté accompanied greed and inexperience, all of which had been imported to Alaska with the boom. Now, too, these boats were being loaded with every gadget available to enable them to find and haul fish as fast as possible. He personally had investigated situations where boats had been so overloaded with their catch that they had flipped and sunk sixty feet from the dock.

In addition to the grueling conditions—the constant cold, light deprivation, incessant machinery noise, and heavy protective foul-weather gear that severely limited a fisherman's hearing and peripheral vision—there was the work itself. De Carteret had seen the crabbers. They were easy to spot. They all had the "Aleutian stare," the ghostly look of someone dispossessed of his senses.

Drugs and booze were definite problems as well. De Carteret had heard the reports about skippers piling amphetamines and cocaine on the galley table, anything to keep the crews working. This was taking things to a terrible extreme. While he admired honest, sensible skippers and their crews, De Carteret also wondered if most of them weren't a bit crazy too.

With all the competition, sabotage was not unheard of either. De Carteret had been in Dutch Harbor a number of times and had seen how freely fishermen exchanged hostilities in the taverns and on the docks. He'd overheard threats and seen enough evidence to know that some of them had actually been carried out, between U.S. and foreign vessels, between competing U.S. vessels, sometimes even in the same company fleet, the result of a personal grudge. He knew what the stakes were all about—young captains, twenty-three, twenty-four years old, going up for one season and returning with enough money to buy a boat of their own and throw in a Rolex or a new truck to boot.

He was sick of these high-seas cowboys—mostly kids, really—killing themselves out there.

De Carteret went to his own desk and called Juneau and Kodiak for updates on the search. Still no survivors or bodies spotted. But there was something new. A sister vessel—the *Altair*—could not be contacted. The search was expanding to include this vessel as well. Apparently, this second Anacortes vessel carried the same number of crew.

"Jesus Christ, that just took your breath away," he remembered.

Late the next day De Carteret was called to Admiral Parker's office. He found Parker facing the view beyond his window, a sweeping vista of Puget Sound, from Mount Rainier, the signature landmark to the south, past the Space Needle and the shipping lanes to the north.

"Fourteen people, John," Parker said. "If they were all lost, if there was a connection, this would be the single worst fishing accident since the United States Coast Guard has been patrolling territorial waters."

De Carteret stiffened.

"One more thing," Admiral Parker said. "They're thinking about calling off the search."

This decision would be made by the district office in Juneau and approved by the U.S. Coast Guard commandant in Washington, D.C. Parker and De Carteret were only bystanders, even though Anacortes, the home port of the *Altair* and *Americus,* was in their district.

Indeed, the following Monday, after searching more than twenty-six thousand square miles of the Bering Sea, the Coast Guard suspended its search and turned the case over to the Marine Board of Investigation, the Coast Guard's highest investigative panel.* Together with the National Transportation Safety Board, the Coast Guard would conduct public hearings into the cause of the disappearance of the *Altair* and *Americus*. In De Carteret's experi-

---

* What the Coast Guard calls "reportable vessel casualties" usually involve single craft. A major marine-accident investigation, involving a senior Coast Guard marine-safety officer, is normally required if a vessel incurs multiple deaths or more than $500,000 damage, calling safety issues into question. The report is then sent to the National Transportation Safety Board for review and comment. From 1978 to 1983, 102 major fishing-vessel accidents were sent to the NTSB for review. Of those vessel casualties, sixty-two involved capsizing, flooding, or foundering, seventeen involved fires, twelve involved grounding, five involved collisions, and eight involved what the NTSB termed "miscellaneous causes."

ence, such a joint investigation and hearing was unique. The National Transportation Safety Board was only called in to actively investigate catastrophes.*

"John, you're going to be in charge," Admiral Parker told him. "And the commandant's office wants the hearings to begin by early next week."

Coast Guard investigations of serious accidents usually took weeks to prepare. But De Carteret did not have to guess at the urgency with which Admiral John Gracey, the Coast Guard commandant, would be pushing for answers. The Coast Guard had been advocating safety laws for a dozen years, and the commercial industry had fought them for just as long. In the mid-1970s, when Senator Magnuson proposed the two-hundred-mile territorial limit and federally subsidized loans to bolster the U.S. fishing fleet, the Coast Guard had proposed testing and licensing captains, inspecting and registering fishing vessels, and making safety equipment such as life preservers and rafts mandatory. But industry lobbyists protested that the margin of profit was already so tight that each dollar spent loading their boats with safety equipment was a dollar that could be invested in catching fish and paying their crews.

That was bull, De Carteret thought. How much is a life worth? What was really at stake was the pride of the fishermen. They fought government intervention of any kind, and well-situated eminencies on Capitol Hill such as Senators Ted Stevens of Alaska and Magnuson of Washington, and Congressman Don Young of Alaska, had given the fishing industry the political backing it needed to keep the Coast Guard at bay. At this point there was not one single law requiring safety equipment or survival measures for any fishing boats in the U.S. commercial fleet.

Backed by hundreds of thousands of dollars in campaign contri-

* It would be six years before another similar joint public investigation would be called. That would be the probe of the *Exxon Valdez,* which ran aground and spilled nearly eleven million gallons of raw oil into Alaska's Prince William Sound. John De Carteret would be summoned out of retirement to help run that investigation too.

118

butions—at a time when that amount purchased political impact—the fishing industry upheld its argument even in the face of labor statistics that showed employment in the industry had risen by forty percent since 1974 and per capita income, adjusted for inflation, remained steady during the same time. In fact, the value of the Alaska fishery had nearly doubled in ten years.

Richard Hiscock, a former commercial fisherman who became a marine-safety consultant, had even offered Congress some figures showing costs to equip vessels carrying four- to ten-man crews with life rafts, survival suits, and EPIRBs. As an example, he stated, the overall costs for a six-man crew requiring a raft, exposure suits, and an EPIRB would be approximately $9,000. When averaged over the ten-year life span of the equipment, the cost would be nominal, about $150 annually per man for ten years.

"That doesn't seem to me to be a high price to pay to save a life," Hiscock testified at a congressional hearing on marine safety in the late winter of 1983, even as the investigation into the loss of the *Altair* and *Americus* was about to begin.

Under federal law, the four-member Marine Board of Investigation—two members from the Coast Guard, two from the National Transportation Safety Board—had subpoena powers to compel the appearance and testimony under oath of anyone it considered a witness or connected to the accident. While the board was not exactly a grand jury, it was patterned after one, though its primary goal was to determine the probable cause of an accident. If the board found negligence or criminal wrongdoing, however, it was bound by law to pass its findings to the proper authorities, in this case the U.S. attorney's office. De Carteret knew the implications. The press would be all over this thing. That made him nervous. But frankly, he welcomed the publicity. He wanted people to know how dangerous it was up there.

De Carteret went back to his office and drew up a priority list of those he would call to testify: the owner of the boats, the designer, builder, and other material witnesses. Within minutes he filled two pages of a legal tablet with a list of prospective "parties in interest."

He also made a list of things he already knew, based mainly on news coverage and what had been passed along from Juneau. That list was very short. The weather had been calm at first. The boats had reputations for being strictly first-class. Supposedly they were superbly equipped and maintained and their crews well trained. Then, suddenly, there were no boats. One was four thousand feet under, and who the hell knew where the other had gone? There were no transcripts of radio calls for help, no EPIRBs. There were no black boxes like those recovered from aircraft wreckage that sometimes convey last-second telltale talk among a cockpit crew. There wasn't a single piece of wreckage to provide a clue. And all the direct witnesses were lost at sea.

De Carteret began compiling a list of unanswered questions: procedures or conditions that might have led to a collision; weather conditions; traffic in the waterway; procedures for standing watch; how the boats were loaded; how they were trimmed; how much fuel they carried. Could each have been overtaken by one of the huge rogue waves the Bering Sea was famous for? Were there reports of icebergs or debris? Were there foreign vessels operating in the area, including foreign military vessels? . . . The list grew quickly.

Theories as to what caused the accident were already circulating throughout the fishing community. Among the more unlikely theories espoused around the docks and taverns of Dutch Harbor was that the boats might have been sabotaged by "foreigners." De Carteret could not discount sabotage as a possible explanation, however remote. The *Altair* and *Americus* would have been competing with Japanese, Taiwanese, Norwegian, and Soviet factory trawlers. In the early 1980s U.S. intelligence agencies reported that the Soviets were outfitting some of their trawlers with military electronic-intelligence tracking devices—a story the newspapers had seized upon—and President Reagan had made his "Evil Empire" speech less than six months before the boats went down, ratcheting up old tensions.

Siberia-based Soviet nuclear submarines were, in fact, operating in the Bering Sea. The Coast Guard had spotted them. One sub that snagged in the nets of a U.S. trawler almost sank the fishing vessel. That story had been in the papers as well.

De Carteret gave little credence to the sabotage theory, but it had made its way to the corridors of Capitol Hill in Washington, D.C., too. Senator Henry M. Jackson, a ranking member of the Senate Armed Services Committee, requested a full-scale investigation that would involve the National Security Council. The CIA was alerted to be ready to send U-2 spy planes aloft.

"Jesus," De Carteret half-joked to colleagues in the hallways of the Federal Building in Seattle, "they want an excuse to go to war?"

De Carteret scanned the list of others who would serve with him: the two NTSB investigators, Herb Collins and Doug Rabe, were seasoned marine-accident specialists. Each had acquired thousands of hours sifting through wreckage, analyzing facts, and challenging theories to help diagnose the causes of some of the nation's worst water-commerce catastrophes, many of which involved multiple deaths. Rabe, a former Coast Guard officer and a naval architect, had headed an investigation in Tampa, Florida, in which a bulk-cargo vessel collided with a bridge, killing thirty-five people. More recently, he'd led the investigation into the sinking of a New Jersey fishing vessel in which eight people had died. De Carteret found his background reassuring. The final member of the team, Coast Guard Lieutenant Commander Paul Larson, had posted a fine record of investigating more than three hundred fatal marine accidents in fourteen years of service. He had been stationed in Seattle since 1979, and De Carteret, who'd worked with him on dozens of cases, trusted him completely. He had already made up his mind that Larson would be his point man throughout the investigation.

"Just one goddamn survivor, that's all I need," the Coast Guard captain said to himself. This was his show now, and although it was probably too late to pin an admiral's stripe on the outcome, the case was definitely high profile.

CHAPTER 8

GLENN TREADWELL HAD TRIED TO STAY AS INCONSPICUOUS AS possible during the memorial service at the high-school gymnasium for the crew of the *Americus*. He still had not spoken directly to Hendricks about his own observations of the *Altair* and *Americus* as they left Dutch Harbor; he voiced suspicions only to Brian Melvin. But Treadwell would not be able to avoid speaking up for long. On Wednesday, February 23, the day after the memorial service, he received a subpoena to appear at the Federal Building in Seattle to testify before the Marine Board of Investigation. Brian Melvin was also subpoenaed, as was Jeff Hendricks.

Hendricks understood the implications; he could ultimately be charged with negligence. He could be sued, lose his company, his standing in the town. He immediately called and retained Doug Freyer, a prominent Seattle attorney whose expertise in the field of marine accidents was widely regarded throughout the Pacific Northwest. He had a reputation for being a detail-oriented, straightforward, and fierce advocate.

Hendricks also called his boat designer, Jacob Fisker-Andersen, to learn that he, too, had been summoned to testify. Fisker-Andersen had designed seventy-five boats during the past fifteen years, many of them similar to the *Americus* and *Altair*. The designer told Hendricks he had seen the television footage of the *Americus* floating upside down. He, like Hendricks, had noted that there seemed to be no scoring marks on the hull. Would that eliminate a possible collision or explosion? Probably. At least that was his opinion for now. In fact, he said he had no clue as to what had caused the loss of the two boats; both had been planned with wide margins of safety. It couldn't be a stability problem, he pointed out. The *Alyeska* was presumably loaded in the same manner and suffered no problems at all.

Hendricks was not reassured.

On Friday, February 25, De Carteret held a news conference. He informed the reporters that a Coast Guard investigator from Anchorage had been dispatched to Dutch Harbor and that the board had already issued subpoenas. He gave the names of Melvin, Treadwell, Hendricks, Fisker-Andersen, and others, including the boat builders and Hendricks crew members. The board would hear testimony from these witnesses for three days, he explained, and then reconvene in Dutch Harbor for more testimony from local witnesses. He pointed out that the *Americus* had been through four seasons in the Bering Sea and the *Altair* two, in all types of weather. He commended the owner's reputation of maintaining the boats in good working order. He reiterated how difficult it would be to account for a sudden capsizing with no call of distress.

"But sometimes it doesn't take much to foul up the stability of a ship," he said, drawing on his own experience and implying nothing about the A-boats. He wanted that understood. "If a sea comes aboard and a hatch is open, this can do it. Tanks belowdecks that aren't full can also be the cause. There are many, many things,'' he told them, without repeating the long list of questions he had made for himself, questions about how fourteen young men could have died during a momentary calm in the Bering Sea.

Meanwhile, a collage went up near the trophy case at Anacortes High School in tribute to the six *Americus* crew members—all but George Nations—who had graduated from there. Within a week the *Altair* would be declared officially lost, and seven names and snapshots of its captain and crew would be added to the collage. School administrators were amazed to find that three hundred students had signed up for special counseling from a grief specialist they had hired. Later that week the Seahawks basketball team dedicated its first state-championship playoff game to the crews of both boats. The team played listlessly, and lost.

One citizen, Eleanor Wynn Wolf, wrote a letter to the editor of the *Anacortes American* recalling how difficult it had been to light a candle in the wind at the Seafarer's Memorial during the outdoor vigil and suggested installing an eternal flame at the memorial. Maria Petrish, the Anacortes Chamber of Commerce manager and daughter of a prominent local fisherman, who had also purchased a candle and tried to light it, informed the newspaper that a plan was already under way. The Cascade Gas Company (Lloyd Bass's employer) had volunteered to run the line for free, the city agreed to patch the asphalt, and the Port of Anacortes, at the bidding of Francis Barcott, one of its directors, would pick up the twenty-five-dollar monthly gas bill.

Reverend Hilary Bitz began his Sunday, February 27, service by asking: ''What does it mean in a theological sense when fourteen young men are lost at sea? . . . What does this do to our notion of God?''

Bud and Lois Awes bought a headstone for Richie, had LOST AT SEA inscribed on it, and placed it in the family plot at the Grandview

Cemetery on the hill overlooking the town, the harbor, and the Cascade Mountains.

Eve Northcutt considered the same idea and dropped it. "What good would it do?" she asked herself. "Paul wouldn't be up there. He's at the bottom of the ocean." And then she changed her mind and placed a headstone next to her husband's plot. On one of her first ventures out after that, a neighbor approached her in the supermarket. "Eve, I'm so sorry, so sorry. How many children do you have?"

She said she had four.

"You're so lucky," the neighbor said.

"How many do you have?" Eve asked.

"Two," the neighbor said.

"How many would you give up and consider yourself lucky?" Eve Northcutt snapped, welling up with tears. She rushed home, went into Paul's room and sat on his bed, feeling guilty for snapping at her neighbor and thinking that maybe she had stepped outside too soon.

Less than two weeks after the *Altair* and *Americus* were lost, Suzanne Knutson, Ron Beirnes's daughter, stood on the dock at Dakota Creek Industries and broke a champagne bottle against a big blue steel hull to christen the newest A-boat, the *Arcturas*. Her husband, Doug, who would be its captain, and Jeff Hendricks stood alongside. They were among only a handful of participants at the subdued ceremony.

Elsewhere on the docks and in the taverns around town, the Soviet sabotage theory was still making the rounds. But the old fishermen—Del Cole, Francis Barcott, and Bill Lowman—kept their own counsel. They had watched the boats being built and watched them sail north. Each had formed his own opinion.

CHAPTER 9

On Tuesday, March 1, 1983, in a small, stark conference room in the basement of the Federal Office Building in Seattle, the first hearings in what would become the longest joint Coast Guard–National Transportation Safety Board investigation in history began. Television cameras from local stations, cluttering the front of the room and the aisles, were trained on three tables before them, awaiting the arrival of Captain John De Carteret, the presiding officer. The tables, arranged in the shape of a horseshoe, were flanked by an American flag and another with sixteen red-and-white vertical stripes, that of the U.S. Coast Guard. Lieutenant Commander Larson was already seated at the center table. He would be responsible for the schedule and testimony of dozens of witnesses, plus the hundreds of field reports and documents that would accumulate during the nearly two-year investigation. Seated to his left were the two NTSB investigators, Rabe and Collins.

The room held thirty seats. On this day every one was filled: with reporters, fishing-industry professionals, insurance investigators, and families of lost fishermen. Jody Gudbranson was there, sitting with her mother, Crystal Sadlowsky. Wayne Melvin was there, in support of his son Brian. Al Littlefield and George Boles were there, as was Doug Knutson, now senior captain in the Hendricks fleet. Jeff Hendricks and his legal team sat nearby. During the moments before De Carteret entered, the room was silent and tense.

What the crowd did not know—and what De Carteret had just learned—was that yet another ship had gone down in the Bering Sea. The Seattle-based *Fly Boy* had capsized and sunk during the previous night. This was the fifth vessel—including the *Altair* and *Americus*—to go down within thirty days. Four crewmen had survived, one had died. Even though De Carteret was accustomed to maritime disasters, these statistics were remarkably high for the first month of the season. He walked briskly to his table, sat, faced the audience, leaned into the microphone, and began.

"This investigation is intended to determine the cause or causes of these casualties to the fullest extent possible. . . . This investigation is also intended to determine if there is evidence that any incompetence, misconduct, unskillfulness, or willful violation of the law on the part of any licensed officer, pilot, seaman, employee, owner, or agent such as the owner of any vessel involved or any inspector, officer of the Coast Guard, or other officer or employee of the United States, or any other person, caused or contributed to the cause or causes of these casualties. . . .

"Parties in interest are not necessarily suspected of wrongdoing. Rather, they are those persons who, under the existing evidence or because of their position, may have been responsible for or may have contributed to one or both of these casualties. . . ."

De Carteret ended his opening statement and asked that all stand

silent for a moment in a gesture of respect for the crews of the
Americus and *Altair*.

Jeff Hendricks was the first "party in interest" called. Commander
Larson, a cordial-looking man with an unimposing physique,
watched intently as the owner of the *Altair* and *Americus,* accompanied by his lawyers, rose from the audience and walked stiffly to the
witness table, where he raised his right hand, swore to tell the truth,
and took his seat. Larson noticed that Hendricks briefly scanned the
crowd before him, peppered with his own neighbors, and quickly
withdrew his gaze.

De Carteret had also sensed Hendricks's nervousness and tried
to put him at ease. He began simply, asking Hendricks for a rough
biography of each vessel—how much fuel and how many crab pots
they could carry, where the pots were located on deck and how they
were stacked, how much water each of the boat's four crab tanks
held, how often the boats were overhauled. Hendricks appeared to
relax as he recited the technological aspects of what he knew.

Doug Freyer, Hendricks's lead attorney—a lean man in his early
forties, whose shaved head shone in the television lights—commanded the microphone next. He was determined to remind the
panel, as often as he could, of the reputation of the Hendricks fleet.
He asked Hendricks to detail Ron Beirnes's and George Nations's
histories at sea, even before De Carteret had a chance to ask Hendricks to vouch for their capabilities.

"From your experience would you say you considered them
careful operators?" Freyer coached.

"Absolutely," Hendricks answered.

De Carteret sat back in his chair, peering over the top of his dark
glasses. He was clearly irked at being preempted right off the bat.

Hendricks told the panel Beirnes and Nations were his brothers-
in-law and business partners, and that he and each skipper made a
point of hiring young men from the Anacortes area because they felt
it was important to give local residents an opportunity. He said it

was company policy to promote crew members through the ranks, from deckhands, to engineers, to captains, citing Doug Knutson, Brian Melvin, Glenn Treadwell, and Kevin Kirkpatrick as examples. "We have had very little turnover in personnel," he said, without a trace of irony in his voice.

De Carteret asked about possible drug use and drunkenness. Hendricks offered the company's written terms of employment, stating that the company would tolerate neither.

Rabe, the NTSB's stability expert, asked about each captain's mode of operation and the company policy for working at sea in bad weather. Hendricks said he had personally sailed the *Antares* through seventy-mile-an-hour winds and thirty-foot seas, far worse conditions than those encountered by the *Americus* and *Altair* when they went down.

Freyer broke in again. "Did the *Antares* ever take a roll and then hesitate before righting itself?"

"Never," Hendricks said.

Rabe continued. "Could you explain to us what cross-tanking is?" The question seemed out of the blue. Hendricks looked startled and turned to Freyer for help. Rabe explained that he wanted to know how the vessels might have been trimmed and ballasted.

Freyer nodded, urging Hendricks to answer.

"Where she is light in the water, it is a bit better to work if she is ballasted down," Hendricks said, explaining that the four thirty-three-thousand-gallon crab tanks, each capable of holding the equivalent of sixty-five tons of seawater, were sometimes filled with water after the crab pots had been unloaded to make up for the sudden loss of as much as eighty tons from the deck.

"Have you or your captains ever cross-tanked your boats?" Rabe persisted.

Hendricks said that George Nations had begun experimenting with the technique the year before, during long trawling or crabbing trips to St. Matthew Island, two hundred miles north of the Pribilofs. As they burned fuel and unloaded pots, the boats would become lighter, so they would take on water in the empty crab tanks for balance.

"Was this condition accounted for in the vessel's stability letter?" Rabe queried.

Hendricks said it was not. "As soon as you burn one gallon of fuel off . . . you are no longer under those conditions," he said, emphasizing that balancing a boat depends more on logic than mathematical formulas.

The next round of questions was based on interviews Coast Guard investigators had conducted at the dock in Dutch Harbor immediately after the fishing vessels were missing. Larson was particularly interested in how much fuel the *Altair* and *Americus* had been carrying when they left port on February 14.

Citing his own records and those from the *Sea Alaska* processor, Hendricks estimated that both the *Americus* and *Altair* had each burned ten thousand gallons of diesel fuel on the trip from Anacortes to Dutch Harbor, about one-seventh of their total capacity. On February 13 the *Americus* off-loaded 28,000 gallons of fuel to the processor and the *Altair* unloaded 27,730 gallons. This stockpiling was done, Hendricks explained, to avoid paying higher fuel prices later on.

Hendricks's calculations showed that when each vessel sailed from Dutch Harbor, it was carrying fifty percent of its fuel capacity. With regard to stability, each boat had relinquished 136 tons of ballast, while adding nearly eighty tons of crab pots on deck. Thus it was important that the remaining fuel be properly distributed. The lower down the weight was located in the vessel the better, operating on the same principle as a keel to a sailboat. But flooding the crab tanks would not completely compensate for the lost weight, since the crab tanks were not positioned as deeply in a vessel as were the bottom fuel tanks. What Hendricks did not say was that flooding the crab tanks also caused water to spill across the decks, adding new weight and lowering the freeboard—the distance from the gunwales to the waterline. In particularly heavy seas, with seawater being taken on deck, this practice could, in fact, diminish stability.

Larson asked from which tanks the fuel had been transferred. Hendricks said he assumed from wing tanks in the bow, as a matter of company practice. He did not have the records and doubted that they existed, but he would check.

Rabe took note of this, as did Larson. If fuel had not been transferred from the smaller wing tanks, but from the big double-bottom tanks instead, the vessels would have given up considerable ballast.

Larson then asked Hendricks for his own theory as to why no Emergency Position Indicator Radio Beacon was heard from either vessel. He answered that it was a company policy to store the devices in the wheelhouse, to guard against thieves in Dutch Harbor. Once out to sea the skippers usually mounted the beacons in brackets outside the wheelhouse, where they could break free, float, and transmit their location. But, Hendricks said, he had no idea why no signal was heard from either of his vessels.

During his time at the witness table Hendricks offered nothing but what he knew to be facts, and Larson appreciated his straightforwardness. He also sensed that as the questioning continued, Hendricks was growing less tense and less defensive. Initially, he had been alerted by Hendricks's nervousness. From his own experience questioning skippers who were in debt and being chased by the IRS, whose boats, after a couple of bad seasons in a row, had mysteriously sunk, he looked for signs of suspicion, particularly when someone couldn't look him straight in the eye. He had watched Hendricks closely, looking for signs that the vessel owner knew more than he was letting on. But Hendricks honestly appeared to be as baffled as anyone else.

Later that afternoon Jacob Fisker-Andersen, the A-boats' designer, was called to the table.

Courtly, slightly rumpled, with a thick accent, the fifty-six-year-old Dane recounted his credentials as a licensed naval designer with more than thirty years of experience, not only in the U.S. but in Great Britain as well. At the panel's request, he described how a boat was "inclined" to determine its center of gravity and inherent stability and the maximum angle, called the "righting arm," at which it could heel over and still right itself. A twenty-five-member international maritime conference had recently recommended that fishing vessels should be designed with a righting arm preferably exceeding thirty degrees and not less than twenty-five degrees, Fisker-Andersen told the panel.

"But twenty-five degrees is acceptable," Fisker-Andersen said. That was the minimal standard he used for the Hendricks boats.

He described in arcane detail how stability equations are arrived at for various load exigencies. He had performed a stability evaluation for the *Antares* when it had been built, he said, and applied it to the *Americus* and *Altair,* which were virtually identical. All the boats were well within their margin of safety with any load, he insisted.

The designer also told the panel that at Hendricks's request, he had calculated the stability of the *Americus* and *Altair* two weeks after the two boats went down. He had even estimated the effects of cross-tanking on his computer, factoring in known and assumed loads of fuel, oil, fresh water, bait, and all the drag gear, which he figured to be an additional 13.5 tons. He had left nothing out. Assuming the No. 1 and No. 2 double-bottom fuel tanks were full, according to recommendations in their stability letters, the boats, he said, could have carried another tier of pots.

"Still they would have been safe," he maintained.

Rabe asked him if this information had been conveyed to the captains.

"No." The typical captain, he said, would not be able to do the complicated computations. But with a handheld calculator, Fisker-Andersen said, he could crunch the numbers in about three hours.

"What information was available to the captains?" Rabe persisted.

Fisker-Andersen thought for a moment. The only stability information was the original computation, he said, the one based on the *Antares*.

"This was before the tons of dragging equipment were added to the boats?" Rabe asked.

"Yes," Fisker-Andersen answered.

"So there was no current stability information available to the two captains, then?" Rabe continued.

"It was not necessary," Fisker-Andersen said, "because the two captains knew the weight of the gear and the weight of the crab pots and could make the simple calculations themselves. It would be a trade-off. I believe the current information was what I and Mr. Hendricks conferred, and it was agreed that fewer crab pots would be carried on board, and I believe those calculations were made with the captains," he said, looking at Hendricks for confirmation.

Hendricks nodded back.

Rabe asked if Fisker-Andersen had any opinions as to what might have happened then.

"It is a complete mystery to me" was his response.

Brian Melvin looked as edgy as a caged animal when he was sworn in the next morning. Nonetheless, facing the Coast Guard brass, investigators from Washington, D.C., lawyers, insurance representatives, industry representatives, the television cameras, and reporters, the twenty-five-year-old captain held his own. He spoke of his previous experiences with George Nations and Ron Beirnes aboard the *Americus* and *Altair* in the Bering Sea. He carefully recounted the events in Dutch Harbor, how he had run to the Pribilofs to lay a load of pots, returned to port, boarded the other A-boats, shared a meal with the *Altair* crew—including his own brother—and watched it depart.

"It looked normal," he said, answering the obvious question from Commander Larson.

At Larson's request Melvin then reiterated, in greater detail, a chronology of the events that led up to and followed the departure of the *Altair* and *Americus* from Dutch Harbor on February 14: how he had run to the Pribilofs to drop 208 pots, twenty below the capacity as recommended in the stability booklet, returned to port, off-loaded 38,915 gallons of fuel, and loaded 175 crab pots onto his own boat. He recalled hearing the Coast Guard emergency broadcast and searching for the overturned hull, then making the run to the Pribilofs to rendezvous with the *Altair* and *Americus,* only to be called back by the radio message that one of the A-boats might be down.

He told the board how he had dumped some crab pots to make room on the *Alyeska*'s deck for a possible rescue operation and then turned the boat back toward Dutch Harbor to search again for the hull. He told them the exact time the *Alyeska* came in contact with the hull and the exact location on the chart. He told the board that the bow of the hull appeared to be riding lower in the water than the stern. He said he could see no hull damage. He recalled watching a wave smack the stern of the hull and the bow rising and everyone on board the *Alyeska* seeing the emblem and the insignia of the *Americus*. He gave the exact time the *Alliance* came alongside and re-traced his own efforts to start a grid-pattern search to locate survivors. Finally, he recalled getting a call from Treadwell and returning to the hull in time to see it sink stern first.

Asked to describe his own loading conditions, Melvin said the first time he had sailed out of Dutch Harbor with 208 crab pots on board, the *Alyeska* was carrying fuel in the double-bottom tanks and the crab tanks were empty. When she sailed the second time, the double-bottoms had been drained, but the crab tanks were pumped full. This time, he carried 175 crab pots.

Doug Rabe then asked Melvin if he had consulted the forty-page stability booklet before loading crab pots onto the *Alyeska*.

"No," the young captain said. "There isn't a page in this booklet for every variable." However, he did keep the one-page stability letter, the general guideline for loading, posted in the wheelhouse. The actual booklet, with all its calculations, was kept in his stateroom. When loading, he said, "I rely on my own judgment and experience."

Rabe noted his understanding that this was Melvin's first trip as skipper of one of the A-boats. Then he handed Melvin a copy of the stability booklet Fisker-Andersen had prepared for the *Antares*. He asked him if he could find any instructions in it that would correspond to how the *Alyeska* was loaded and trimmed when it had left Dutch Harbor the second time.

Melvin fumbled through the booklet, turning page after page. But he could find no corresponding load conditions. He closed the booklet, looking defeated and bewildered.

"I'm not trying to put you on the spot or trick you in any way, but I just want to find out how to make the booklet more helpful," Rabe said. "You're the man that needs to use the information."

Melvin felt a rush of anger and fought for self-control. He again cited his experience and judgment, his particular feel of the boat he commanded. At that moment he was speaking for the commercial fishermen he respected, Ron Beirnes and George Nations included. They didn't need a goddamn booklet, he thought to himself, and they didn't need the government to tell them how to run their boats . . .

"You can't have a boat full of fuel, full of water, and full of gear," he said firmly, trying to parry what he took to be Rabe's assault on his competence.

Rabe then asked Melvin if he had ever cross-tanked the *Alyeska*.

Melvin was glad for the question. "No," he said. The *Alyeska*'s crab tanks were different in size, he explained. Filling some of them with seawater while leaving others empty would cause the boat to list.

Once again, board members asked Melvin if he had an opinion. Was there anything unusual at all he could think of?

He pondered, rolling things over in his mind one last time, weighing what he knew and what he suspected and reminding himself that he was under oath.

"No, nothing," he said at last.

Glenn Treadwell was the last member of Hendricks's crew to be called to the witness table. Stiff and self-conscious in his suit and tie, he hoped he looked less nervous than he felt.

"Answer directly, but don't volunteer any opinions," he recalled Hendricks's lawyers admonishing him before the hearings began. As he sat down, he cautioned himself once again about volunteering too much. He looked back at his wife, Evelyn, and at Janice Nations beside her. Anything he had to tell Jan he would do privately, he thought. Not here. Not in front of the U.S. government and reporters.

Just let me get through this, he reminded himself, knowing full well the direction the questions were taking the investigation.

As they had the others before him, the board asked Treadwell to summarize his background, to provide details of his professional history with the Hendricks fleet, to recall details of how the *Altair* and *Americus* were loaded and trimmed when they left Dutch Harbor, and to recount his own search for the missing vessels. He obliged, sticking to what he had witnessed firsthand, avoiding conjecture. Even when he was asked if the *Americus* had been crosstanked when she sailed, Treadwell couldn't say for certain and didn't volunteer what he suspected: that she probably was.

Once Treadwell had satisfied Larson's more-general questions, the Coast Guard officer asked him why he had taken the extra time to dump crab pots before returning to the reported location of the overturned hull for a possible rescue.

Treadwell felt the color drain from his face. He knew what

Larson was after—he wanted to know if Treadwell thought that the boats had been overloaded to begin with.

"If we wouldn't have done that," he said, unable to conceal his annoyance, "we wouldn't have had any room on deck to be of any help."

"Were you concerned about your failure to establish communications with the *Altair*?" Larson asked.

Of course I was concerned; I was damn scared, Treadwell thought. But he answered, "Not at that time," explaining that when they were fishing, the captain in the wheelhouse was usually concentrating on the work on deck.

Treadwell told the board how he came alongside the *Americus* and stood by while the *Alyeska* searched for survivors. He described the hull, the waves, and how, when the vessel went down, the bow pointed skyward to reveal the familiar American flag and winged emblem of the *Americus*. His voice cracked as he recalled the two life rings and then the empty life raft surfacing several minutes after the *Americus* went down. He looked at Jan Nations again and could hardly bear to continue in her presence. Slowly, he described the search for survivors, retracing the drift he and Brian Melvin thought the *Americus* might have taken, then recalled their decision to leave the search to the Coast Guard.

Larson asked if he had an opinion as to what happened.

"None whatsoever," Treadwell answered. Despite his suspicions, he was being honest. At this point, he was still taking inventory of any number of fatal mistakes Ron and George may have made, and had not come up with a satisfying conclusion himself.

Other witnesses followed that afternoon: Bob Gudmundson, the Dakota Creek shipyard manager, furnished dry-dock inspection and maintenance records for the Hendricks fleet and detailed the three separate stages of trawling-gear retrofittings the *Americus* and *Altair* had undergone through January 1983, just a month before the vessels sailed for the last time to Dutch Harbor.

The boats, he insisted, "were very well maintained."

Kaare Ness, a highly respected Seattle fisherman who shared ownership in ten boats that sailed the Bering Sea, testified that he had never experienced instability on the vessel he operated, the *Viking Explorer,* designed by Fisker-Andersen and built by Dakota Creek as a twin of the *Americus* and *Altair.*

"It's really a mystery to me," he said, when asked his opinion of what went wrong.

James Goldade, a surveyor for the Insurance Company of North America, which held $60,000 premiums on the *Americus* and *Altair,* told the board that he had surveyed at least four thousand boats in his career, including at least half the boats in the entire Northwest crab fleet. He had watched both the *Americus* and *Altair* being built and tested each vessel for stability in 1981. After a three-hour tour of each vessel, he did, however, admit to finding a flaw. Playing to the drama of the moment, Goldade paused and said, "One of the *Americus*'s life rafts was overdue for inspection. . . . Otherwise, if I had to rate them from one to ten, they'd be ten. . . . The maintenance on them was tip-top. They are the last vessels in the world you'd expect to go down."

Fisker-Andersen, the designer, grinned.

After two days and half a dozen witnesses, the investigation was getting nowhere in Seattle. In his corner office on the top floor of the Federal Building, John De Carteret collected his team and told them they would be heading for Dutch Harbor within the week. They would interview dockworkers, fishermen, anyone who might have witnessed something unusual about the vessels or who might have overheard anything that could help explain the loss.

"Shit. What have we got?" he asked. "I think everyone out there was answering as honestly as they could. All we have got so far is fourteen people dead. And a lot of families who are asking for answers."

It seemed to De Carteret that Hendricks was being honest. He appeared just as anxious as the board members to discover how fourteen of his employees were lost. So far they had learned that the vessels had added a certain amount of weight on deck after three retrofittings for trawling gear—how much weight would have to be determined. They would also have to determine which tanks had been emptied of fuel and the effect on each vessel's stability. What struck De Carteret most was the fact that neither vessel had been reinclined for new stability variables after the retrofittings. Apparently stability was a seat-of-the-pants thing, even in a so-called top-of-the-line fleet; cross-tanking at their own discretion, the captains seemed to have no regard for a designer's rules for loading vessels in certain conditions. But De Carteret knew the captains of the *Americus* and *Altair* were not unique. Men who made their living from the sea were simply not going to follow rules dictated by men who had never set foot off land.

That night, at home in Anacortes, Glenn Treadwell told his wife, Evelyn, that he and Brian Melvin had decided to go back up to Dutch Harbor to finish out the season and to try to figure out themselves what had gone wrong with the *Americus* and *Altair*. Evelyn was not happy.

"The sea did not do this," Glenn said. "That's all I can say for now, but I'm pretty certain. It was no accident. I mean it just didn't come out of the blue. I've walked those decks. Seven-foot seas do not knock those boats over." And then he told her what he suspected: how George had probably cross-tanked the *Americus* and Ron had likely flooded all the crab tanks of the *Altair* and how that might have affected the boats' stability. He told her that Brian Melvin had flooded all his tanks too, something he had learned from Ron Beirnes. He described how the *Americus* and *Altair* appeared to be riding low in the water when they left Dutch Harbor, especially in the stern, even though he could still see the boot stripe above the water. What he saw that night confused him, he said. He was not completely certain of anything. That was why he hadn't volunteered his concerns during his testimony. Certainly, he was not ready to talk to Jan Nations about his suspicions. Not yet. But, Evelyn had to understand, he was completely confident things were not the same on the *Alliance*.

Treadwell then called Pat Barbarovich, his engineer, and told him to get the rest of the *Alliance* crew ready.

Across town Brian Melvin was having much the same conversation with his wife, Tammy. He reassured her that he would not take any risks with the crew of the *Alyeska*. If anything, this had made him a better fisherman. In fact, he said, he had already taken just about every precaution, including carrying fewer crab pots the second time out. He would carry even fewer this time, but he had to go back to finish the season and to try to figure out what had happened. He owed it to his brother, he said, and Tammy understood.

Meanwhile, Jeff Hendricks called Jacob Fisker-Andersen and asked him to conduct a computer recalculation accounting for the additional weight of the trawling gear to the *Alyeska* and to determine the number of crab pots she was capable of carrying in the best and worst conditions. Still, what caused the *Altair* and *Americus* to capsize remained elusive. If there was a fatal flaw somewhere in the fleet, Hendricks believed the obligation was his, not the Coast Guard's, to find it.

CHAPTER 10

A HERD OF PRINT AND TELEVISION REPORTERS HAD COME ALL THE way from Seattle to cover Lieutenant Commander Larson and his investigators when they arrived in Dutch Harbor the following week. The reporters had already scoured the town and sent their dispatches south via telephone or satellite hookup. With the snow-covered mountains as a backdrop, they recreated a picture of a town at the end of the world, complete with accounts of hundred-mile-an-hour winds. "This place is small, it's muddy, there are no paved streets," one television reporter said on camera. "It's closer to Russia than Seattle." Not to be outdramatized, another, while the camera panned the bay and sea beyond, quipped, "The Bering Sea—only bachelors should be allowed to fish here." The reporters roamed the docks to the Unisea Inn and the Elbow Room to scare up quotes there too, and Dennis Petersen, a crabber, gave them a succinct appraisal: "It's a hard life. Every year you lose fifteen to twenty guys. Both my brother and I have been overboard, and we know what it's like. I don't care what kind of model you come up with, you're not going to solve the problem, I don't think. When it's your turn to go, you go."

The investigators boarded the *Alyeska* on March 10, a little over three weeks since the overturned hull of the *Americus* had first been spotted. Larson asked to see the vessel's stability report and wasn't surprised when Melvin retrieved it from under a stack of magazines in a drawer of his stateroom. It appeared never to have been opened. The investigators also boarded at least two vessels similar to the *Americus* and *Altair,* to measure the decks and depth of the crab tanks and the distances from the deck to the waterline. In public hearings they interviewed other captains, including Buster McNabb, who had carried divers on board his *Golden Pisces,* only to abort a rescue attempt. They interviewed Ken Griffin, the marine biologist, who told them he had so much confidence in the boats that he had chartered the *Altair* that previous summer to do surveying work for the Alaska Department of Fish and Game. They interviewed the dock foreman and the dockworkers who had unloaded fuel and loaded crab pots. They took the names of people who saw the *Altair* and *Americus* take their last leave from Dutch Harbor, yet no witness recalled anything unusual. In fact, the witnesses said, the *Americus* appeared to be riding high, considering all the pots and trawling gear she was carrying; she was riding right at the red boot stripe, right where she ought to be.

After three days the investigators convened in private once more. They agreed that most of the people they'd talked to had been straightforward and yet had provided no insights—with the exception of Dean Brenengen, an engineer who had supervised the fuel transfer from the *Altair, Americus,* and *Alyeska* to the *Sea Alaska* processor. His records showed how much fuel had been transferred, but he could not say for certain which fuel tanks were drained.

Larson asked him specifically about the instructions Larry Little-field, the *Americus* engineer, gave him for unloading fuel. "He said something about a front tank with eight or ten thousand gallons" was all Brenengen could remember.

Larson checked the blueprints for the vessels. There was no front tank capable of holding eight to ten thousand gallons on the *Americus, Altair,* or *Alyeska*. The forward wing tanks had already been drained, according to what Hendricks had told them. The only tanks placed forward in the vessel were the big double-bottom tanks that the stability booklet instructed the captains to keep full, espe-cially under the loads the *Americus, Altair,* and *Alyeska* were carry-ing. Larson called De Carteret in Seattle and told him about this minor revelation.

"At that point any discovery was progress," De Carteret re-membered thinking. He instructed Larson to wrap up his business in Dutch Harbor and head to Anacortes, to tour the Dakota Creek boatyard and talk with people who had converted the *Altair, Ameri-cus,* and *Alyeska* from crabbing boats to hybrid crabber–trawlers. In the meantime, De Carteret had decided to call in another stability expert. His name was Bruce Adee, and he was a professor of me-chanical engineering at the University of Washington in Seattle.

"What is his specialty?" Larson asked.

"Capsizing," De Carteret answered.

"How does he do that?" Larson asked.

"With models," De Carteret said. "The guy works with models."

That night, March 11, the Seattle-based *Arctic Dreamer* capsized and sank approximately eight miles northeast of Dutch Harbor. The crew of six was rescued after floating for several hours in survival suits. The next day the Seattle-based *Sea Hawk* was moving crab pots from the fishing grounds off Umnak Island in the Aleutians when ice began building on the deck and crab pots. The captain ordered the crew to begin chipping the ice. Hours later, about 1

P.M., the rudder suddenly turned hard to starboard. The captain reduced speed, disengaged the autopilot, and tried to turn the rudder back to port. The vessel did not respond. The captain increased speed, and when he did, the *Sea Hawk* turned sharply to starboard into the trough of a wave. The boat overturned approximately eighty miles west of Dutch Harbor. One crew member was lost. The *Sea Hawk* was the eighth vessel lost since the season began four weeks earlier. Already, twenty-one crewmen had been lost in the Bering Sea and Gulf of Alaska. This number was higher than the seasonal average for the last five years.

In the half-light of an early March afternoon, Dutch Harbor felt like a ghost town to Brian Melvin. The investigators had left, and except for a few reporters, the waterfront was strangely quiet. On the *Sea Alaska* dock, the *Altair*'s and *Americus*'s crab pots, clearly labeled with the names of the two boats, were still stacked and arranged for their return.

Melvin climbed aboard the *Alyeska* and checked the wheelhouse, where the sideband radio still displayed the channel for calling the *Altair*. He stood for a moment, trying to mentally process all that he needed to do. When he climbed down to the dock, a television crew was waiting for him. He recognized the reporter from the Seattle hearings. He was from KOMO, the Seattle ABC network affiliate.

"How does it feel to be going back out knowing your brother and others are gone out there?" the reporter asked.

Melvin's first inclination was to shove the whole TV crew off the dock. But he tried to maintain his composure while the camera was running. "It's going to be hard to get back into the swing of things. It'll never be the same as it was," he said. But he was going back out, he said firmly, "because that's what I want to do. That's what those guys would want us to do."

When the *Alyeska* and *Alliance* made the turn at Priest Rock at 8:00 A.M. on March 14, their crews stood in silence. In the wheelhouse of the *Alyeska,* Melvin said his personal good-byes to his friends and reserved a few more words for his brother. In the *Alliance,* Glenn Treadwell said good-bye to George Nations, and swore at him for having taken Jeff, his own son, along with him. When the vessels were about three hours out of Dutch Harbor, the crews tossed a wreath into the water, near where they had last seen the *Americus* almost a month before.

Minutes later, one of the crew spotted an orange blur on the water. Treadwell grabbed the binoculars; it was floating off the starboard bow. He throttled the *Alliance*'s engine way down and ordered one of the deckhands to stand by with a gaff. He swung the boat on a parallel course, as he would to land a crab pot. The crew member snared a deflated life raft, torn and moldy. One of the deckhands hosed it off, and when he did, the stenciled name ALTAIR emerged from the green sea slime. From where he stood in the wheelhouse, Treadwell could see the name. He felt nauseous. This course to and from Dutch Harbor was one of the busiest sea corridors in the world. For them to find the *Altair*'s life raft—what were the odds? Treadwell couldn't even imagine.

Jesus, he thought, were they just passing over the position where the *Altair* had gone down?

He called Melvin in the *Alyeska.*

"Brian, you're not going to believe this shit! It's happening again. We know where the *Altair* went down."

Melvin checked the position on the chart—54 degrees 24 minutes north latitude, 166 degrees 53 minutes west longitude—less than five miles from where the overturned hull of the *Americus* was first spotted.

Melvin got on the radio and called Jeff Hendricks back in Anacortes and told him what they had found and where. He also told him that the raft was missing all its gear and was too damaged to determine if it had ever been occupied.

Hendricks's guess was that no one had used the life raft. As far as where the *Altair* went down . . . He knew what the currents and tides were like up there. The *Altair*'s life raft could have drifted in any direction over the past month, easily covering five miles or more fifty times over. Or it might not have drifted at all. The raft might have popped loose from the bottom just as the *Alliance* was about to pass over the sunken hull.

Jacob Fisker-Andersen greeted Hendricks's news of the life-raft remnant with a long pause. Finally, he spoke. "A collision," he said firmly.

He also told Hendricks that, as he had asked, he had recalculated the stability of the *Alyeska* with a computer program, allowing for the added weight of the trawling gear. The numbers were a bit imprecise, he said, since the vessel was still in Dutch Harbor and he had not been able to conduct a full incline experiment. Nonetheless, these new calculations showed that the *Alyeska* weighed thirty-five tons more than he had accounted for in her original stability letter, and that the additional gear would have raised her vertical center of gravity by about a foot. Therefore, with her bottom fuel tanks full, she was capable of carrying a maximum of only 180 crab pots— forty-eight fewer pots than she was capable of carrying before the trawling gear was added.

Brian Melvin had carried 175 pots when he sailed out of Dutch Harbor on February 14 with his crab tanks flooded and the *Alyeska*'s big double-bottom fuel tanks empty, a trim configuration that would allow the smaller, lighter vessel to carry 116 pots at the most. In truth, the trim was so dangerous it was not even accounted for in the stability booklets.

The implications for the *Americus* and *Altair* were just as boggling. Because both vessels were slightly larger and heavier than the *Alyeska,* it was possible that recalculations would show their weight gains to be even greater than that of the *Alyeska*. Fisker-Andersen reduced the maximum number of pots they were capable of safely carrying from 230 to 227. But that capacity was for optimal weather with the double-bottom tanks full and the crab tanks empty.

Had Ron Beirnes and George Nations sailed the *Altair* and *Americus* with 224 and 228 crab pots respectively, as presumed—

nearly fifty more crab pots than Melvin had sailed with on his second trip out of Dutch Harbor—and their bottom fuel tanks empty and crab tanks full or cross-tanked, their trim configurations could have been even more dangerous than that of the *Alyeska*.

Hendricks was stunned by Fisker-Andersen's new stability calculations. The implications made the designer's collision theory sound gratuitous, at best. But he said nothing argumentative over the phone. As soon as he hung up, Hendricks radioed Brian Melvin and ordered him to leave Dutch Harbor with no more than 175 pots and to maintain full bottom fuel tanks. But Melvin did not have to be told. He was unsettled enough by the *Altair* and *Americus* and his own lucky escape from death. He had already taken every precaution he could think of.

CHAPTER 11

THE EARLY-MORNING FOG HAD BARELY LIFTED FROM LAKE Washington, but Bruce Adee and his two graduate-student assistants had been on the water for hours. From their Boston Whaler they were observing an unmanned, eight-foot-long model boat floating twenty yards in front of them. It had the pragmatic, hard-working profile of a modern fishing vessel; its wheelhouse was forward and there was plenty of deck space aft. The model weighed approximately six hundred pounds and was made of sheet metal. Adee had built it himself, for one purpose: capsizing. He had rolled his little vessel hundreds of times, for clients such as fishing-vessel builders, insurance companies, the National Oceanographic and Atmospheric Administration, the Coast Guard, and for the general sake of scientific inquiry. With an undergraduate degree from Princeton and a Ph.D. in engineering from the University of California at Berkeley,

Adee specialized in marine architecture—more specifically, in the science of stability. Or, as he sometimes put it sardonically, recognizing "the point of hopelessness," when a vessel violates its margin of stability and rolls over.

Adee guided the model by remote control. He could set and change its course, increase or decrease its speed, and, most important, he could send a signal to an electric motor to raise or lower a lead block mounted on a rotating shaft boring upward from the center of the hull. In this way he could simulate the loading and the trim of any large fishing vessel by simply changing weights and lowering or heightening them on the shaft. He could add or subtract other weights too, distributing them above or below the deck to more closely replicate a vessel's loading conditions.

Adee had induced his model to suffer more rollovers than any vessel afloat. Its value, among other things, was in being able to establish a curve that could be used to predict when the rollovers might occur and to furnish information so that vessel captains would know their parameters of safety. He had launched his model under various loads, courses, and conditions. His goal was to replicate every conceivable combination of circumstances and events in order to pinpoint the final factor that transformed the entire mass into what he was looking for: "a catastrophic demise."

Adee's headquarters, the Department of Mechanical Engineering, occupied a low, rectangular, concrete-and-glass building among a cluster of other unremarkable buildings on the lower campus of the sprawling University of Washington in Seattle. Within the cluster were the schools of electrical engineering, nuclear engineering, computer science, and physical engineering. Lower-campus jocks were not, as a rule, tied to fraternities or sororities or much interested in athletics or student government. Birkenstocks and pocket protectors reigned, not as fashion accessories, but out of pure practicality. Anyone connected with the lower campus, student or faculty member, was by association considered a geek.

At thirty-nine, lean, square-jawed, and youthfully handsome, Adee did not outwardly fit the geek stereotype. In his fifteen years as a professor he had earned a reputation as a serious academic and had written enough high-profile papers to rise above the publish-or-perish terrorism. His research grants brought in respectable amounts to the university. He had advised the multinational conference that had set international voluntary stability standards for hull design; he had consulted with boat builders; he had worked with claims investigators for insurance companies and accident investigators for the Coast Guard. He had been on the docks from Seattle to Alaska, had examined hundreds of boats, and had spent thousands of hours among fishermen.

Currently, Adee was working with the National Oceanographic and Atmospheric Administration to forecast forces that would cause fishing vessels to capsize. Out of this might come the national legislation the Coast Guard had once been pushing to regulate fishing vessels. Adee knew how powerful the industry lobby had been in opposing any government meddling.

The professor was working in his third-floor office on the third Saturday of April when Lieutenant Commander Paul Larson came calling. The tiny office was so crowded with books, boxes, and files that Larson jokingly wondered to himself whether Adee had come in to work that weekend or if he'd haphazardly trapped himself in and been unable to find his way out. Seeing no room to even lay down his briefcase, Larson suggested they meet downstairs in the lounge.

Jeff Hendricks epitomized safety-consciousness, Larson explained to Adee as he snapped open his briefcase and pulled out the files on the *Americus* and *Altair*. Hendricks, said Larson, had seemed forthright in giving the investigators whatever they needed. On the stand he seemed genuinely distraught over the loss of his brothers-in-law and crew.

Larson handed Adee a fuzzy photo of the overturned *Americus*'s hull floating in the Bering Sea.

Adee held the photo close. No structural damage was evident. The bottom looked freshly painted and the propeller was in a full forward pitch, meaning the boat had been running at full speed or near full speed. Then his eyes focused on the rudder. He traced it with his finger and told Larson to look at the position of the steering device: The rudder was hard to starboard. Whoever was at the helm had made a radical move, most likely reacting to a catastrophic situation.

"Did somebody make a mistake?" he asked aloud. "I think so," he said. "We'll have to reconstruct everything."

At the time of their meeting the fishing season was barely two months old, and already twelve boats had gone down in the Bering Sea. Adee had been keeping track. Every year for the past five years, in fact, the numbers of lost vessels had been climbing, and so had the fatalities. "Some of those captains think seamanship is being able to crash through the waves," Adee told Larson. "These fishermen take the view that if you do not consider yourself invulnerable to death and your boat invulnerable to the sea, then you and your boat must be weaklings.

"Fishermen are fine about some things," Adee continued. "If the lightbulb is not working, they fix it. They like to fix things, mechanical things. But stability is another matter. They just don't get it. They are looking to make immediate fixes. If you look at the boat at the dock, it just doesn't normally tell you whether it is unstable."

The following Monday, Adee and his assistants went back to Lake Washington to reenact the rollover of the *Americus*. Even armed with the possible numbers and combinations of loads and trims furnished by Larson—including an additional ton that fresh paint would have added to each vessel—Adee was aware of the handicaps: no witnesses, no recovered wreckage, and a misleading stability report from the *Antares,* a vessel no longer afloat. The report had not been revised even after tons of trawling gear had been added.

"They use the same design, the same patterns to cut the steel. They use the same steel," Adee told his assistants. "They reason that all the boats are the absolute same. What a rationale! No two boats are ever the same."

Adee loaded his model boat with lead weights relatively equal to the 228 crab pots plus the extra tons of trawling gear carried by the *Americus* out of Dutch Harbor the morning of February 14. Weights had been added and subtracted, fore and aft, to simulate the diagonal cross-tanking of the crab tanks, and others had been removed near the model's keel to resemble the lightness caused by empty bottom fuel tanks. He set his model on a southeasterly course so that the breeze from the southwest would send the light chop off the lake against the model's beam, as the Bering Sea had chopped at the beam of the *Americus* after she had passed Priest Rock and headed for the Pribilofs.

For three days Adee and his assistants varied each combination of weights slightly and recorded each change in the model's stability. He ran tests that took into account Fisker-Andersen's new computer inclining calculations. He took the model just to the point he expected it to capsize, then he gingerly raised the weight—and therefore the center of gravity—half an inch higher, feeling more tense with every passing minute, as if he had lighted a fuse. He would watch for the initial telltale sign, the first wobble, the beginnings of a lean. When nothing happened, he would adjust the remote control again to raise the weight on the model higher, notch by notch. When the little vessel failed to roll, he pulled the Whaler alongside while one of his assistants added and shifted more weight. After several hours and dozens of combinations, they still could not make the model capsize.

At the end of the third day, as he and his crew carried the model up across the beach and hoisted it onto a trailer, Adee reminded himself and his graduate students that theirs was an inexact science.

The next morning Adee drove to the Federal Building in downtown Seattle, where he told Larson and De Carteret that he had failed to make the model capsize. Every conceivable combination of weights had been tried, he said. He had worked up to the stability threshold gradually, he told them, and then exceeded it. "And still I couldn't roll the damn thing," he said. "From what we have here, it appears these boats were not just stable, they were incredibly stable."

De Carteret was chagrined as well. He, too, had been trying to make the *Americus* sink. At night, at home, he had been throwing every conceivable equation into a Macintosh computer program that could factor probabilities in split seconds. Each time, the *Americus* refused to capsize.

"Long after my wife was asleep, I'm up with my stability software program going. I move fuel around. I add more crab pots. I add weight and take it off. And I still can't make the goddamn thing sink," he recalled. "This thing's going nowhere. Others, you know that they were overloaded. Others, you have survivors. We got nothing."

On his desk was a stack of letters signed and ready to send. The one on top bore the name and Anacortes address of Al and Judy Littlefield. The heading was in capital letters: PRESUMPTION OF DEATH.

The letters bore the seal of a notary public. There were fourteen in all, one for each crew member of each boat. He had prepared them, he said, "because the son-of-a-bitch coroner up in Alaska won't issue death certificates. If the families have any money coming to them, they can't even begin to collect until someone tells them their sons or husbands are really, truly dead."

In addition, under the Jones Act—a sixty-year-old law based on nineteenth-century British sea laws—when a single, able-bodied man died at sea, the maximum he would be entitled to was an average of one year's wages.

"When you think about it, if we can't find any negligence, all these guys are entitled to is about thirty to forty thousand dollars,"

De Carteret said. "But if we find negligence, then it's going to be a free-for-all for the lawyers."

If the board found that the boats were unseaworthy when they left Dutch Harbor and if it appeared that Jeff Hendricks had willfully contributed to their condition, they were bound to pass their findings along to the U.S. attorney's office. The government could then make a case for criminal negligence; if negligence was established, wrongful-death lawsuits would surely follow. The payouts to the families of the crew members could be in the millions.

Under a somber sky, just after noon on Wednesday, April 20, three hundred Anacortes townspeople gathered silently on the marina dock as Delmar Cole in the *Radio*, Francis Barcott in the *Ethel B.*, Bill Lowman in the *Zig-Zag*, and nearly two dozen other fishing vessels circled the neat little harbor beneath Cap Sante. One by one, boats of all sizes passed by the memorial to the town's lost seamen. As they did, Reverend Hilary Bitz, the Lutheran minister, and Reverend George McLean, the Catholic priest, raised their right hands to acknowledge and bless them.

The blessing of the fleet was a ritual nearly as old as fishing itself. The Catholics argued that it began in the Mediterranean and Adriatic. The Lutherans claimed its origins lay with the Viking ships. Earlier still, historical evidence points to the fact that native tribes observed blessings when they sent dugout canoes into Puget Sound. In recent years, however, the blessing had fallen by the wayside, as local boats fishing in local waters had become as much of an anachronism as the ceremony itself. The reason it was being resurrected now, for the first time in twenty years, was clearly seen in the faces of Eve Northcutt, Lloyd and Jean Bass, Bud and Lois Awes, Wayne Melvin, George Boles, Punky Harvey, Jody Gudbranson, and a sprinkling of others who had lost someone on the *Americus* and *Altair*.

At the end of the ceremony, a newly installed eternal flame was lighted at the memorial dedicated to the Anacortes fishermen who had died at sea. Within the week, the fourteen names of the lost A-boat crew members would be added to the other ninety-six already there.

CHAPTER 12

On June 9, six weeks after Al Littlefield was informed by Captain John De Carteret's office that his son was presumed dead, he received a $30,000 settlement offer from Jeff Hendricks's insurance company. The condition of acceptance would be his signature on a release of presumption of liability and an agreement not to sue Hendricks.

Littlefield was furious. Two days earlier Hendricks had met with the Littlefields and other family members of the *Americus* and *Altair* crews to update them on the investigation and to let them know that as far as he was concerned, the estates of his crew members would be entitled to whatever was fair. "But dollars don't replace loved ones," he added. At the time Littlefield felt Hendricks was being sincere, and he thought, He's lost almost as much as any of us.

When he received the settlement offer, however, the loss of his son Larry felt codified and terribly reduced. A commercial fisherman since he was twenty, Larry had spent 450 days at sea fishing for Hendricks's company. He was making close to a hundred thousand dollars a year, owned his own home, stayed out of trouble, and was engaged to be married. "And this is it? This is what my son is worth?" Al Littlefield shouted in his own living room, frightening the dogs.

Wayne Melvin was angry too. He was so angry that he was going to refuse any settlement at all. There was nothing the insurance company could come up with that could change things, he said. He wanted no part of any settlement for the life of his son Brad. Instead, he called Shannon Stafford, a Seattle maritime-law specialist recommended by Paul Luvera, Anacortes's leading personal-injury lawyer.

Crystal Sadlowsky decided to call Stafford too, even though her daughter Jody Gudbranson had been offered a considerably larger settlement because she was a wife with a dependent. "My daughter's world went down with that boat," Crystal said.

Two weeks later the Coast Guard Board of Investigation resumed its public testimony. By his own request Jacob Fisker-Andersen was the first to testify. For the record he stated publicly what he had already informed Hendricks and the board—that, based on his latest computer calculations, the *Alyeska, Americus,* and *Altair* had each sailed with a greater lightship weight than he had accounted for in his original stability letter and therefore should have carried fewer pots. Still, the designer insisted that even these revised conditions were not enough to have caused the two vessels to capsize, and he presented his own theory: "I have been determined to find out why these two vessels disappeared. . . . I am of the firm opinion that the vessels did not capsize. . . . I have determined that these two vessels collided."

De Carteret shot Lieutenant Commander Larson a sharp glance, barely concealing his disdain for the designer's facile conclusion.

Even Jeff Hendricks appeared taken aback. A goddamn collision? De Carteret thought to himself. He had been expecting something like this.

Fisker-Andersen outlined his theory. The two vessels had been on virtually identical courses. Their crews were tired. The photograph of the *Americus* showed its rudder at hard right and the propeller pitched forward in full-speed position. This indicated only one thing, he said: the *Americus* was in an evasive action.

"I wasn't sure of this theory until they found the *Altair* life raft two miles from where the *Americus* sank," Fisker-Andersen told the board. The proximity of the life raft confirmed it all for him.

Larson interrupted. He wondered if Fisker-Andersen knew how far a life raft could drift during the month that had elapsed between the sinking of the *Americus* and the discovery by the *Alliance*.

"Nobody knows that," the designer snapped. Because it had left Dutch Harbor earlier than the *Americus,* he continued, the *Altair* was running at reduced speed. Then, about forty miles out of port, the *Americus* overtook the *Altair,* passing closely alongside.

"This created a vacuum effect," he said, explaining that when two boats run close by each other, the water between them moves at a higher speed than the water outside them. This creates low pressure on the outboard sides of the boats, which, in turn, acts as an airfoil, lifting and pushing both boats toward each other. Hence the collision.

De Carteret leaned forward, barely containing his anger. He said he was "slightly surprised" by the boat designer's theory, again noting that there were no damage marks on the overturned hull of the *Americus.*

Other forces could have been at work, Fisker-Andersen countered. A big wave could have slammed into one of the boats at the precise moment the vacuum effect occurred, creating enough force to capsize both boats. A tired or inexperienced crew member at the helm might not have noticed the two boats were drawing dangerously close to each other.

"Do you believe, with the experience of both captains, the crews would be so tired the helmsmen wouldn't watch the radar?" asked Herb Collins, one of the two NTSB investigators.

"You would have to ask someone else. If I had worked all day and had to leave at two A.M., I would be tired," Fisker-Andersen replied.

A murmur of derision, directed toward the investigation panel, rose from the portion of the audience made up of insurance-company representatives and lawyers. To them the collision theory was the one that ought to fly. If it could be proved that Ron Beirnes, George Nations, or a member of their crews caused the collision, the focus on the liability for the accident would narrow, as would their own potential liability. Such proof could reduce payouts to crew-member families and lessen the pressure for safety reforms.

The fishermen in the audience, too, were deeply concerned that the Coast Guard was using these hearings to come down around their necks. The agency had been trying to regulate their industry, urging laws that would force them to carry expensive safety equipment, pay for unnecessary training and certification, even license captains to run fishing vessels. The Coast Guard wanted them to turn their vessels over for spot safety inspections and force them to pay huge fines or put up money to meet what they felt were unreasonable safety standards. Their own insurance premiums were also likely to go up if this investigation came down hard on the industry as a whole. Any way you looked at it, the results could drive thousands of fishermen right out of business.

De Carteret called a lunch break. Reporters rushed him as he left the room. What was his response? Was it a collision?

"That's one of a hundred things that could have happened to the vessels out there," he answered matter-of-factly as he stepped into the elevator to return upstairs to his office. Inside, his guts were churning. The commandant's office in Washington, D.C., had called that morning. They wanted a progress report and he had little to pass along. De Carteret had counted on Bruce Adee to be his trump card, but the professor remained uncertain.

After lunch, Jeff Hendricks was asked whether he gave credence to Fisker-Andersen's theory.

His vessels did sometimes rendezvous at sea, he said. "It's conceivable that something of importance could have been left on one vessel or the other," he said, perhaps a crabbing position chart, a piece of equipment, even a training videotape or movie. But he also volunteered that standard operating procedures called for both captains to use radar and approach at greatly reduced speeds.

Larson noted the answer. Hendricks might acknowledge Fisker-Andersen's collision theory as a possibility, but he wasn't necessarily endorsing it. That was a good sign. We haven't lost him, Larson thought, or, at least, he's staying open-minded and not trying to cover his own ass.

Hendricks also explained why no other boats had picked up radio messages between the two vessels. The *Americus* and *Altair* were equipped with scramblers, which were used "one hundred percent of the time" when the vessels were heading to the fishing grounds. This prevented competing boats from getting a fix on their positions or their courses. Anyone listening would have heard only gibberish, he said.

Bruce Adee looked tense as he marched across the floor to the witness table later that afternoon. Once seated, Adee enumerated his qualifications for the record and delivered a lengthy discourse on the fundamentals of stability, avoiding the arcane, as De Carteret had instructed him to, for the sake of the press and the laypeople in the audience. Painstakingly, he took the board through twenty separate loading scenarios, each minimally different from the others but with consequences wide enough to be significant to the boats' overall stability, just as a single protein in a strand of DNA might be to the color of one's eyes. In just a few instances, he found, the loading might not have met the minimal international criteria for stability.

"But I believe both vessels were inherently extremely stable. . . . We may never know what actually happened." He could see De Carteret blanch. "However," he continued, "I believe that what happened to one vessel happened to the other." Adee had, in fact, developed a hypothesis by process of elimination but until this moment had kept it to himself.

"Synchronous rolling," he announced. "Even small waves could have caused the two boats to sink."

Synchronous rolls, Adee explained, occurred when the hull design and the waves were in conflict. Instead of one long pendulum swing of the hull, there could be a series of short, sharp, incremental heels, each building up on the previous one. Instead of righting itself, a vessel might list, harder and harder. Even in small seas a vessel could capsize easily, he said. "It would take only a few rolls of the vessel."

"How did this occur?" De Carteret asked.

"Because a boat was made unstable," Adee said. He asked for a slide projector.

The lights dimmed. His first slide showed the hull of an overturned vessel, an inverted American flag clearly visible on the bow.

"This is the *Americus,* taken by a crewman aboard the Russian trawler *Svetlaya,* which was standing by on February fifteenth. Several witnesses have testified that they spotted no hull damage."

He flashed a new slide showing the stern of the overturned hull.

"Note the rudder. It's hard over to starboard. The steering action of the rudder seems to play an important role once a vessel gets into a dangerous situation. The tendency is to put the rudder hard over as a vessel capsizes, in the opposite direction, as one would swerve an automobile. Steering actually makes the situation worse. . . ."

Larson remembered Adee focusing on the rudder from the first glimpse of the photo he had shown him in March.

"We have found with our model experiments that turning the rudder hard over, as you'd expect, generally tends to contribute to the capsizing. The initial effect is to further upset the vessel. In fact, it seems possible that this could have happened with the rudder position of the *Americus* as shown in the capsized position. . . ." Adee could tell he was getting ahead of himself, but he had already started down the path. "The best thing we've found to do when a person at the helm perceives he's going to capsize is leave the rudder amidships . . . cut the power . . ." The vessel's natural stability, he explained, "would have a better chance of saving the vessel than trying to correct imminent capsize."

A muffled snort came from somewhere in the audience. Someone was scoffing at him. De Carteret glared and grabbed the gavel. Adee continued.

"With synchronous rolling, sailing with the winds and seas off the starboard beam, water could have come on deck on the starboard side. The vessels could have heeled into the waves and not have had sufficient stability to return upright.

"I think if this did occur, initially, the crew probably would not have perceived anything greatly out of the ordinary because the boats still have some significant amount of initial stability, so their small-angle rolling would not have been greatly affected," he continued. "They may have perceived getting a bit lower and a period of rolling a little longer but probably would have thought that the vessel was more sea kindly under those circumstances.

"But it wouldn't be until they got to a large angle of heel where they would feel the vessel was sort of hanging at the edge."

"What then?" De Carteret asked.

"It had to be catastrophic and it had to be sudden," he said.

"Is this your conclusion, Doctor Adee?" De Carteret asked.

Bruce Adee paused, looking around the room. Besides the members of the board of investigation he knew no one except Jacob Fisker-Andersen, yet he could see that every face was tense with expectation.

"We have a long way to go before we can begin to understand the events contributing to the dynamics of this incident," he replied, choosing his words carefully. He explained that adding thirty tons of trawling gear could not be simply offset by subtracting crab pots. The value of the relative weights were different. They were in different locations. "This affected the metacentric height differently," he said, then concluded simply, "Our stability calculations are static without considering the complex forces found during the actual loading and at sea."

De Carteret thanked his star witness and announced that further independent stability tests would be conducted by the investigation panel and its consultants.

Bruce Adee packed his briefcase as the crowd filed out. De Carteret approached him. Dressed in a starched white short-sleeve shirt, with epaulets and gold bars, he looked more casual on this June afternoon than he had in his usual blue dress uniform. But what was on his mind was very firm.

"We have simply got to have some answers next time we come back in here," he told the professor. "We owe it to the families. Shit, these vessels are still going belly up out there."

CHAPTER 13

Oɴᴇ ᴍᴏɴᴛʜ ᴀғᴛᴇʀ ᴛʜᴇ Cᴏᴀsᴛ Gᴜᴀʀᴅ–NTSB ᴀᴅᴊᴏᴜʀɴᴇᴅ ᴛʜᴇɪʀ second hearing in Seattle, investigators began their next probe by crawling through a vessel named the *Morning Star* as it was tied to the dock at the Dakota Creek boatyard in Anacortes. The boat's owner, Dave Stanchfield, had come in for routine maintenance, but because his vessel was a twin of the *Americus,* Bruce Adee and Paul Larson had talked him into letting them use it for stability tests.

Stanchfield had heard rumors that the investigation was going nowhere. He himself had already testified before the board because he had known Ron Beirnes and George Nations and because he had once been a skipper of Jeff Hendricks's *Antares.* Stanchfield figured he owed them something and so had given up his ship. But now he was growing impatient, and that was not a good thing. Under normal circumstances he was not the most affable of fishing-boat captains, a tall, burly man with a flaming-red beard and volcanic eyes. His reputation was founded on the decibel level his voice could attain and the speed, force, and accuracy with which he could hurl a coffee cup from the wheelhouse when something went wrong on the deck below.

Stanchfield, thirty-seven, had started fishing in his late twenties in Alaska after serving in the Navy. He had wanted to go to college, and fishing was going to pay his way. But after two seasons he was making too much money to go back to school. Besides, he loved the rugged, independent life. So he lost himself in Kodiak and stayed. When he wasn't working on deck, he was working on the dock, and when he wasn't working, he was having a high time at the local bars.

Stanchfield had been perfectly positioned when the king-crab boom hit Kodiak. Oscar Dyson, the dean of the Kodiak crab-boat owners, gave him his first job and taught him to run a crab boat. Later, he hired on with Bart Eaton, another legendary skipper. By 1975 Stanchfield was running a boat and making $200,000 per season.

"I almost lost my life that year," he recalled. "The owner of the boat I was running never gave me a stability report. So we just loaded until we felt we couldn't load any more. I remember it was the last day of the season and we were loaded with king crab and we were pulling the pots back up and stacking them on deck. It was real calm.

"We had been fishing deep, so we had lots of line out. We loaded everything up and were heading back, and on our way back the wind came up. It got up to seventy miles an hour and the waves got up to twenty feet and the tide was running against the wind, a typical situation. We went over three huge waves and I looked out the back of the wheelhouse window and the waves were four or five feet high over the back deck. You couldn't see the railings. We were just buried. It scared the shit out of me.

"We were all alone out there. There was no one else to save us.

. . . I just throttled back and kept the bow into the waves. The last twenty miles we fought for our lives. . . . And, I'll tell you, if we had a stability report, it would have showed that we should not have been carrying so many pots and coming in with our crab tanks full and all those pots aboard. It was just plain stupid.''

In 1978 he accepted an offer from Jeff Hendricks to take the *Antares* into the Bering Sea. He remembered being impressed by how well built she was, how stable, how well she performed. He made a promise to himself to get his own boat as soon as he could afford to. He wanted it to be built by Dakota Creek Industries in Anacortes and wanted it to be as similar as possible to the *Antares*. At the end of the season he commissioned the boatyard to build the *Morning Star*. She came off the line right after the *Americus*.

Now, armed with the *Antares* stability report—the only one ever actually performed on the Hendricks boats or any similar boats, including the *Morning Star*—a small team of Coast Guard investigators led by Larson and Adee was tearing up his vessel to get a better understanding of the basic hull of the *Americus*.

Stanchfield thought that was a pretty backward way to go about business and told them so. But Larson and Adee reminded him that his vessel was the only tangible thing they had. They're reaching, Stanchfield thought, and he wished them luck.

What Adee and Larson were after was the lightship weight of the *Morning Star,* the bare-bones basic hull—essentially, the body without clothes. To measure this, all the fuel and crab tanks would have to be emptied, all the heavy trawling equipment would have to be dismantled and weighed separately, all the crew's gear and personal belongings and all the ship's stores and equipment would have to come off, down to the very last cable. When they got to pulling out his personal belongings and piling them on deck, however, and after Adee had made a crack about finding his bronze baby shoes, Stanchfield began to get impatient. "They were literally crawling along on their hands and knees through the innards of the vessel. I could hear them banging and yanking down below and I wasn't liking it one goddamn bit.''

Late one night, around midnight, the investigators were struggling to move a spare net onto a scale. They figured it weighed between two hundred and three hundred pounds. Stanchfield stood by for a moment, watching them try to drag the unwieldy net along the deck. Finally, he'd had enough.

Adee remembered, ''He stomped across the deck, grabbed the net, lifted it, gathering it to his chest, and he climbed up on the scales with it, glaring at us. And he wasn't even breathing hard.''

Adee sensed that the investigation team better step it up before Stanchfield gathered them up in his arms, walked to the edge of the dock, and dumped them into Puget Sound.

After the vessel was almost stripped, Adee and Larson measured the *Morning Star* amidships from the waterline to the deck, and they measured her length and width. They dangled a pendulum from the mast and, with a crane, moved one-ton weights around the decks, following the arc and distance of the pendulum's swing and measuring the angle of each reaction to a weight change. This gave them the *Morning Star*'s inclination to roll. Each night, back in Seattle, Adee fed the numbers into his computer program at the university, comparing them to the stability report of the *Antares*. From those numbers he tried to make the correct extrapolations to duplicate the *Americus* the moment she sailed into the Bering Sea on that last fatal voyage.

And as the work progressed, the numbers astounded him.

By the time they had stripped the *Morning Star* down as far as possible, measured her, and calculated her displacement, they found she was actually 55.6 tons heavier than the *Antares,* or at least 55.6 tons heavier than what the stability report stated the *Antares*'s lightship weight was supposed to be. That would mean she was 55.6 tons heavier even without the addition of trawling gear that Fisker-Andersen had eventually accounted for in revising the stability booklet for the *Alyeska* after the two A-boats went down.

Adee drove back up to Anacortes, astounded at his new findings. One last time the investigators crawled through Stanchfield's vessel, looking for something, anything, any combination of things that could have caused the discrepancy. The difference in the vessels was just too great. They were obviously missing something.

"I was really shaken," Adee remembered. "In the *Morning Star* we had virtually the same vessel as the *Antares*. Yet our numbers just didn't add up. We were way off. I felt we were no closer to the answers, maybe farther away."

He drove back to Seattle. That night he went to Fisker-Andersen's house, where the two men pored over Adee's data. Fisker-Andersen was stunned; Adee was saying that his stability calculations for the *Antares* and hence the *Altair* and *Americus* were based on a nearly fifty-six-ton mistake—Fisker-Andersen's mistake. If what they had discovered was true, the *Antares, Morning Star, Americus, Altair,* and *Alyeska* had all sailed with an overwhelmingly uncertain sense of gravity. How could any of them have sailed and survived the Bering Sea? But the *Alyeska* had survived, as had Stanchfield's *Morning Star,* the designer reminded Adee. He suggested that Adee go back to the drawing board and recalculate the weights. But Adee could see signs of self-doubt creep across Fisker-Andersen's face. Adee knew what Fisker-Andersen was thinking: A fifty-six-ton mistake could ruin him.

Adee returned to Anacortes. The next step on this complicated trail would be to see if there was a discrepancy between the in-scale plans for the *Antares* and *Morning Star* and the actual hull of the *Morning Star*. If they matched, then how could anyone explain the nearly fifty-six-ton difference in weight between the two vessels? He wanted to be certain he had considered every explanation before calling De Carteret.

Bob Gudmundson, one of the partners at the Dakota Creek shipyard, met him at the gate and led him to the barn-sized building that housed the mold loft, where designers and draftsmen drew vessels to scale on plans laid out on the floor. When Adee and Gudmundson arrived, the original plans for the *Antares* were already spread out before them. With tapes and calculators they crawled across the floor, measuring the drawings of the *Antares* and then the *Morning Star*. They set their tapes at the rail amidships and measured its distance to the waterline. They calculated each hull's cubic-foot volume under the water and multiplied by the water's density, which yielded the respective displacements or weight of the hulls underwater.

Both matched Fisker-Andersen's original calculations.

Then they performed the same measurements on the hull of the *Morning Star*. Again a match. The drawings were correct.

Captain De Carteret exploded when he heard the news of the weight discrepancy between the *Morning Star* hull and the *Antares*'s stability report.

"That is too goddamn much tonnage to give away," he said flatly. He ordered Adee to recalculate every figure. Before they came out publicly and said that the boats were actually 55.6 tons heavier than anyone was aware of, before the reputations of the designer, the boat builder, and the owner were wrecked, before there was a stampede to the lawyers, De Carteret wanted to be certain the investigators' conclusions were solid. Besides, he reminded Adee, even when the professor had plugged in the *Alyeska*'s added tonnage to his model, he couldn't capsize it.

But Adee reminded him he had not plugged in an extra 55.6 tons during those early tests. He had only accounted for Fisker-Andersen's recalculations due to the addition of thirty-five tons of trawling equipment. "Find another vessel," the Coast Guard captain said. "Do another calculation." De Carteret immediately called the press together again to tell them that the hearings were being postponed indefinitely, at least through the rest of the summer.

On August 17, the 107-foot crabber *Ocean Grace* had just passed Priest Rock and was heading out into the Bering Sea. The captain had set the course for the fishing grounds off St. Matthew Island, about 350 miles to the northwest. A large population of king crab had been discovered in the area. Under pressure from the crabbing industry and backed by consumer demand, a short king-crab season was opened. Dock prices were what they had been in the "pots of gold era" of the 1960s. Earlier, there had been some problems with the vessel's steering, but they had been temporarily repaired. The *Ocean Grace,* loaded with fuel, water, and a load of 112 crab pots, still seemed to handle sluggishly in the seven-foot seas on her stern. The captain ordered the aft crab tank filled with seawater. When the tank was filled, the rudder seemed to respond better, but the engineer was concerned about the heavier load. To confirm his fears, the portside of the vessel dipped underwater from a little ahead of midships nearly all the way to the stern. Only the last ten feet of stern were riding out of the water.

This is what the engineer later reported: "She laid over a little bit . . . on a normal swell, but she just stopped there. She didn't come back. On the next one she went a little farther. Well, that got everybody startled and everybody came piling out of their staterooms. . . . I didn't say anything. I was just trying to feel the boat . . . thinking, well, okay, she should start coming back. And she never did."

The engineer of the *Ocean Grace* was the only survivor of a crew of five.

The Coast Guard took approximately twenty-four hours to discover the reason the *Ocean Grace* capsized. She had been carrying twice the number of crab pots her stability booklet called for. When the captain flooded the aft crab tank, her righting arm—the angle at which she would roll and recover—had been cut in half. What followed were the synchronous rolls Adee had described at the hearings.

Two weeks later the ninety-seven-foot crabber *Golden Viking* had just retrieved and loaded 102 crab pots southwest of St. Matthew Island and was heading on a northwesterly course in calm, five-foot seas with eight-foot swells. The winds had just started to kick up to approximately thirty miles per hour out of the northeast when the vessel developed a slight port list. The captain ordered the engineer to check for slack water in the crab tanks, but none was found. The captain then ordered the engineer to transfer fuel from a port tank to a starboard tank. As the fuel was being transferred, the vessel listed to starboard. The list was so dramatic, the captain ordered the engineer to transfer the fuel back to port.

The *Golden Viking* continued on. The sea was moving in from the northeast and striking the vessel off starboard, halfway between the bow and amidships. When he reached the fishing grounds just south of the island, the captain began a slow turn to port, exposing the *Golden Viking*'s starboard flank to the sea. A big wave that crested and broke over the rail pulled it severely over. Frozen blocks of fresh bait broke loose and slid against the starboard bulkhead, contributing to the list. There was panic on deck. Water rushed through the forecastle door and into the pilothouse and through the air vents. The captain increased the speed and steered hard to starboard, but this sudden maneuver sent the listing vessel careening into oncoming waves. Another phenomenon Adee had described.

The *Golden Viking* held for a second and then went over. Two of six crew members were lost.

The following Monday, September 5, the *Golden Viking* was discussed in detail during Admiral Parker's briefing at Coast Guard District Headquarters in Seattle. Captain De Carteret appraised the details routinely, just as he had the details following the loss of the *Ocean Grace* two weeks earlier: The rapid shift of the vessel during fuel transfer from port to starboard was a sign of poor stability. The large angle of the *Golden Viking*'s heel when water swept over her deck was a sign of a low metacentric height. The emergency action the captain took accelerating and steering hard to starboard to right the vessel confirmed what Professor Adee had predicted during the hearings on the *Altair* and *Americus*. Finally, the *Golden Viking* was carrying nearly forty pots more than the safe limit noted in its stability report.

Again, De Carteret noted, that one was obvious. The *Golden Viking* catastrophe was a direct result of a disregard for its stability recommendations. The *Americus* and *Altair* had come nowhere near such huge violations of their safe-load limits—even according to Fisker-Andersen's revised stability calculations.

The admiral looked at De Carteret. "How's your investigation going?"

De Carteret could only demur.

That fall rumors had begun to circulate in Anacortes: The Coast Guard investigation was pointing to the conclusion that the A-boats were unstable; the boats had been overloaded and were lucky to have made it out of Dutch Harbor. The word was being passed from stool to stool at the taverns and the Elks Club and along the aisles at the Thrifty supermarket. Stability was being assessed by the customers who stopped into Al Littlefield's Texaco station, by customers of the gas company that employed Lloyd Bass, and by those who received their mail each day from George Boles. On the docks, too, the fishermen talked openly among themselves. "Damn fools," they called the captains and crews of the *Altair* and *Americus*. From his office at Alyeska Ocean Seafoods, Jeff Hendricks tried to handle every phone call from the families personally: "No, we still don't know what happened," he repeated. He tried to look his remaining skippers—Doug Knutson, Kevin Kirkpatrick, Brian Melvin, and Glenn Treadwell—in the eye. The rest of the time, he tried to avoid most everyone else in town.

Recently, however, Janice Nations, his sister-in-law, had begun to look beyond Hendricks for answers. She had been spending a lot of time in Evelyn Treadwell's kitchen. There, she could be silent or make small talk, depending on how Evelyn, her friend of nearly twenty years, read her needs. Evelyn knew firsthand that George had been difficult. She had been around the Nations family enough to know that sometimes Jan's gumption was the only apparent force holding things together.

Since Jan had lost George, she seemed to be coming around more often. Evelyn sensed that Jan wanted to talk to Glenn and he to her, but both had balked. By the late fall Evelyn began urging Glenn to tell his best friend's widow what he knew about the tragedy.

Finally, during one of Jan's visits, he stepped inside the kitchen and invited her upstairs to his den. There, photos of fishing vessels hugged the walls—heroic snapshots of the *Alyeska, Alliance,* and the other A-boats crashing through mountainous seas. Glenn had installed a bar there too, where he and George had often holed up to drink beer and take in the view of the harbor and the Cascade Mountains beyond, while their wives were visiting downstairs or out shopping. Often the quality of their time together was measured by how close their empty beer cans came to the brim of an industrial-strength plastic garbage can.

Jan stood silently, waiting for Glenn to speak. He popped a beer, took a long sip, and began to talk: He felt like a criminal, he said. The Coast Guard investigators had made him and Brian feel like they had done something wrong because they hadn't rushed to rescue the crew of the *Americus.*

"We did all we could," he told her. He had said that at least a dozen times before.

He took a deep swig and stared out the window. Then he turned to her and began to tell her what he had been adding up and keeping to himself for nearly a year.

He described how the boats looked when they took off from Dutch Harbor, how they were loaded, how they rode in the water. "It was overwhelming. I was overwhelmed. But what was I supposed to say?" he remembered telling her. "Was I supposed to tell George he shouldn't have a stack of crab pots so high? That he should have checked the fuel to see where the boat was light? Should I have questioned him about the water flowing out of the crab tanks?" He took another swallow of beer and continued.

"Ron and George caused those accidents. It wasn't the boats. This was preventable," he said. He'd been thinking about it for a long time, challenging his own memory, and he was ready for her to pummel him with denials too, ready for her to escape back downstairs in tears. But she stood there, looking calmly at him. "This was not an accident," Glenn continued. "You cannot call it an accident. An accident is when something happens you can't foresee, when two or three things go wrong. You can't see them coming. This was no accident."

She looked past him. Maybe she was looking through the window, he thought. Maybe she was looking at the harbor or the mountains, or maybe she was looking at nothing at all. After what seemed a long time to him, she said, "Glenn, I know. You've been letting this on a little at a time."

He started to say something more, but she cut him off, thanked him, then turned and walked back downstairs.

Treadwell lit a cigarette and stayed there, looking out the window, wondering if he had said enough or said too much, wondering if he was absolutely right about what he said. Eventually, he convinced himself he was. And then wondered again about what the hell really happened out there.

As each of the Anacortes families approached the deadline for accepting the insurance settlements, division grew within the ranks. A majority of those who were offered the $30,000 agreed the amount was not enough. Wayne Melvin, on the other hand, after his initial anger, decided to accept it. He was the only one. He wanted no part of any monetary negotiations or legal entanglements when it came to his son Brad, he said. Besides, Brian was still working for Jeff Hendricks, and Wayne did not want to make things more difficult than they already were.

Shannon Stafford, the lawyer for the families, told them that Jeff Hendricks's lawyers had filed petitions in court to limit the owner's liability. For the most part, Stafford would try to ensure that each family received the $35,000 the law said the relatives of single seamen were entitled to. He also assured them he would search for circumstances that would suggest the crew members deserved more. He would stay abreast of the Coast Guard investigation and keep his clients informed. But for now, they were not to settle.

Al Littlefield lingered after the meeting. He had been thinking, he said, that both the *Americus* and the *Altair* had to have been overloaded. He had heard that they had no up-to-date stability reports and that neither Ron Beirnes nor George Nations had supervised the loading of the vessels.

"I have been thinking that there was a good chance those boats left port in a dangerous condition," he told Stafford. "They should have known. They had to have known."

On November 2, 1983, partly to counter Hendricks's lawyers asking the families of the victims to sign away their right to sue and partly to signal that his clients intended to push for larger settlements, Shannon Stafford cited negligence and filed a $1 million wrongful-death claim against Jeff Hendricks and his company, Alyeska Ocean Inc., on behalf of Al Littlefield and the other family members, except Wayne Melvin, Nancy Beirnes, and Janice Nations.

CHAPTER 14

SINCE THE END OF SUMMER, WHEN HE COMPLETED HIS SURVEY OF the *Morning Star*, Bruce Adee had been desperately trying to find an explanation for the 55.6-ton discrepancy between the vessel and its twin, the *Antares*. Still, every time a new test was conducted, the discrepancy was reconfirmed: In January of 1984, when Jacob Fisker-Andersen finally performed a physical stability test on the *Alyeska*, it showed the vessel to be actually sixty tons heavier than his original calculations (versus the thirty-five-ton discrepancy he had found with his computer program ten months earlier, in March 1983); in May of 1984, Adee himself surveyed the crabber *Viking Explorer*, yet another twin of the *Antares*, *Americus*, and *Altair*. It, too, was nearly sixty tons heavier than the A-boats' recorded weights.

Finally, after fifteen months of tests and revised calculations, the break he had been hoping for simply came in the mail. The slim package was from Charles B. Fortson, a marine surveyor out of Panama City, Florida; it contained several photographs accompanied by a note. *I hear you're involved in the investigation,* Fortson wrote. *I'm sending you these because they give you a good profile of the ship.*

Fortson had been encouraged to forward the photographs by Norm Holmes, a marine surveyor from Kodiak who had been retained by the Insurance Company of North America on Jeff Hendricks's behalf. Adee remembered that Holmes had been one of the first investigators of any kind to go to Dutch Harbor after the two boats were lost and had seemed straightforward and guileless in his research, regardless of his ties to Hendricks's insurance company.

When Adee had first talked with Holmes in Alaska, Holmes had advanced the idea that the A-boats might have been overloaded. Holmes had mentioned hearing that the boot stripe showed the *Altair* to be riding lower to the water in the stern. But Adee wasn't certain what Holmes had meant.

The package of photos might not clear anything up, Fortson wrote, but they at least offered a good look at the *Altair.* Taken in 1982 after the second of three conversions had added nearly twenty-two tons of trawling gear to the *Altair,* the photos showed the vessel in perfect profile. According to Fortson, at the time of the photo she was being chartered by the Navy on a surveying job in Puget Sound. Judging from the lack of her wake, Adee concluded the *Altair* was under way at approximately half speed in calm seas.

Adee shuffled the photographs like playing cards, then combed them with a magnifying glass. Each showed the blue hull and the red boot stripe. He picked the clearest image and focused hard on the stripe. Previous measurements came to mind. He reached for a ruler and laid it on the photo, measuring the distance from the top of the stripe to the water; it was greater than he had come to expect, but this didn't entirely surprise him. When these photographs were taken the *Altair* was probably running with empty crab tanks and was not fully loaded with fuel. There were no crab pots on board either, since she was on a surveying job.

Adee made some quick calculations and entered them into his software program, which already contained stability quotients for the *Altair*. When he punched up the totals with the final keystrokes, the numbers told him that the *Altair* was running about as high as she should be under the loading conditions he had entered. Nothing new to be learned from that exercise.

Adee sat back, baffled, staring at the image. He put his ruler to it again, this time measuring the distance from the boot stripe to the deck rail. He plugged the numbers into the computer, and again everything matched the original design.

What was he supposed to be looking for? He was about to call Norm Holmes in Alaska for help when he glanced at a more recent photo atop a pile on his desk. It was a photo of the *Altair* as she was leaving Anacortes for Dutch Harbor in February of 1983. She had already undergone her third and final conversion for trawling.

There was enough of a profile to make some measurements. Adee applied his ruler and scaled off the marks between the boot stripe and the deck railing fore and aft. Once again he fed the scaled numbers into his computer. This time the results were different. According to his scale, the *Altair*'s red boot stripe was a foot higher than in Fortson's photographs. More precisely, it appeared to be a foot higher than the stripe on Fisker-Andersen's 1977 outboard profile blueprint of the *Antares*.

The answer was almost overwhelming in its simplicity. If the *Altair*'s boot stripe had been painted a foot higher, then, sailing under loaded conditions with the waterline meeting the top of the stripe, she would in fact be riding a foot *deeper* in the water than she should have been. Adee knew that there were no uniform guidelines as to where boot stripes should be painted on a vessel's hull, and that owners sometimes repainted the stripe at different heights for various reasons. He also knew that every inch a vessel rode lower in the water corresponded to a 7-ton weight gain. The computer told Adee that this extra one-foot displacement at the waterline implied a difference of approximately sixty tons in the weight of the vessel itself; finally, the discoveries he had made in reinclining the *Morning Star* and *Viking Explorer,* and his theory that the *Altair* and *Americus* were actually 60 tons heavier than their stability booklets indicated, were confirmed by the *Altair* itself. What struck Adee most was how much sooner the sixty-ton discrepancy could have been discovered and how simply. If the *Altair*'s boot stripe had not been raised before she sailed that Valentine's Day, the vessel would have been riding a foot below the waterline, obvious to anyone looking that she was dangerously overloaded. Of course the boats looked normal when they left the dock in Anacortes. By moving the stripe a foot higher, someone had created a fatal illusion.

Adee recalculated other loading factors, plugging in values for the extra 35 tons of trawling gear, the nearly 230 crab pots each of the A-boats was carrying, and the empty bottom fuel tanks. Under these conditions, the righting arm for the *Altair* could have been as little as 7 degrees—23 degrees less than the recognized safe minimum. In other words, Adee said out loud to himself, "in any kind of sea or with any kind of turns, the boats would have rolled over. The stability reports didn't relate at all to the real vessels those guys were sailing."

The captains and crews of the *Altair* and *Americus* sailed out into the Bering Sea that last time, as they had always done, in the comfort of complete ignorance. The only difference between the two boats, Adee thought, was that if the *Altair* had flooded all its crab tanks, the vessel probably rolled over quicker and sank faster than the *Americus.*

Bob Gudmundson, the A-boats' builder, confirmed what Adee suspected. The boot stripes of both the *Americus* and *Altair* had been raised in January of 1983, just a month before they left for Dutch Harbor. They had been painted a foot higher, he said, to protect the hull against corrosive marine algae. Adee could hardly believe that the lives of fourteen men could have rested on something as simple as a paint job. Gudmundson insisted, however, that the boot stripes never served as reference points. The key was the original stability report done on the *Antares*. That was what was applied to every subsequent sister vessel that came off the line.

Still, Gudmundson could not account for what made the *Morning Star,* the *Viking Explorer*—even the *Alyeska*—sixty tons heavier, and neither could Adee.

Yet the facts were there. The boats were carrying an extra sixty tons even before the trawling gear was added. If any of them had undergone inclining tests, the numbers would surely have come up. If there had been laws requiring stability tests or reassessments of a vessel's inclination after any kind of conversion or weight adjustment, the A-boat tragedy—and countless others—would likely have been averted. Had Hendricks been required by law to order the *Americus* and *Altair* to be retested after each conversion, no doubt he would have instructed his captains to load their boats differently.

Adee was ready to face a public hearing. De Carteret, he knew, had been hoping that his research might yield the ammunition to push for unprecedented regulations of the commercial fishing industry. Perhaps now, Adee thought, he could hand De Carteret something conclusive.

On Wednesday, December 19, De Carteret reconvened the joint Coast Guard–NTSB hearing. During the twenty-two months that had elapsed since the overturned hull of the *Americus* was first discovered, 488 commercial fishing vessels were lost and 240 fishermen died—more than one-third of them in the Bering Sea and Gulf of Alaska. More than half of those deaths in Alaskan waters were caused by vessels capsizing.

In Seattle, the hearing room in the Federal Building was packed as De Carteret called Adee, the first witness. Adee could see the tension on Jeff Hendricks's and Fisker-Andersen's faces. And he could see it on the faces of the families who had come to see if finally the government could assign a reason for their losses.

Step by step Adee took the investigation board and the audience through his analysis. He recounted the tests with his model; he elaborated on measuring and surveying the *Morning Star* and *Viking Explorer,* and he described in great detail the blueprints and misleading numbers for the *Antares.* He described all possible combinations of loading conditions. Then he pulled Chuck Fortson's 1982 photos of the *Altair* out of his briefcase and placed them against the easel behind the witness table. With a pointer he explained how he had come to learn that the boot stripe had been painted higher on the hull after the vessel had been retrofitted in 1983 and how investigators had been using misleading calculations for its overall weight.

The truth, Adee said, turning away from the easel, ''was that the boats were probably doomed at the dock. . . . I believe the major contributing factor of the resulting capsizing or the loss of these vessels was the lack of static stability because the vessels were heavily loaded.''

Adee could see the effects of his words register with the audience. He tried to avoid eye contact with the lost crewmen's families but couldn't; he had just told them their sons or husbands had been killed by the hands of their own captains.

Jacob Fisker-Andersen asked to take the witness chair. He tried unsuccessfully to effect some damage control, telling the board that he had recently tested another vessel and found the weight discrepancy between that vessel and the *Antares* to be only twenty-five tons, not sixty. A twenty-five-ton weight gain was not enough to capsize one of the A-boats, his estimates showed. It would depend on exactly how the vessels were loaded. One factor would not be enough. It would have to be a combination of mistakes. He also said his own analysis of the boot stripe marked it only four inches higher, not a foot higher, than it was previously.

The implication—and he wanted the audience to understand this—was that the cause for the loss of the two vessels might very well lie with the two dead captains, who had responsibility for supervising the loading of the crab pots. That was assuming, of course, that a true cause could ever be arrived at.

Hendricks was called to the stand next. He confirmed that the *Altair*'s boot stripe had been painted higher. He confirmed the added weight of the trawling gear and the number of crab pots each vessel was carrying on February 14, 1983. He regretted that neither vessel had undergone an independent stability test after the gear had been added. Each of his remaining vessels was now being tested, he assured, and every future vessel would be tested as well. And any time any significant alteration occurred on any of his vessels, he would ensure they were reinclined and their stability guidelines were updated. He said he was determined to revisit every outstanding possibility: the possibility that the double-bottom fuel tanks had been emptied and could not provide ballast, that the crab tanks of both boats had been flooded, or that Nations had cross-tanked his vessel. He was appealing to the board, not so much to raise doubts about Adee's conclusions as to imply that the truth was still eluding them.

Hendricks wanted to establish one other point: He wasn't in Dutch Harbor when the *Americus* and *Altair* sailed for the last time; he couldn't know for certain what had happened.

De Carteret tried to read the faces of the victims' families. *Jesus, he's asking for the benefit of the doubt, and they want to give it to him,* he thought.

Back in Anacortes, Jeff Hendricks tried to get on with business. He still had what was left of a fleet. A new crab season was about to begin. But he was haunted by his lack of certainty.

"The families were looking at me for answers," he remembered. "They were looking right at me."

The hardest moments came when the workday was over and he was alone with his own thoughts.

"I'm a certified diver," he said. "I should have gone up there right away rather than staying down here. I could have gone over the side, rapped on the hull . . .

"Was I negligent?" he remembered asking himself over and over again. "Am I or am I not the cause of this tragedy? If I am, and I can construe that I am, am I to be the sacrificial lamb? What good would that do? It wouldn't do any good to go around town holding myself open and saying, 'I am a killer.' "

In order to gain some distance, Hendricks anointed himself skipper of the *Andrew McGee,* his newest A-boat, and asked Glenn Treadwell to be his relief skipper. Treadwell was grateful. The trip would offer some release from the pressure of running his own boat. Besides, Hendricks had traded Treadwell's boat, the *Alliance,* for the *Andrew McGee.* A job as relief skipper was the only suitable position for Treadwell left open in the fleet.

Rather than fishing in the Bering Sea, Hendricks had decided to work in deep water off Washington State. They would be prospecting for sizable schools of brown crab. Opening a new crab fishery in waters closer to home would allow the A-boats to keep working when the Bering Sea seasons were closed.

Hendricks also had an ulterior motive for bringing Treadwell along. He among them knew George Nations the best. If there was anything unusual that Treadwell had noticed about Nations or spotted on the *Americus* or the *Altair* during that last trip out of Dutch Harbor, anything he could remember, anything he hadn't told him or the investigators, Hendricks wanted to know. He was hopeful this trip might jog Treadwell's memory—in private, away from home.

The *Andrew McGee* sailed out of Anacortes on a sunny late spring day in 1985 and headed west out the Strait of Juan de Fuca toward the horizon. The swells were low and even for the day-and-a-half-long trip. When Hendricks finally idled the boat over possible new crabbing grounds, he and Treadwell relaxed at the railing, staring into the sea. As the boat rolled lazily, water washed over the deck and back out through the scuppers.

Suddenly, Treadwell pointed at the deck.

"That's what the *Altair* looked like. She had water rolling across the deck, coming out the tanks. That's how she looked when she left."

Finally he told Hendricks everything he had been piecing together from memory. The *Altair* and *Americus* had probably emptied their bottom tanks, as had Brian Melvin on the *Alyeska*. Ron Beirnes had also probably flooded all his crab tanks. She was sitting low in the water, he remembered now. It was no normal lay. She looked like she was overloaded. So did the *Americus,* Treadwell said. She was not quite as low, but very low still. She must have been cross-tanked.

Hendricks asked the obvious. Why hadn't Treadwell come out with this at the hearing or before now?

He wanted to protect Jan Nations, he said. And Nancy Beirnes. It wasn't up to him to tell them their husbands had killed everyone. He couldn't sit there and start in on all this in front of the reporters and the Coast Guard. Besides, Hendricks's attorneys had instructed him to answer directly only what was asked. He was to volunteer nothing he wasn't sure of.

Jeff Hendricks stared into the water. He thanked Treadwell. Nothing else was said.

A few weeks later, just days after they'd returned to Anacortes, Treadwell received a telephone call. It was from Doug Freyer, Hendricks's attorney.

"Jeff called me," the attorney said. "He said he thinks you'd better talk to the Coast Guard."

Finally, nearly two years to the day after he first testified, Glenn Treadwell, as close to an eyewitness as anyone could be, would offer the Coast Guard investigation some relief. He reached into his memory and experience as a fisherman, and Adee, the scientist, spun it into calculations on his computer. Treadwell had finally enabled the investigation to transcend speculation.

Even with Treadwell's insights, they would never be able to say precisely what happened out there—when it happened, where it happened, and what occurred, second by second. But Treadwell did offer something concrete that everyone could agree on. Mistakes had been made at the dock. By flooding the crab tanks, the *Altair*'s stability was substantially diminished. By the same token, the *Americus* would have been similarly affected had George cross-tanked his vessel.

In town, the news of Treadwell's revelations was greeted with a mixture of renewed sorrow and relief. On the docks where the old fishermen were spreading their nets, Ivan Suryan, a native of Croatia who had immigrated to Anacortes from the Dalmatian Coast in 1939, offered his own opinion: "Those A-boats were taking big chances. . . . They thought they were stronger than God's power. You have to respect the power of the sea. The sea has the power. You're just trying to make a living at it. . . . Those guys on the A-boats were young and crazy and after big money. . . . They thought they were so big and strong in those big boats. The thing is not to respect how big and strong you are. It is to appreciate how fragile you are."

CHAPTER 15

On April 8, 1985, twenty-five months after the investigation had begun, the longest inquiry of its kind in Coast Guard history came to a conclusion. It was not announced at a public hearing, and the families and parties of interest involved first learned of the results only when they received copies of what was officially titled a "Marine Casualty Report" by Captain John De Carteret.

The published findings were these: Whether the vessels were only twenty-five tons overweight, as Jacob Fisker-Andersen suggested, or sixty tons overweight, as Professor Bruce Adee had determined, the *Americus* and *Altair* were found to be unstable and unseaworthy. No single cause or overriding factor was blamed for the loss of the two vessels and their fourteen crew members. Rather, a combination of factors was cited in a carefully worded statement:

The following factors are identified as having contributed to apparent unstable conditions on board Americus *and* Altair.

1. Drag-gear conversion
2. Apparent weight gain above and beyond the drag-gear conversion
3. Crab-tank flooding
4. Fuel distribution

Hendricks, Fisker-Andersen, and the Dakota Creek builders were completely exonerated. Cross-tanking of the *Americus,* the report said, contributed to deck submergence, causing the vessel to heel quickly. For the *Altair,* with all four crab tanks flooded, the effect was much more dramatic. The *Altair* was likely to have capsized faster and sunk quicker than the *Americus.* It was only because the seas were extraordinarily calm that the *Altair* made it as far out of Dutch Harbor as she did, the report suggested.

Furthermore, it also suggested, *Though stability of the* Alyeska *was not evaluated, it is concluded her stability characteristics were dangerously minimal due to her sailing with empty double bottoms and all crab tanks flooded. It appears that the lighter crab-pot loads on* Alyeska, *compared to* Americus *and* Altair, *made the difference between survival and capsizing.*

Brian Melvin read the report and could only think back to those moments during the ice storm when one of his crew members had broken out the survival suits and he had ordered them put back. Those thoughts had not left him and he knew they probably never would. What, exactly, was the difference between survival and death? A single seven-hundred-pound crab pot? Two? Three? Was there any reason for him to be back in Anacortes and his brother at the bottom of the Bering Sea?

He called Glenn Treadwell and arranged to meet him at the tavern. As always, they sat with their backs to anyone who might approach them.

"They still can't say for certain what happened," Melvin said, staring into his glass. "But I can imagine the water rushing in, through the doors, the vents . . . the blackness, the cold . . ."

Treadwell remained silent. When Melvin had finished, when they had gone back over the entire experience together—the loss of the A-boats, the inquisition in Seattle, the conclusion—Treadwell looked at his friend and said, "It is an honor to be here with you." These were not the precise words Treadwell was looking for. To say he felt lucky to be there would have been more to the point. But that would have been clumsy. Besides, the point had already been made.

Indeed, the board issued a general admonishment to all fishermen, noting that "There is convincing evidence that commercial fishermen in general lack an appreciation of principles of stability. This investigation demonstrated that there was a critical failure to utilize information (stability booklets) readily available for determining safe loading."

Shannon Stafford, the attorney representing the families of the victims, read the board's findings carefully. He had been aggressively conducting a parallel inquiry in civil court, questioning many of the witnesses, including Treadwell and Melvin, whom the Coast Guard–NTSB had interviewed. The captains of the *Americus* and *Altair* had engaged in various degrees of negligence, he believed. He also believed Jeff Hendricks was well aware of the dangers involved in commercial fishing and had not done all he could. Stafford could keep pressing for larger settlements on behalf of the relatives of the unmarried victims even though maritime laws governing liability in wrongful death cases were very tight. But building a case that ran contrary to the Coast Guard findings would be very difficult, he believed, and would likely prove futile, involving hours of further testimony and inflicting more pain on families who were already emotionally exhausted. He called Al Littlefield and advised him that while he could still make an argument for larger settlements, in light of the results of the Coast Guard–NTSB investigation, going forward with a wrongful-death suit and trying to establish Jeff Hendricks's liability would serve no one's best interest.

Rabe, the NTSB investigator, concurred. "I'm not a lawyer, but I can honestly say that these people didn't act in a way that disregarded something they knew. They could and should have done more. But they didn't take shortcuts just to get out of the harbor on time. It was obvious to me from talking to the witnesses, even the owner, that none of them had a good understanding of stability."

The panel's strongest indictment was leveled at the fishing industry and the government itself:

> The absence of jurisdiction over commercial fishing vessels does not allow for the imposition of regulations which apply to the inspected segments of our Maritime industry. The practices of not verifying the displacement of follow-on sister vessels and of not reevaluating stability characteristics after major modifications seem to be common. In the case of the *Morning Star* and the *Alyeska,* even though modifications were made and the stability booklets were revised, it was done only on paper. The aforementioned practices reflect the absence of an industry standard to the extent that a lax approach to decision-making defines the industry standard.

That was a political statement De Carteret insisted on.

In the name of the *Americus* and *Altair,* the Coast Guard and the National Transportation Safety Board investigators jointly recommended:

1. Inclining all new commercial fishing vessels and conducting weight surveys on all other vessels in the same class.
2. Inclining and surveying every vessel that underwent major modifications.

3. Surveying every vessel two years and five years after construction to check for possible weight gains.
4. Standardizing hull markings to define uniform waterlines and load lines.

Finally, the panel recommended that the Coast Guard should request the authority from Congress to establish competency standards and require licenses for captains of every fishing vessel of a certain minimum length and tonnage. This authority would require that captains take a Coast Guard–approved or –administered course and pass a Coast Guard examination.

De Carteret felt strongly that his investigation would at last give the Coast Guard the impetus to demand safety reform on Capitol Hill. Finally, a commercial fishing tragedy had made national news, focusing the media on the nation's most dangerous unregulated occupation. Jeff Hendricks had suffered enough, De Carteret believed, and so had the community of Anacortes. He decided against recommending that the U.S. attorney's office initiate its own investigation into possible negligence on the part of the boat owner.

The Marine Board's recommendations were sent to Admiral J. S. Gracey, commandant of the U.S. Coast Guard. Gracey would decide whether to push the Coast Guard's backing of reform legislation on Capitol Hill. But he also knew the limitations of his own power. He served at the pleasure of the President, and the laissez-faire attitude of the Reagan Administration encouraged deregulation, not government intervention. Gracey had been fighting just to maintain the status quo on his own budget, which was being eaten up by the presidential mandate to conduct a war on drugs and sea-going smugglers. To send a full-blown and costly enforcement mandate to Elizabeth Dole, the secretary of transportation, to pass along to Congress would have been a fool's errand. Gracey had been down that road before without success. But even should his recommendations make it to Congress, they would surely meet dead ends there as well.

In the Senate the paperwork would have gone to the Committee on Commerce, Science, and Technology. In turn, it would have been passed to the subcommittee on merchant-marine activities and to certain doom. The chairman of that committee was Ted Stevens, Republican from Alaska. Stevens's two sons were crab fishermen. He was an avowed friend of the industry and an ardent opponent of regulations. In the House of Representatives, the Committee on Merchant Marine and Fisheries would have parceled out the recommendations to various subcommittees for review. Don Young, the Alaska Republican, was a prominent member of several of them. Like Stevens, Young opposed governmental intervention. He had campaigned and been elected on the timeless words of fishermen and Alaskan frontiersmen: "Leave us alone."

In the end, Admiral Gracey's recommendations were tepid compared to the board's proposals. He ordered a republishing and redistribution of a ten-year-old Navigation and Vessel Inspection Circular reiterating the international criteria for fishing-vessel stability. The circular, which would go to designers, owners, and builders, suggested that fishing-vessel owners voluntarily incline all new vessels and conduct weight surveys on all others in the same class. The board's recommendation that surveys be conducted two years and five years after vessel construction was rejected as too costly, as was its recommendation to standardize load line and waterline draft marks. Gracey reasoned, as had Gudmundson, the Anacortes boat builder, that line marks by themselves did not adequately reflect a vessel's stability; a more proper approach would be to consult the vessel's stability booklet. Finally, Gracey rejected the recommendation that fishing-vessel captains be required to pass exams to earn operators' licenses. Instead, a safety task force was called for to establish a "Safety Awareness Education Program." This was to be "a viable alternative to licensing. . . ." Gracey added, "Being voluntary, it will require no legislation, will have no disruptive effect on industry, and will not require an increase in Coast Guard resources.''

De Carteret was outraged. He was also powerless. He had kept his own outrage at what he believed was a general disregard for safety rules in check all through the hearings. In the interest of safety reform he had guided the board toward coming up with conclusions that might benefit the whole commercial fishing industry. That was his motivation—to make work safer out there. And now the head of the Coast Guard was rejecting his recommendations outright.

Now there were no more outlets for De Carteret's anger. Instead, on the same day that he learned of the commandant's decision, De Carteret, a career Coast Guard officer for more than twenty years, drove home to tell his wife he had decided to resign. He would submit his resignation within the year.

In June, National Transportation Safety Board Chairman Jim Burnett sent a letter to the Coast Guard commandant reminding him that ''the use of voluntary training and manuals to improve the poor safety record in the industry was started as early as 1968, but has not been successful'' and suggested there was ''no justification for inaction.''

The letter went unheeded.

Professor Adee, too, was infuriated by the impotent response his research had generated. But his work for the Coast Guard was finished. He appeared on national television and in public meetings throughout the nation, and each time his speech was the same.

''These lives should not have been lost if, technologically, these boats had been operated safely. Even carrying what they were carrying, they could have been operated safely. The early theories— wind shear, tidal waves, collisions, icing—those are acceptable risks. You could say, 'The sea rose up and smote those people down'—people have been saying that for thousands of years—but there was no honor in this. This is just tragic. . . . Someone knew those boats were unstable and they accepted that risk. Now, to say that they will accept voluntary standards and abide by them . . . that is just tragic.''

His public statements generated a number of threatening letters. Most of them were unsigned. They were obviously written by or on behalf of local fishermen. Underneath the harsh language, the strident message was more or less the same: *Keep your head out of our business*.

PART THREE

"All through the dark the wind looks for the grief it belongs to."

—*W. S. Merwin*

CHAPTER 16

A ̲ ̲ ̲LL THROUGH THE SUMMER OF 1985, PETER BARRY, JUST TWENTY, had been writing letters home to his parents, Bob and Peggy, in Washington, D.C. Peter was a Yale anthropology student, and this summer job was his first major adventure. One of fifteen thousand summer workers in the Alaskan fishing industry, he was hired to run a high-pressure hose cleaning fish slime in a Kodiak processing plant. The job was more monotonous than physically demanding, but it gave him a chance to explore Kodiak and the nearby Kenai Peninsula in his time off. His first letters home were exuberant, filled with details of awesome scenery along the trails into the John Muir Wilderness: spotting gigantic Kodiak bears, camping under soaring trees and mountains, sport-fishing for trout and salmon, and digging clams along the beaches.

In a letter Bob and Peggy Barry received from their son in late

July, Peter told them his fortunes had taken an ironic twist. There had been a strike at the processing plant and he had refused to cross a picket line. Exploring the docks looking for work, he met Gerald Bouchard, captain of the seiner *Western Sea*. Bouchard needed a deckhand and offered Peter the job. Peter would be working harder on the *Western Sea* than he had in the plant, but he could make much more money in the six or seven weeks remaining before school started, and if the weather cooperated, he would get to see an even greater Alaskan panorama. "Because I'm the least experienced, everyone is telling me what to do," Peter told his mother in a phone call from Kodiak, after three days of preparing gear and getting ready to sail. "But I don't mind. I expect it." And he told her what they were calling him. "Greenhorn."

The last letter Peter Barry sent home had a different tone. He had been at sea for just a few days, but he was concerned: The boat didn't seem right; neither did the captain. The whole operation seemed shady. He had wanted to get off at the next port, but the captain told him he would not get paid if he left the boat. And that, Peter feared, was the least that might happen to him.

Days later, on August 20, fishermen spotted the body of a young man floating off Kodiak Island. He couldn't have been in the water too long, they guessed, because a soggy letter they retrieved from a pocket of his jeans was still legible. It was addressed to Peter Barry, and it identified the young man's fishing vessel as the *Western Sea*. The boat had left the dock less than one week earlier.

In the search that followed, the Coast Guard sighted only minor wreckage close to where the young man had been found. The boat itself had disappeared. Apparently, there were no suvivors among the *Western Sea*'s six-man crew, though only two other bodies were discovered. One was that of Stewart Darling, a twenty-five-year-old summer worker from Bremerton, Washington. The other, recovered three weeks later, was Captain Gerald Bouchard's.

Two days after he was notified by the Coast Guard of Peter's death, Bob Barry arrived in Anchorage to claim his son's body.

Distraught and angry, he was determined to find out what had happened. He questioned resident fishermen, dockworkers, and he spoke by phone to the two Coast Guard officers who staffed the marine-safety office in Kodiak. One of the officers was brutally candid: "That boat never should have been allowed to leave the dock. . . . But our hands are tied."

Barry flew to Kodiak seeking more information, and what he learned on the docks shocked and infuriated him. Scott Dennistown, the crewman Peter had replaced, told him the *Western Sea* was a leaky and rotten wooden boat, built in 1915. It had no pumps to handle leaks, no EPIRB to transmit an automated distress signal, and its radio was underpowered. The boat had no life rafts or survival suits—only child-size life preservers. Dennistown had been afraid of the captain too. That's why he quit.

When he returned to Washington, Bob Barry was exhausted and bereft. Gradually, however, his anger took hold. He needed to find out more about the circumstances surrounding his only son's death. Barry had been U.S. ambassador to Bulgaria and was about to go to Sweden as head of the U.S. delegation to the Conference on Disarmament in Europe; his calls connected and his questions got answered.

Through connections to marine insurers and fishing-industry sources, Barry found out that the *Western Sea* had left Seattle without any financial backing for the season. He learned that the captain, also the ship's owner, had a reputation for loading his vessel so heavily with fish that the decks would be awash when he reached port; those who had tied up alongside Captain Bouchard said he took macho delight in the risk. The captain, then, was taking a gamble on the salmon run on the backs of a young, inexperienced crew.

A few weeks later, Barry got a call from the Coast Guard in Kodiak. A toxicology exam performed on Bouchard's body showed that he had been loaded with cocaine the day the *Western Sea* went down.

Despite every horrifying discovery Barry made about the *Western Sea*, there was "no actionable misconduct, inattention to duty, negligence, or willful violation of the law or regulation" on the part of the captain, according to the Coast Guard report. Possession of cocaine, it did note, was the only illegal activity. Barry was stunned to discover that there were no laws requiring commercial fishing vessels to be seaworthy, safely operated, or outfitted with any survival gear other than life jackets. He also learned that the death rates among commercial fishermen nationwide were seven times higher than the national average for all industrial occupations, and twice as high as mining, the next most hazardous occupation, a statistic the Coast Guard was well aware of. Barry traced the official records of the Coast Guard's halfhearted efforts to get congressional appropriations for enforceable safety laws and, incredulous, reviewed the results of the A-boats investigation and the laissez-faire response Admiral Gracey had issued only two months before Peter's death.

"It was as though everyone had given up on safety," Barry recalled. "My son, Peter, was a victim of this inexcusable neglect."

Barry channeled his fury into a letter to Admiral Gracey: *I believe the voluntary approach to fishing vessel safety is completely inadequate to the problem, and that the Coast Guard is being intellectually dishonest by claiming that it will be successful,* he wrote. *I find it sadly ironic that the memorandum covering the report of the* Western Sea*'s sinking consists of claims for the effectiveness of the voluntary approach. It is obvious that the voluntary approach would never have had the slightest effect on the owner–operator of that vessel.*

Barry received no response to his letter, and in the fall of 1985 he had to leave Washington for Stockholm, where he would spend months helping negotiate principles for the ban on nuclear weapons. Peggy stayed behind with their teenage daughter, Ellen, and grew increasingly despondent. A tall, handsome woman of fifty, with thick, gray-blond hair and the sharp features she had passed on to her son, Peggy Barry tended to be reserved, even though Washington's diplomatic protocol demanded sociability. Now, though, she had no reason to venture out. She seldom opened the blinds and could hardly bear to answer the condolence calls that poured in after Peter's death.

One phone call, however, did break Peggy's depression. Rosemary Hofer's son, Christopher, had been a crew mate of Peter's on the *Western Sea*. "I had no idea of the danger until this happened," Rosemary said, and Peggy Barry recognized the anguish in her voice.

Other families of the *Western Sea* crew, she discovered, had been asking the same questions she and Bob had, and they, too, called to share their outrage. Among them was Lisa McClain of Idaho Falls. Her twenty-four-year-old husband, Chris, had also disappeared when the *Western Sea* went down, leaving her alone with their two young children. Bob Darling, another parent, was galvanized by his son's death. "I can't bring my son back, but I can do something," he said. A woman named Mary Finch Hoyt called: Peggy Barry recognized her name immediately. She had been White House press secretary to Rosalynn Carter, and in 1978, while she was serving in the White House, her son Stephen died when the lobster boat he was working on went down off the coast of Rhode Island. No bodies were ever recovered, but the hull was located and the National Transportation Safety Board had investigated. There had been no public hearing and no cause was determined, but investigators discovered that Stephen's boat carried no EPIRB that might have sent out emergency locating signals. Thereafter, the NTSB recommended that the Coast Guard require EPIRBs on all fishing vessels.

"That was seven and a half years ago, Peggy," Mary Hoyt said. "Nothing has happened. Nothing has changed."

The more Peggy Barry listened to the families of victims, the more determined she became. She found herself picking up the phone and making calls too, her resolve growing, although for how long and to what end she could not be certain. For the moment she was simply learning how widespread the grief was and how heedless the government seemed to be.

Peggy began collecting everything she could find on marine safety. She signed up for courses taught by marine-safety experts and met with industrial-safety proponents and editorial writers for newspapers and magazines. She attended congressional hearings on reforming insurance for commercial fishing vessels and drafted statements to send to lawmakers and the press. She sought a meeting with Ted Stevens, Alaska's senior senator, and was granted an audience with an aide who told her, "You know, your son didn't know what he was doing up there."

Some years later Peggy found out that Stevens's predecessor, a maverick Democrat named Mike Gravelle, had gotten a call in his Senate office from another mother. Her son was interested in a summer fishing job in Alaska, she told him. Could he recommend it?

Gravelle made some calls and consulted several old-time Kodiak-area fishermen.

"Tell your son to look for work elsewhere," he told the woman. "People say it's just too dangerous and no one's paying any attention to safety."

Some days later, Jacqueline Kennedy called back to thank him and to say her son, John F. Kennedy, Jr., had been persuaded to take a safer summer job on a ranch in Montana.

Peggy Barry was learning that naïveté and indifference to safety were the biggest killers on the high seas. In the space of four months her home had been converted into a national clearinghouse for like-minded people who she vowed would not suffer fruitlessly. She was determined to see a law enacted that would curtail the astounding number of deaths at sea, and the grief she saw everywhere around her.

———

Ironically, no one from Anacortes had contacted Peggy Barry. As the memorial by the marina attested, Anacortes was used to losing its young men, sometimes three or four in a season. The men who fished did so by choice and were lucky to get good-paying jobs. For them the risks were acceptable. Danger, death, and grief, then, were natural elements of the community.

Even if the town had wanted to take action, there would have been no clear place to direct its anger. Towns like Anacortes that depended on sea commerce could hardly afford to take on the fishing industry that helped sustain them. Moreover, by placing most of the responsibility for the *Altair*'s and *Americus*'s capsizing on Beirnes's and Nations's loading practices, the Coast Guard had virtually exonerated Hendricks, Fisker-Andersen, and the boatyard. Gradually the people of Anacortes were forced to carry on as usual, or at least to keep their resentment to themselves.

On their lawyers' advice, the victims' families decided not to pursue a $1 million wrongful-death lawsuit against Jeff Hendricks. Al Littlefield even told people how relieved he was, Hendricks being, he believed, a decent man who had suffered along with the rest of the townsfolk. Ultimately, the relatives of the single crew members accepted an increased offer of $45,000 each by Hendricks's insurance company. The wives of Tony Vienhage and Lark Breckenridge received more than $500,000 each, and Jody Gudbranson, Troy's wife, received even more because she had a child.

The awards for Nancy Beirnes and Janice Nations were rumored to be far greater, but the settlements were not made public. Additional insurance interests paid off as well because of the equity interests of the captains' wives in the vessels.

Time moved forward: Valentine's Day, 1986, the third anniversary of the A-boat tragedy, passed without public recognition in town. That day, Eve Northcutt descended the stairs to her son Paul's room, sat alone on Paul's bed, and told him as she had done every night since he disappeared to mind himself wherever he was. Jody Gudbranson looked at herself in the mirror, at the dark lines around her eyes, and vowed she would bring herself back from the brink for the sake of her daughter, Rochelle, and out of loyalty to Troy. Rick Harvey wrote a sentimental note to his daughter, a jaunty little girl he and his wife, Suzie, had named Randi, after Rick's brother who died aboard the *Altair*. Al Littlefield raised a glass of Crown Royal to his son Larry, took a small drink, and, with tears running down his face, sat and turned the pages of the family photo album.

As he had nearly every day, Jeff Hendricks took measure of his recurring guilt and avoided anyone in town for whose grief he held himself responsible. Recently, he had bumped into one of his neighbors, one of a lost crew member's relatives, as she was walking out of the supermarket. He had a chance to say something, but what was the right thing to say? He could think of nothing, so they nodded to each other and simply said, ''Hi.'' Maybe their eye contact was enough, he thought. He hoped so, and walked on.

Since the tragedy Hendricks had not completely climbed into a hole, as some people predicted he would. Vowing privately to make amends, he became president of the North Pacific Vessel Owners Association, a nonprofit fishermen's coalition that began as lobbyists. With his backing and the help of the Coast Guard, the association developed the first volunteer safety program in the nation. Initially, the program met with skepticism. Leslie Hughes, the association's executive director, had joked how the hallway had to be recarpeted from time to time because so many fishermen came in dragging their feet. By 1986, however, on any given day at Fishermen's Terminal in Seattle, more than a dozen fishermen could be found taking courses in navigation, safety, stability, fire fighting, and first aid. Hendricks had made the courses mandatory for his own employees and campaigned hard to compel other vessel owners to enroll their crews.

Meanwhile, Hendricks continued to manage his fleet as efficiently as he could. Brian Melvin remained a first-rate skipper and money-maker; Hendricks had given him some equity in the company. In the seasons following the A-boats' disaster, however, it was clear that Glenn Treadwell was losing his edge. He had become overly cautious, which didn't necessarily make him a safer skipper. Given the circumstances and his experience in losing his best friend, it was understandable. Nonetheless, Hendricks knew that any weak link could be a liability. He let Glenn go.

By the fall of 1986, Hendricks had recovered enough financially—the value of the A-boats was more than $3.2 million each—to begin expanding his fleet again. He was about to launch newer and bigger boats capable of trawling for larger masses of fish. Eventually, his own sons, Rod and Todd, would run the new boats for him. Corey Nations, George's only remaining son, would be working for him, as would Glenn Treadwell's son Kevin. Hendricks was still determined to keep the company together and to generate new opportunities for Anacortes's young men.

Still, even with the passage of time some townspeople remained resentful. Doug Knutson, for instance, still held Hendricks responsible for the unseaworthy state of the *Americus* and *Altair* when they left Dutch Harbor. After several seasons running the *Arcturas,* Hendricks's top new boat, he would resign in a dispute over his crew's share of a season's catch, telling Hendricks that his management style was "bullshit." He complained that Hendricks had taken to running the company by fiat without consulting other members of the remaining family, including his sisters-in-law, Nancy Beirnes and Jan Nations.

The holiday season approached, and as usual, the Knutson family received an invitation to the Hendricks company Christmas party. Knutson had no intention of accepting, but his wife, Suzanne, prevailed for the sake of her family. They arrived late and Knutson, by his recollection, had only one drink. Still, word spread around the dance floor that he was bad-mouthing Jeff Hendricks to anyone who would listen.

"I had about enough," Hendricks recalled. "I was carrying so much around inside of me. I just erupted. I walked over and picked him out of a chair and threw him to the floor and said, 'You've been saying so-and-so about me.' "

Knutson remembered the incident differently. "He walked up to me from behind and said, 'Merry Christmas, asshole,' and sucker-punched me."

A small brawl ensued and the fighting moved outside. In a flurry of punches, Knutson sent Hendricks and Hendricks's brother-in-law, Mike Atterberry, to the ground. As he leaned over the two of them, Knutson blurted out what had been on his mind for months: "You're a killer. You killed those people!"

Hendricks, Knutson, and Atterberry spent most of the night in the Skagit County jail. By the next morning the surface had calmed, the lawyers had negotiated a truce, and the town had already buried the incident.

CHAPTER 17

PEGGY BARRY'S GRASS-ROOTS CAMPAIGN FOR SAFETY ON THE HIGH seas had its predecessors. While Peggy gathered force for her own cause, Sarah Brady was publicly campaigning for gun control after the near-fatal shooting in 1981 of her husband, Jim, President Reagan's press secretary, and congressional support was mounting for a bill that would regulate handgun purchases. Candy Lightner, following the killing of her thirteen-year-old daughter by a drunk driver in 1980, had knit a powerful web of other grieving parents into Mothers Against Drunk Drivers, arguably one of the most influential social-reform movements of the decade; in less than one year her group managed to achieve rigorous drunk-driving laws in most states.

Peggy knew that the plight of commercial fishermen might appeal less to public sympathy than high-profile issues like gun control or alcohol-related deaths. Still, throughout the winter, while her husband was in Europe, Peggy Barry campaigned hard—through an ever-growing list of political and journalistic contacts—to pressure lawmakers for mandatory safety measures.

"Everyone seemed to have been in the dark about this," she remembered. "It was so shameful. Maybe the people in positions of power wanted to be in the dark."

A government that had turned its back on her cause wasn't her only source of frustration. From the outset she was typecast by the fishing industry as a "privileged outsider" and therefore an intruder. "Fishermen have been dying for years, then one Yalie dies and the whole world seems to get up in arms," one lobbyist cynically told a reporter for *National Fisherman* magazine, an industry trade publication. He was speaking for many people who resented the attention generated by the letter-writing campaign of a diplomat's wife pleading for a forum on marine safety.

One grateful recipient of her letter barrage, however, was Representative Gerry Studds, a Democrat from Massachusetts. Studds was a gentle-spoken but fierce liberal, and a pain in the side of the Reagan Administration. A former schoolteacher, he was first elected to Congress in 1972, and because he represented the coastal communities from Gloucester to New Bedford, he was appointed chairman of a key subcommittee of the House Merchant Marine and Fisheries Committee. His panel oversaw wildlife conservation and the environment.

Studds was often at odds with fishermen because of his hard-line pro-environment stances. He believed in regulating fishing seasons and making certain fishing grounds off-limits. Most recently, he insisted that dolphins be protected from tuna fishermen. Although he was often accused by fishermen of imposing his own liberal prejudice against them, in truth he was mindful of his constituents, the thousands of fishermen who had fished the shallow banks off New England for generations.

Throughout his career Studds had met with dozens of family

members who had lost relatives to the sea. As a result he had been trying to reform compensation laws in favor of seamen injured or killed on fishing vessels. But for the past eight years the insurance industry opposed him at every turn. Vessel owners did as well, but for one reason only: Studds insisted that mandatory safety regulations be included with insurance reform and that all fishing vessels carry adequate safety and communications equipment. Each time he had pushed for these reforms—the first national laws ever proposed in the history of the U.S. commercial fishing industry—the industry had pushed back, citing overwhelming costs and holding fiercely to their traditional abhorrence of governmental intervention.

Studds's most powerful adversary was Representative Don Young of Alaska, a Republican four years his senior in the House. Every year Young received approximately one-fifth of his total campaign contributions from lawyers and lobbyists representing the fishing and sea-transportation industries. He knew that his seat would remain safe as long as he fought hard for his homegrown fishing industry. Even after Studds was named head of a subcommittee that governed commercial fishing resources, Young could command enough committee and subcommittee votes to kill any safety initiatives before they reached the floor of the House.

Still, Young could not prevail over the rise in insurance costs. Huge losses in Alaska, highlighted by the A-boat tragedies, had driven insurance premiums so high that policies were nearly out of reach for half the Alaskan fleet. On a typical vessel with a crew of seven, the premiums had risen from $34,000 in 1976 to $169,000 in 1986, and deductibles had risen from $1,000 to $17,500 per incident in the same amount of time. Industry lobbyists were pleading for insurance relief just so their clients could stay in business. The boat owners' goal, then, was to put a cap on premiums as well as on liability claims against owners and insurance companies. Naturally, others in the food chain—personal-injury lawyers in particular—opposed it. The Trial Lawyers Association of America was mounting a furious campaign against any measure that would limit their settlements and therefore their fees.

Studds's subcommittee was studying a variety of compensation bills to present to the House. The most tepid of these, and therefore the least distasteful to the opposition, was the bill proposed by Representative Walter Jones, a North Carolina Democrat and chairman of the Committee on Merchant Marine and Fisheries. While the Jones bill provided for sizable cuts in insurance premiums, it also provided for limits on compensation awards to injured or deceased crew members as long as the owner and operator of the vessel complied with certain minimal safety standards. These standards would be voluntary for vessels built before 1987 and mandatory for vessels built after 1987 or whenever an insurance reform measure finally was signed into law. Similar legislation would be introduced in the Senate, where another Alaska Republican, Ted Stevens, was preparing to fight back. Like Young, Stevens received heavy campaign contributions from the fishing industry. His son, as it happened, was captain of a crabbing vessel.

It was the insurance crisis that had caused the subcommittees to first meet in the fall of 1985, but every member, whether in the House or Senate, knew that these ongoing hearings would grease the skids for the debate and possible drafting of the country's first fishing-safety legislation.

Studds knew that demanding even minimal mandatory safety regulations in exchange for insurance reform was like marching with one of the opposing armies to the crossroads of Gettysburg. He knew that proposing such regulations in the midst of an insurance reform fight would be unpopular. Still, he sensed the time was approaching for a decisive battle. Peggy Barry, he hoped, might be just the weapon he needed. In letters written throughout the winter of 1985–86, she had framed the problem perfectly. What the fishing industry, the insurance industry, the legal industry, the Coast Guard, and Congress were facing, she insisted, was the issue of freedom: "The freedom to die or the freedom to kill."

Studds invited her to meet him in his office on Capitol Hill in early February.

In his first meeting with Peggy Barry, Studds's hopes were confirmed. He was immediately impressed by her eloquence, resolve, and sense of urgency. She had come prepared with a list of witnesses ready to testify at any congressional hearing. Through them Studds recognized he might be able to insist that any law addressing insurance reform take safety requirements into consideration as well.

The congressman worked quickly. He enlisted marine-safety consultants and included Peggy Barry among them. He then directed his staff to draw up a bill, and he prepared to horse-trade and twist arms in the corridors of the House.

Within weeks after the opening session of Congress, Studds's bill was introduced to the House subcommittee, along with five others calling for insurance reform. Studds's bill was exceptional in its demands. It was the only proposal that would require all fishing vessels, regardless of when they were built, to carry emergency radio beacons, lifeboats or life rafts, visual distress signals, communications equipment, and survival suits if the vessels were fishing in northern waters. Nearly every fishing nation in Europe insisted on these standards, and as a result the mortality rates of Great Britain, Denmark, even of Norway, a country whose fleets fished in the North Atlantic and North Pacific and Bering Sea, were far lower than that of the United States.

Congress, the Coast Guard, and the commercial fishing industry had never been confronted by such a bold initiative. Ironically, Jeff Hendricks had required this equipment on all his vessels, including the *Americus* and *Altair,* from the day they hit the water.

On April 17, just weeks after Studds's staff drafted his sweeping reform, the first of what would be three separate hearings was convened on Capitol Hill. These sessions would serve as the forum in which lawmakers would gather public input in order to draft a law that would best address the calls for insurance reform. Initially, it appeared that this would be an arcane legislative exercise with a low public profile. But Studds was determined to raise public awareness by leveraging safety issues into the debate. In addition, to ensure the broadest possible input, nine regional hearings would be scheduled during the next twelve months in coastal cities where fishing played a prominent economic role. Studds himself would host several hearings in villages within his coastal district to better gauge his constituents' support for and opposition to safety regulations.

On the morning of the first hearing Studds was dismayed, but not surprised, to see that only a handful of the subcommittee members had bothered to show up on time. The audience was sparse and scattered. To Studds, the scale of these potentially historic hearings suddenly began to appear insignificant. Young, he knew, had been working on his colleagues in Congress—successfully, it seemed.

Mario Biaggi, the gruff New York Democrat and chairman of the full committee on merchant marine and fisheries, gaveled the session open with a clear look of disdain. Studds knew that Biaggi felt he was trying to slipstream his own reform into an ongoing debate over insurance costs and, now, the Jones bill. While the commercial fishing industry might embrace the lenient Jones bill, the Studds bill could snarl any legislation on insurance reform, and Biaggi, who represented the seat of some of the nation's biggest and most powerful insurance companies, resented Studds's maneuver.

"I agreed to this meeting on fishing vessels only because of the immediacy of the problem—that is, availability of insurance at reasonable rates—but, I must emphasize, not at the expense of the fishermen," he said sternly.

Studds followed. From the podium he looked at his fellow panel members and identified his opponents. He noticed Young's absence without surprise, thinking to himself that his adversary was probably somewhere else in the building carrying out his own battle plan. He recognized nearly a dozen powerful lobbyists for the fishing and insurance industries in the audience and guessed there must be $500,000 worth of campaign contributions out there aligned against him. He spoke for nearly ten minutes, carefully outlining the provisions of his bill and the reasoning behind each provision.

"I am convinced that some limits must be placed on the liability of boat owners in personal-injury cases and that fishing vessels must become safer places on which to work," he concluded, peering over his reading glasses. "The problems of insurance and safety are linked: Both lives and livelihoods are at stake."

It was now time for rebuttal, but Young still had not arrived. Instead, Representative John Miller, a Republican from the state of Washington, asked permission to read a statement on Young's behalf. The two were allied on many issues, although the A-boats were from Miller's home state and he had been horrified by the loss.

Predictably, Young's statement said that he was committed to "moving legislation forward" that would alleviate the insurance crisis for fishing-vessel owners, as long as that legislation did not interfere with the freedom of fishermen to make their living. "We have heard numerous reports that commercial fishing is a dangerous occupation. I don't know any fisherman who would disagree," Young stated in his letter. "My concern is that we are attempting to legislate safety, rather than letting the fishing industry resolve its own problems.

"We cannot create a risk-free society. If we try, we may find ourselves legislating the commercial fishing industry out of business. While my heart goes out to all those who have been lost at sea and to their survivors, we have to accept the fact—as fishermen have done for hundreds of years—that the sea and nature are unforgiving, and no matter what we may mandate through Congressional action, fishermen will continue to risk their lives to provide us with the food that we eat."

Young had laid down the gauntlet. He was trying to characterize safety reforms as grandiose liberal measures that ran beyond the scope of Congress's responsibility. He wanted safety proposals jettisoned so that the committee could get on with its real work: to satisfy industry lobbyists with concerns over mounting insurance bills.

Studds was seething. What Young wanted was what Congress had been delivering for years—a laissez-faire approach to marine safety. As the subsequent opening remarks wound down, Studds was planning his next move. It would not be an open letter to the committee nor a prepared speech. He would introduce real human evidence of the need for safety laws. At the next hearing, he would introduce Peggy Barry.

Two months later, chairman Biaggi gaveled open the second subcommittee hearing. Studds noticed that the audience had grown, especially those opposed to mandatory safety standards. Obviously Young and his staff had been busy. There were no subsistence fishermen or father–son operations in the audience that day, but bigtime lobbyists representing big interests instead—the American Trial Lawyers Association, the American Institute of Marine Underwriters, the American Tunaboat Association, the Eastern Fisheries Association, the Pacific Seafood Processors Association, and the National Federation of Fishermen.

As he inventoried the opposition, Studds glanced to the rear of the room, where Peggy Barry, Bob Darling, Rosemary Hofer, and Mary Finch Hoyt sat, waiting to testify.

Before the witnesses appeared, though, Biaggi asked for the subcommittee's written statements to reiterate their positions. While they were not meant to be taken as votes, they did reveal the inclinations of each member. Had they been tallied, Studds knew the majority would have been leaning toward voluntary safety standards and the lenient Jones bill. Again, Young was absent, but Studds clearly felt his presence. Still, while Studds may have been in the minority, he had allies in the room that day as well. Two representatives from Washington State, John Miller, the Republican who'd read Young's statement at the last hearing, and Mike Lowry, a Democrat, had not only been shocked by the loss of the A-boats, they had been upset by the board of investigation's conclusions that both the *Altair* and *Americus* were made unstable by human error, especially by their crewmen who died at sea. Each had been outraged by Admiral Gracey's dismissal of the recommendations of the investigation board. In efforts to draft his own marine-safety bill, Lowry had contacted Captain John De Carteret earlier that winter for help. De Carteret simply repeated what the board had recommended to the commandant of the Coast Guard—that fishing vessels should be inspected and fishing-vessel captains should be tested and certified for competence.

With Studds's encouragement Lowry and Miller had met with Peggy Barry and others who had lost sons at sea. The result was yet another bill—unusual in that it was nonpartisan—which contained the provisions of the Studds bill and in addition called for Coast Guard inspections of all fishing vessels and stability tests for all vessels that underwent any major modification. The Lowry-Miller bill essentially resurrected the recommendations sent to Admiral Gracey by the joint Coast Guard and NTSB investigation board a year earlier. As such, it was the most demanding piece of legislation being proposed.

On this day Rear Admiral J. William Kime, chief of the Coast Guard's Office of Merchant Marine Safety, took the stand to represent Gracey's point of view, which had not changed. In his statement Kime reiterated the Coast Guard's official view that fishing-vessel captains were in the best position to make safety decisions and that overarching mandatory safety regulations would hamper them and be difficult to enforce.

"A voluntary program would be as effective as regulation," Kime said, "with little difference in the cost to fishermen, much less costly to government, and would achieve the desired results more rapidly."

Evaluating each of the bills, Kime announced that if the Coast

Guard were put in a position of advocating any of them it would be the Jones bill, because it called for voluntary crew training as an incentive for lower insurance rates. The Studds bill was less desirable, he said, and the Lowry-Miller bill was simply "at odds with this philosophy" of deregulation.

During the ten-minute recess that followed, Peggy Barry, Mary Finch Hoyt, and Rosemary Hofer vented their exasperation at the Coast Guard and assessed their opposition.

"It's like a mountain," Peggy Barry said, growing nervous. Her time on the stand was quickly approaching and the opponents were there in ranks, row after row of them, with the apparent blessing of the Coast Guard.

When the hearing adjourned, Admiral Kime returned to the stand. Biaggi had been called away, leaving Studds the acting chairman. Turning to Lowry, Studds invited him to respond to Admiral Kime's remarks.

Lowry, sharp and intense, had been spoiling for a fight all day as he listened to the positions of the Coast Guard and lobbyists from the fishing and insurance industries. Waving a pencil in the air, he repeated the figures that made the commercial fishing industry the nation's deadliest occupation, adding that, "Mining has a lot of problems. . . . It has government inspection required. Timber, which we have out where I am from, is an extremely hazardous business, and the government takes a position of responsibility about the deaths and injuries of people in that business."

Anger rising in his voice as he spoke, Lowry went on to point out who exactly was being endangered by the Coast Guard's policy of voluntary safety precautions—not only scores of fishermen, but hundreds of "twenty-year-old summer kids."

Under pressure, Kime tried to defend the Coast Guard's position, reminding Lowry that eleven years earlier the Coast Guard had helped draft a proposal for licensing fishing-vessel captains and calling for full inspections and certification of new vessels.

"We received no support from the fishing industry," he emphasized. "We received not enough support from Congress to bring this into effect, and the reason was that the economic burdens were cited as being too great to justify the potential safety improvements. We backed off that position."

Kime did not refer to the Coast Guard's own figures that cited the increasing fatalities at sea annually or the four thousand yearly rescue operations that were costing taxpayers about $30 million a year. The figures showed that in 1975, the year the Coast Guard drafted the proposal for an inspection and licensing law, ninety-one fishermen died at sea. The number would increase nearly every year. In 1983, the year the two A-boats went down, 145 fishermen died. By the spring of 1986, as the debate on safety was being waged on Capitol Hill, ninety-eight fishermen had already died on the job. A barrage of questions from Lowry finally forced Kime to admit that every year since 1982, the Coast Guard budget for marine safety had been cut thirty percent and the majority of its recent budgets was spent on searching for and interdicting drug-trafficking operations.

Finally, Studds excused Kime and waited for the room to calm down before he introduced his next witnesses. Peggy Barry, Rosemary Hofer, and Mary Hoyt rose at the back of the room. Rosemary's husband, Roderick, and Robert Darling, another bereaved father, accompanied them to the table in front of the dais. Mary Finch Hoyt was called as the first witness.

"I am the mother of Stephen Mitchell Hoyt, who was captain of a seventy-five-foot steel-hulled lobster boat that went down at sea off Point Judith, Rhode Island, in September 1978. Steve and his four crewmen were never found," she began.

She recounted what she had been told by Coast Guard investigators. Her son's vessel had no emergency position transmitting signal, which could have set a rescue into motion. A cause for the accident could not be established.

"Now, that is a pretty hard fact to live with. My son was a very cautious, prudent young man. In fact, the older and younger fishermen at Point Judith went out of their way to tell me that he was doubly cautious about everything and everybody at sea. He had more-expensive and extensive equipment, but he did not have an EPIRB, and I suppose I will always wonder why he didn't spend two hundred dollars or less for that device and how many people today are way out at sea without simple distress notification equipment quite simply because they are not required to have them.

"One does not tend to talk about cost-effectiveness in talking about human life," she said, searching the eyes of the half dozen panel members. "One of the main conclusions of the National Transportation Safety Board was that the Coast Guard should seek authority for EPIRBs for all fishing vessels, and that was seven and a half years ago. And now my friends the Barrys have lost Peter, and the Hofers have lost Chris, and Mr. Darling and many, many others, several hundred families, have been shattered in this time.

"Our tragedy is no less because members of our families were not lost in some terrible plane crash or some massive disaster that freezes the public's attention and mobilizes action. It is almost worse when it is three men here and five men there or seven men there, and it is merely taken for granted that there are inherent risks in going to sea. . . ."

Walking to the witness table, Peggy Barry prayed that her own testimony would sound as confident as Mary Hofer's. Nervously, she straightened herself in her seat, tugged at her blue silk blouse, and struggled to get out the words that would articulate the arguments she had been building since the body of her son, Peter, was found nearly nine months earlier.

"On August fifteenth of last year, the *Western Sea* left the harbor of Kodiak, Alaska, to fish for salmon. Something happened; we will never know what," she began. "But we do know that the wooden-hulled vessel was seventy years old, that some of the structure was rotten, that it probably had a loose hatch cover, that it had only a hand-operated bilge pump, which we hear was in operation every couple of hours around the clock, and that it had a heavy, diesel-powered skiff lashed to the deck, making it top-heavy.

"We also know that there were no life rafts, no EPIRBs, and no survival suits, which in those icy waters are absolutely required to last more than a few minutes. And we know that on August twentieth, the body of our son, Peter, was picked up. He was wearing a life jacket, which is all the survival equipment that's required today and all that may be required by law. He and the rest of his crew who died with him never had a chance. . . . Are you aware," she asked, looking directly at the panel members, "that there are more regulations that apply to small pleasure power boats than to large commercial fishing vessels with crew members? We were not, nor was Peter. . . ."

Peggy Barry then proceeded to dissect each bill, speaking to the merits of supporting the fishing industry while balancing prosperity and liability with safety. She spoke informatively and decisively. "If we could legislate unstable vessels like the *Western Sea* out of existence tomorrow, we would. But our immediate goal is to give the crew a chance, both by warning them of the dangers and equipping them to live on the brink of death."

She paused to collect herself. The room was quiet, and she could sense that her appeal for attention had been sincerely met by the members of the panel.

"Let me close, Mr. Chairman, with a word about the voluntary safety standards as advocated by so many in the fishing industry. Think about whether these voluntary standards ever would have saved any lives on the *Western Sea*. Read the Coast Guard investigation report of the sinking . . . describing the poor conditions of the vessel and the lack of safety equipment. And note that, judging by the autopsy report, the owner/operator had evidently been spending his money on cocaine and on neither survival equipment nor insurance. And then ask yourself if you think his right to engage in commercial fishing without any effective regulation is sustainable, and if you think it is, then ask how you would feel if your son or daughter decided to take up commercial fishing," she said, her voice trailing away. "I thank you."

The room was still hushed. Assured that she had made her point, Peggy Barry looked once again at the panel and then left the table.

Rosemary Hofer followed. With her husband by her side, she told of the devastation her family had suffered with the loss of their son Christopher on the *Western Sea,* a tragedy that could have been averted, she said, if the captain had been compelled to undergo licensing and his vessel an inspection, and if safety equipment had been in place. "My husband and I have committed ourselves to do whatever it takes and for as long as necessary to make people aware of the current situation and the remedies available as a memorial to our son and the others lost in similar tragedies. . . ." she concluded. "We trust you will keep in mind the agony that follows these accidents when you consider the cost and fairness to the commercial fishing industry. These young people have lost two lives, the one they were living and the one they might have had."

As Rosemary Hofer concluded her testimony, Studds felt a momentary elation. These women had achieved what he had been previously unable to: they had put a human face on the issue of maritime safety.

Studds saw this as the perfect opportunity to offer his closing remarks: "Members of Congress are very quick to claim credit for themselves; it may even be the thing that we do best. But one thing you can be certain of, I think, is that mandatory federal safety standards for fishing vessels will be enacted . . . and it will happen to a large extent because of you and your efforts. Those efforts, I think, will turn out in the future, when we look back on it, to have saved lives. . . ."

Peggy Barry, Mary Hoyt, and Rosemary Hofer rose from their chairs and embraced. The next day, as their words were conveyed in stories in the *Washington Post* and other newspapers throughout the nation, Studds felt confident he had scored a major strategic victory.

CHAPTER 18

PETE ZIMNY UNDERSTOOD THE ALLURE COMMERCIAL FISHING HELD for young men and kids. He himself bragged that his fishing career began when he was nine years old, when "my Croatian grandfather strapped me to the mast and told me to watch the water for schools of fish." He boasted that when he was a kid, he could catch shrimp with his bare hands and salmon with a handheld line. His Croatian nickname was Sukula Moi, meaning "son-of-the-eagle." He was so named, he explained, because he had telescopic vision. "I could spot jumping fish from two miles away."

A sinewy man of fifty-one with dark hair and alert, dark eyes, Pete had led an adventurous life. He had joined the Army at fifteen, lying about his age, to fight as a paratrooper in the Korean War. By eighteen he had been discharged and was already running his own fishing boat in Puget Sound. At twenty-five he was running a boat in the Bering Sea—no place to break in greenhorns, he said. By thirty-six, after eighteen years at sea, Pete decided to quit fishing in order to spend more time with his wife and six children. He tried a number of occupations, including various sales jobs that took him away from Anacortes. He was successful at some, others not. But he continued to travel, which led to his divorce. Still, when his eldest son, Mark, told him he had decided to go to sea, Pete had made no attempt to talk him out of it. In just a few years Mark had worked his way up the ranks and, by the age of twenty-six, become skipper of a ninety-six-foot trawler, the *Aleutian Harvester*.

Just before Thanksgiving in 1986 the *Aleutian Harvester* went down in blinding fog in Unimak Pass. The Coast Guard called Pete Zimny to say that its twenty-four-hour search had turned up nothing—no traces of the vessel, no survival gear, and no survivors.

Mark would be the first of two sons whom Pete Zimny would lose to the sea.

After conducting a desperate and exhausting three-day air search on his own, Zimny, heartbroken, stopped to visit old friends in Anacortes before heading home to Edmonds, a town just north of Seattle. One of the friends was Nancy Beirnes, whom he had known in high school. The two consoled each other and vowed to do everything they could to keep their younger sons away from the fishing life. They both knew that would not be easy—already Mitch Zimny and Tony Beirnes, both seventeen and best friends, were planning to partner their own fleet, despite the deaths of a brother and father respectively.

Two months later, on a calm, unusually balmy Saturday in January 1987, Mitch, Tony, and their friend Keith Humenik, sixteen, set out in an eleven-foot fiberglass skiff for Young Island, a small, hump-backed button of land about a mile directly west and in easy view of Nancy Beirnes's beachfront house. There was a small cabin on the island and the kids said they planned to do a little exploring, drop a small crab pot, and jig for rockfish. They had probably brought

along a little beer, beer-can voyages to Young Island being something of a rite of passage for Anacortes teens. It was also not uncommon for Anacortes teenagers to spend the night in the cabin on
Young Island or on the much larger neighboring islands, Burrows
and Allan, where there was plenty of natural cover.

Nancy Beirnes, Joyce Humenik, and Marlys Daniel, Pete
Zimny's former wife, were not unduly worried when their sons did
not return home that Saturday night. When they did not return on
Sunday night, the families made optimistic excuses; the boys were
having a good time and testing their limits; the six-and-a-half-
horsepower outboard motor had conked out; the weather had kicked
up and the boys had done the right thing by staying put and not
risking a run for home. But as the evening passed, their excuses
wore thin. From the front window of Nancy's house, the little islands shimmered darkly against the metallic winter sky. Finally,
since it was too dark and too rough to venture out looking for the
boys themselves, the families called the Coast Guard for help. The
search wouldn't be difficult, they reassured each other; there were
only three islands, and they were so close to town.

On Monday morning the cutter *Point Richmond* was dispatched
from Anacortes and a helicopter was launched from the neighboring
Whidbey Island Naval Air Station. They combed the area all day
Monday and again on Tuesday and found no trace of the boat or the
boys.

As the doorbell rang and neighbors brought food and words of
solace, Paul Daniel, Mitch Zimny's stepfather, tried putting on an
unflinching face while Marlys, his wife, rubbed her hands and
wiped away tears. Casseroles from these same neighbors were still
in the freezer from two months before, when Mark's boat had gone
down in Alaska.

Like Marlys, Nancy Beirnes had heard the words of denial and
hope before. She felt a familiar numbness too, just as she had felt
nearly four years earlier, when she could not reach Ron's boat by
radio. Her daughter Suzanne greeted the guests this time and spoke

for her mother: "We have a lot of family and friends, but when you get right down to it, it's really hard to take. . . . You keep hoping he's out there, but after what we've gone through, it's hard to keep hoping."

Pete Zimny remembered feeling "as if I was walking around dead." Once again he chartered a plane. That he now would be searching for his youngest son within two months of losing his oldest was beyond any nightmare he could ever have imagined. He ordered the pilot to fly back and forth over Rosario Strait while he stared into the empty water. Those who knew him would later claim that the stare had never left him. "I kept telling the pilot, 'I'll pay you extra to get down lower.' Until you search for a lost son you don't know what pain is, what it is to be powerless as a father," he remembered.

When he finally returned to his house in Edmonds, when he was finally alone again, Pete Zimny let his suffering take its own course. He felt defeated and guilty and ignored everything—meals, phone calls, his job, and the half-finished handmade boat he and Mark had been working on.

"I thought that my sons had done something bad," he remembered. "I felt bad that I contributed to their education about the sea. Was it me? Was I to blame?"

He remembered his own early days on deck and on the docks, when the work—mending nets, hauling line—was everybody's work, when the fleet sailed as one family within a larger family. "We lived in the community. We had a responsibility to each other," he remembered. "We were supposed to watch out for each other."

Condolence letters from friends and former neighbors in Anacortes were stacked neatly to one side of his work desk. The newspaper clippings and literature on marine safety he had collected since Mark's death were piled neatly too, with details of how many had died, how dangerous the occupation was, and the lack of safety regulations all highlighted in yellow marker. Alongside were lists of names, phone numbers, and addresses of legislators, congressional delegates, and others he'd been meaning to contact; among them were John De Carteret, Peggy Barry, and Don Young. During his research Zimny had come across newspaper accounts of the congressional hearings on maritime safety. Two articles in particular stood out. One was the account of Peggy Barry's testimony and the other bore a photo of Young, under which ran the following caption: *Alaska Rep. Don Young favors less-restrictive legislation for fishing vessels.* Pete Zimny circled the photo. Then he began drafting a letter to the congressman from Alaska.

Why do you favor less-restrictive legislation for fishing vessels? he began.

Do you advocate safety? Have you read the fishing-vessel accident statistics? Do you have a financial interest in any fishing venture? Are you associated socially with boat owners, boat owners' associations, processors, or banks that have large loans on fishing vessels? Have you talked to the Coast Guard concerning the cost of rescues relating to unsafe vessels? Do you have compassion for the average fisherman?

Who are you protecting? The needy or the greedy? Have you ever fished commercially in the fall or the winter around Kodiak or the Bering Sea? . . .

The questions were rhetorical. Zimny was a fisherman. He had never been to Washington, D.C., but he had a fuzzy concept of how things worked and that money, power, influence were the keys. But he had no idea of how to go about confirming his suspicions.

Next, Zimny wrote to Peggy Barry and included a copy of his letter to Young. He told her the congressman had not responded. She forwarded his letter to Studds, Lowry, and Miller and wrote back to Zimny, urging him to keep up his letter-writing campaign and to keep her up to date.

Zimny promptly wrote again to Young.

Times have changed. When I was a young boy growing up in

Anacortes, Washington, I shrimped with my hands. I would reach down and into the water and catch them by their feelers. I would also put a hand line in the water off the main street dock and catch salmon. Clams and crabs were plentiful along the shore. The commercial fishermen had simple boats and fished the local waters, where sea life was in abundance.

Local fish are not as abundant as they once were. They are almost nonexistent due to overfishing. . . . Therefore the commercial fishermen must fish farther out on the high sea. They must fish in waters that are known to be extremely dangerous. . . . They feel legislators are looking out for safety in the fishing industry as they do in other industries. But if there is no legislation or inadequate legislation, banks, corporation-owned boats, and holding companies are only obligated to follow the letter of the law in regards to safety.

The Lowry-Miller bill, now before Congress, is the very best, in my opinion, considering what there is to choose from. . . .

I hope you have at least read and understood these bills before making your comments. I am of the opinion that you just don't understand the true obligation that you have, ethically and morally, toward the fishermen, young and old alike. . . .

He signed his name, satisfied he had made his point, then thought of another.

P.S. What little financial gain that is realized by not having safe vessels and safety equipment is a sordid gain.

Again, Young did not respond, and again, Peggy Barry had copies of Zimny's letter sent to Studds, Lowry, and Miller. Studds told her Young was working hard to maintain the status quo; perhaps that was why his office let Zimny's correspondence—and others'—languish.

On Capitol Hill, sentiment in favor of regulating the fishing industry was growing. The issue that had begun as a trade-off against rising insurance premium rates had snowballed. Peggy

Barry had used her connections to generate publicity and a political audience, and with Studds's help she and the other parents had gained an emotional edge. Support for mandatory safety regulations, led by Studds, Lowry, and Miller, was gathering momentum. Even Senator Stevens was softening his opposition.

Don Young, a veteran of back-room politics, also understood that the direction of the political winds had changed. The question was no longer whether there would be a safety law, but what its mandate should be. At this point, Young reasoned, his only obligation was to see that the fishing-vessel owners and operators at least got something in return. In that sense, none of the bills before the subcommittee offered much. The Jones bill and Studds bill at least had some give in them. Either was more tolerable than Lowry-Miller, which not only called for mandatory safety equipment, but for licensing captains and inspecting fishing vessels as well.

By the time the third and final hearing was scheduled for June of 1987, Young had already sized up the battle and was mapping his retreat. His goal now was to help shape a compromise bill among the three on the table that would make its way to the full House without too much commotion from the fishing industry. It also meant he would likely have to make peace with Gerry Studds, perhaps even support his bill over Lowry-Miller, if that's what it took.

When he first glanced at the letter bearing the return address *House of Representatives, United States of America,* Pete Zimny thought that Young had finally gotten around to replying to his letter. But the letterhead was that of Gerry E. Studds, Massachusetts, chairman of the Subcommittee on Fisheries and Wildlife Conservation and the Environment. A hearing on fishing-vessel compensation and safety was to be held before various subcommittees of the House of Representatives of the 100th Congress on June 11, 1987. Zimny was invited to appear in Washington, D.C., and to make a statement.

Meanwhile, he had begun speaking out closer to home: "A seven-year-old, if he had enough money, could buy himself a fishing boat, call himself a captain, hire a crew, and go to the Bering Sea, that's how rotten regulations are," he had told reporters from the Seattle papers, whom he tried to enlist in his private safety campaign. Almost immediately thereafter, he received anonymous phone calls telling him to back off or his two remaining sons, Michael and Matt, both fishermen, would be blackballed from the fleet.

By speaking out, he had cast himself outside the circle. He was more like Peggy Barry now, some sort of crusader, no longer a fisherman. So when the letter arrived inviting him to speak before a congressional committee in Washington, D.C., he called his two sons.

"I don't want this attention if it's going to get you guys into trouble with your bosses," he told Michael and Matt separately.

Each told him the same thing: "Go for it."

Pete Zimny went out and bought himself a new suit.

A month before Zimny was scheduled to appear on Capitol Hill, Kevin Kirkpatrick, Nancy Beirnes's son-in-law, who had abandoned the burning *Antares,* was again in the Bering Sea, standing on the deck of a new Hendricks trawler supervising the transfer of a huge net loaded with tons of cod to a Japanese processing vessel. The net was attached to a twelve-strand steel cable. As the net was being hoisted, the strain of the cable increased. Those who were there when the cable snapped said it sounded like a gunshot. The cable whipped in an arc across the deck with such speed and force that when it hit Kirkpatrick, it threw him thirty feet in the air. Those who saw the entire scene marveled that he hadn't been cut in half. As it was, his skull was split open; the crewmen who got to him first thought he was dead.

A doctor on board the Japanese vessel miraculously resuscitated Kirkpatrick and was able to stabilize him enough for an emergency evacuation by Coast Guard helicopter. Doug Knutson, Kirkpatrick's brother-in-law, who was standing by on another vessel, called Anacortes and told Hendricks that he didn't think Kevin would survive the evacuation flight. Hendricks then called Nancy Beirnes and told her the same thing.

Nancy, again distraught, called her daughters Suzanne and Krystal, Kevin's wife. For the third time in four years, a vigil would be held at the Beirneses' household.

CHAPTER 19

IT WAS ONLY 9:00 A.M. AND ALREADY THE SWEAT WAS sluicing down the hollow of Pete Zimny's back. He had wanted to walk from his hotel to the Capitol Building, to cross the Great Mall's vast lawns and tulip beds, and to pass the monuments and ornate government buildings made of stone from the Dalmatian islands of his ancestors. He had hoped to gather perspective before he made his speech to members of Congress, but if the path he had chosen inspired anything, it was only the feeling of his own inconsequence. It was hot. It was muggy. His shirt was sticking to him, and he doubted his decision to have come at all.

When he reached the steps of the Capitol, he looked up as if sizing a peak for the final ascent. He prayed to God for a clear voice and to St. Nicholas, the patron of the Croatian fisherman, for guidance. A guard at the top of the steps, though, told him he had the wrong building and redirected him. Zimny hoped his prayers would be better answered on the witness stand.

The hearing room was virtually empty when Zimny stepped through the door. It was not what he had envisioned, not grand like everything else, but small. He felt less intimidated. The names of the members of the subcommittee had already been placed on the dais; he made a note of Young's position.

Around 9:35 people began trickling in, and Pete Zimny could tell there wasn't a fisherman among them. They all carried brief-cases. They all looked like lawyers. Members of the committee strode in casually and he noticed how relaxed, how jovial, everyone seemed. This was not right, he thought. He was here to talk about the deaths of his sons at sea.

He was glad to see Peggy Barry when she arrived. They had met briefly the evening before, and she had taken him on a short tour of Washington. But now, in a crisply tailored suit, even Peggy looked like a lawyer, he thought. She looked comfortable too, like an "insider," not an "outsider," as Zimny felt himself to be.

Seated next to Peggy in the back of the room, Zimny watched as the panel members took their seats. He was still waiting for Representative Young to appear when a small man wearing reading glasses called the meeting to order. This was Gerry Studds.

Scanning the room, Studds was awed by how quickly the audience had grown since the first public hearing fourteen months ago. Most, he knew, were there to fight against his proposed safety reforms. The Association of Trial Lawyers of America, who stood to lose millions of dollars in retainers or billable hours in a safer industry with fewer accidents, represented the greatest opposition. In fact, they had already managed to kill the provisions of Studds's bill that capped liability claims even before they were heard by a full committee. There were other opponents in the audience as well. August Felando, president of the American Tunaboat Association, which represented nearly two hundred vessels and 3,500 crew members, appeared frequently on Capitol Hill, where he extolled the safety record among the California-based tuna fleet and had already helped persuade California Senator Pete Wilson to oppose fishing restrictions. Earl Krygier, the executive director of the Alaskan Trollers Association, was there too, representing thousands of smaller subsistence fishermen—Don Young's constituents—who fished closer to shore and insisted that safety requirements for them should be different than those directed at larger vessels that fished out in deeper, colder water. What seats remained were crowded with representatives from the insurance industry. Already that year, the Pacific Marine Insurance Companies of Alaska and Washington, a combine that held policies on twenty-four thousand commercial fishing vessels, had gone into receivership and was being administered by a government-appointed overseer. There were estimates that thirty percent of the entire fleet was sailing without their owners bothering to purchase any insurance at all.

This third and final day of hearings, then, marked each interested party's last chance to publicly sway congressional opinions and, they hoped, to shape a bill that might least affect their pocketbooks.

Studds scanned the dais, noting his colleagues flanking him—Jones of North Carolina; Lowry and Miller of Washington; Davis of Michigan; Boxer and Shumway of California; Bennett, Lipinski, and Bateman of New Jersey—and tried to count their votes. His own agenda that day was compromise. He knew that his own bill, though favored over the strict demands of Lowry-Miller's, was still not as popular as the weakest bill, sponsored by Jones. What he hoped to achieve by the end of this hearing was a sort of middle ground between his and Jones's demands for safety requirements. At the very least, Studds hoped to secure some political sentiment for making life rafts and EPIRBs mandatory.

As he opened the hearing, Studds was given some cause for hope. In their introductory remarks several committee members expressed, for the first time, an interest in including some concession to new safety requirements in order to ensure insurance reforms. Most importantly, though, even Don Young offered some support, couching it vaguely in a statement read in his absence. This statement carried a different tone from Young's others: "I am also concerned with how best to handle safety issues," it read. "Although we cannot create a risk-free society, we must ensure that appropriate safety legislation is adopted. . . ."

On the dais, Gerry Studds tried hard to keep his own smile in check. Young had certainly seen the tide turn, he thought, and now he was scrambling for high ground. This was collateral Studds could use.

Watching Peggy Barry stride confidently to the witness table, Pete Zimny told himself to walk the very same way when it was his turn. Still, he felt his own pulse pounding in his ears.

"Last year I appeared before you speaking only for my husband and myself," Peggy began. "This year I have learned how many we speak for. . . . We speak for a great many who could not be with us here today, and for those who have written or called from all over the country to share the frustration and pain of having lost a loved one to the sea and not having been able to do anything to alleviate the situation. . . . But by far the most important, we speak for the crew members of the U.S. fishing fleet, for the injured seamen who have contacted us, and for all those whose lives are presently endangered by the lack of proper safety measures.

"We have been referred to as 'outsiders'. . . . Who are the insiders? The trial lawyers, the PR men for the commercial interests? . . . It's all these insiders who you have seen saying that safety is the ultimate responsibility of the man on the boat. . . . And that's fine, as long as the safest possible workplace has been provided and that the man on the boat has been adequately prepared. . . . That is all we're asking for, not miracles."

There should have been applause, Pete Zimny thought, anything but the rustling of papers, the snapping shut of a briefcase, the scratch of chair legs on the floor. But the next sound he heard was that of Studds calling his name.

He moved stiffly to the stand, sat down, and started right in, giving himself no time for fright. His voice obliged, sounding strong as he began.

"I hail from a fishing family, three generations of fishermen: my grandfather, father, brother, uncles, and cousins. I have four sons who fished, crewmen to captains. Their livelihoods have been in many different areas of fisheries—Dungeness crab, king crab, tanner crab, brown crab, salmon, herring, reef netting, gill netting, seining, trolling, bottom fish, otter trawl, midwater trawl, joint ventures, and processing. . . ." He reached for the water glass in front of him, but his hand trembled. He wondered if anyone noticed and set the glass down without taking a drink. "Thank you for the opportunity to express our opinions on the proposed legislation. . . ." he continued, his eyes directly on his carefully prepared notes. "Safety is a very large—"

Studds interrupted: "Excuse me, sir, I apologize. Could you pull your microphone just a little bit closer?"

"Yes, sir," Zimny said, jolted. Pete Zimny then put aside his notes and looked up, sweeping the faces of the panel with his dark eyes, coming to rest for a long second on the empty space behind the placard that read REP. DON YOUNG.

"Every other advanced country in the world has been or is licensing their fishermen. We feel it is appropriate at this time to license captains and crews in safety routines. This will promote professionalism, safety, and the lowering of the liability insurance in the long run. At the present time, on a two-hundred-ton fishing vessel, there are no or minimal federal or state license requirements for the captain. . . . There are more requirements for a person to obtain a moped license."

Faint laughter erupted, but Pete Zimny did not appreciate it. He went back to his notes.

"I personally have seen the derelict hulls of Louisiana shrimp and scallop boats, parts of wooden salmon boats, scattered along the beaches of Unalaska, Umnak, and along the Aleutian chain. The ones I didn't see had sunk into the deep.''

He swept the dais again with his eyes. "In the last five years I have personally lost five very good friends," speaking of George Nations and Ron Beirnes, among others. "My daughter lost her fiancé, and two of my sons were lost in boating incidents that might have been prevented if fishing-vessel safety requirements were in effect.''

In closing, Zimny thanked the hearing members and Peggy Barry. "Last but not least," he concluded, "thank you to the people, the mothers, fathers, brothers, uncles, sons and daughters, and friends whose feelings are drafted into this testimony.'' Then he sat back in the chair, exhaling deeply, relieved at knowing he had held the panel's attention. He glanced at Peggy Barry and found affirmation in her eyes.

Over the next three hours Pete Zimny listened to almost every witness after him speak against mandatory stability tests, inspections, licensing, and other tenets of the proposed liability and insurance reforms. As the day closed, he began to wonder if he had been heard at all.

On the flight back to Seattle he remembered what he had told Nancy Beirnes five months earlier in Anacortes, when both their sons were missing. He would do whatever he could. At the moment, though, he felt that he had not done enough.

In small increments, though, Peggy Barry's and Pete Zimny's goals were gaining concrete support. Testifying before a Senate committee considering its own version of a marine-safety law three months later, Barry cited a recent court decision in Portland, Oregon, where a judge ruled that the owner of a vessel that sank off the coast, with the loss of three crew members, not only had "an absolute and undeniable duty" to provide adequate lifesaving equipment such as a life raft and survival suit for each crew member, but also had been negligent for having no stability test conducted after his vessel underwent a conversion and added heavier gear. The judge had fined the vessel owner $1 million.

"He was not providing a safe workplace, which is all we're asking for," she told the Senate panel.

Throughout the fall the separate bills were revised, rewritten, and reshaped, enduring assaults from all sides. By the close of 1987, 116 commercial fishermen had died at sea, the largest number since 1983, the year the A-boats were lost, when 145 commercial fishermen died. By the winter of 1988 it was becoming clear that some sort of safety bill would emerge in the spring. Studds had pointed toward a deadline, and he was joined by a growing number of colleagues on the Hill who were hearing from constituents, thanks in part to the public testimony of Peggy Barry and Pete Zimny and others.

In the halls of Congress, deals were cut and compromises struck. The trial lawyers even managed to shelve provisions that would have limited insurance liability. Ironically, those provisions had begun the debate four years earlier, even before safety measures were introduced. Now, however, safety was the imperative.

In the end the Lowry-Miller bill, calling for mandatory inspections and stability tests, was subsumed by the more lenient Studds bill, which, in turn, was subsumed by the even more lenient Jones bill, the only one the Coast Guard said it could support. The proposals for licensing and training captains and crews, the proposals for registering and inspecting all fishing vessels and requiring stability tests—all the elements Captain John De Carteret, Peggy Barry, and Pete Zimny had pleaded for—had been gutted.

Studds had not argued with the compromise legislation. He had battled long enough to appreciate the value of gaining ground where none had previously been held. Peggy Barry, who shared the news with Zimny and other relatives of lost crew members, had to agree.

On June 28, more than a year after Peggy Barry and Pete Zimny had testified, the U.S. House of Representatives passed a bill setting safety standards for commercial fishing. Even Don Young had stood to speak in its favor.

All vessels, the bill stated, would be required to carry life rafts, survival suits, and emergency radio beacons. Mandatory safety training would be required, and a $5,000 penalty could be imposed for failure to comply. The Coast Guard was ordered to intervene and terminate any unsafe operation of a fishing vessel, although the definition of unsafe was left for further interpretation. A seventeen-member advisory committee was to be formed to help draft further safety regulations, including a plan for licensing vessel operators and inspecting their vessels. Of the seventeen members, ten were to represent the fishing industry, one was to be a naval architect, one was to be an insurance underwriter, one a vessel builder, one an educator, one an admiralty lawyer, one a safety advocate, and one from the general public. Peggy Barry would become vice-chairwoman of this committee. Plans for inspecting vessels and licensing operators were to be submitted to Congress by the secretary of transportation within two years from the date the act was signed into law.

The Senate passed the bill by voice vote on August 11. On September 9, without ceremony, President Ronald Reagan signed into law the Commercial Fishing Industry Vessel Safety Act, the first comprehensive commercial fishing safety bill in the nation's history. By that date, 843 commercial fishermen had died during his six years in the White House. The *Washington Post* editorialized that it was "a good law bought at an awful price."

The congressional victory, however, was far from complete. To blunt the outrage from the industry, a two-year grace period for imposing the regulations would be allowed. During the following twelve months, 102 commercial fishermen died at sea. The next year the numbers dropped to seventy, but one of those fatal accidents shed light on the Coast Guard's inaction and became a prominent factor in hastening the enforcement of safety laws.

The accident seemed no different from those Congress had heard about in hearings the previous years. In clear, calm weather on March 22, 1990, the 162-foot fish trawler–processor *Aleutian Enterprise* capsized in the Bering Sea. Nine crewmen ranging in ages from nineteen to twenty-eight were lost. Twenty-two others were rescued, many of them suffering from acute hypothermia, some near death. The vessel was owned by Seattle-based Arctic Alaska, the nation's largest fishing company, which for nearly a decade had been waging an intensive public relations and lobbying campaign professing to lead the industry in advocating and voluntarily adhering to good, safe operating practices at sea. At the time the company appeared to be leading the fight against government regulations.

But now Arctic Alaska was hit with the worst commercial fishing disaster since the loss of the *Americus* and *Altair* seven years earlier.

The combination fish-catching and processing vessel already had a near full load of pollock on board and was hauling in the last net— weighing approximately fourteen thousand pounds—when the net tore, dumping the contents on deck. The vessel listed approximately five degrees to port, hesitated, and, because it was already heavy with fish, rolled further. Seawater crashed over the bulwarks and flooded the processing area, just below the main deck.

As the flooding continued, the vessel listed harder. Crewmen below scrambled to get to the main deck. Some hollered and beat on closed doors to awaken off-duty sleeping crew members. In the wheelhouse, the captain, twenty-six-year-old Mark Siemons, switched to the emergency frequency on his radio in the wheelhouse and transmitted a MAYDAY. The vessel capsized two minutes later. Those who made it out frantically crawled up the side and kept crawling across the upturned bottom as the vessel continued to roll like a log.

Despite his youth, Siemons had earned a remarkable reputation as a fisherman. But he had no safety training. The vessel had survival suits, but many crew members had no idea where they were and most had never practiced putting them on.

The *Aleutian Enterprise* sank within three minutes of capsizing. Some crewmen jumped from the hull. Some were washed into the sea. The water temperature was reported to be between thirty-two and thirty-four degrees. Those who made it into the water clung to nets, floats, anything they could grab to stay afloat. There had been four life rafts on board, but one did not inflate and another had to be manually inflated in the water. The other two life rafts inflated, as they were designed to, but bottom side up. Some crewmen were able to right one of them, while others threw themselves on the inverted raft as it was.

Two sister ships, the *Northwest Enterprise* and *Pacific Enterprise,* were fishing within two miles of the *Aleutian Enterprise* and reached the scene inside fifteen minutes of its MAYDAY call. Had the two vessels been farther away, many of the remaining twenty-two crew members, including Mark Siemons, would likely have died.

Eighteen months had passed since President Reagan signed the Commercial Fishing Industry Vessel Safety Act into law, and the Coast Guard still had not issued regulations putting the law into effect. In addition, two months had passed since a federal advisory committee, with Peggy Barry as vice-chair, had submitted a plan for inspecting vessels and licensing operators to the Coast Guard. Peggy Barry was frustrated. The Coast Guard seemed to be ignoring the plan. Yet, because it involved the country's largest fishing company, the *Aleutian Enterprise* disaster gave Peggy Barry a nearly perfect platform to push for putting safety regulations into effect. When the mother of one of the men who died on the *Aleutian Enterprise* called her for help, Peggy urged Studds to call a hearing into the Coast Guard's progress as soon as possible.

The hearing took nearly a year to convene. In the meantime, 250 fishermen had died at sea. Now, in the summer of 1991, Peggy Barry found herself in the same House hearing room where she had begun her crusade more than five years earlier. This time, however, she provided the smoking gun that would point to the owner's responsibility and force the Coast Guard and federal government to enforce safety laws.

In her testimony she pointed out ways the fishing industry had maneuvered around the law: Skiffs, for instance, were being substituted for life rafts, and she reminded the panel that her own son had died on a boat whose skiff had been chained to the deck when the vessel sank.

Fish processors such as the *Aleutian Enterprise,* she pointed out, carried large crews and were much larger than strictly fish-catching vessels. Because of their size, they were subject to the same laws that applied to merchant ships. Any fish processor over two hundred gross tons was, by law, required to be registered with the Coast Guard, and its operators were required to be licensed.

Peggy Barry referenced a letter to the editor of the *Alaska Fishermen's Journal,* written in response to the sinking of the *Aleutian Enterprise*. It detailed the way vessel owners and purchasers routinely paid off marine architects and surveyors to register their boats at just under two hundred tons in order to avoid costly licensing fees.

"I would like you to listen to this," she said, taking her time, allowing her pause to register. " 'The 160-foot *Kodiak Queen* is 478 tons. The 162-foot *Aleutian Enterprise* was 195 tons. This 199-ton farce has gone on too long. How many more lives will be lost before we stop looking the other way?' "

Within weeks after Peggy Barry's testimony the mandate of the 1988 Commercial Fishing Industry Vessel Safety Act was published and distributed by the Coast Guard. The forty-page government pamphlet reflected the tireless commitment of Bob and Peggy Barry, Pete Zimny, Robert Darling, Rosemary and Rod Hofer, Mary Finch Hoyt, and hundreds of other relatives of lost seamen. For the first time in history the American fishing fleet was required to put to sea with regulations posted in the wheelhouses stating that

life rafts, survival suits, and emergency radio beacons were mandatory. To sail without them was to risk being fined.

After the conclusion of the *Aleutian Enterprise* hearings, the Coast
Guard turned the case over to the Justice Department. There was
evidence that not only the captain but the company, Arctic Alaska,
had criminally conspired to increase its profits at the expense of
safety and men's lives. If the case went forward, it would be the
first time in history that a Coast Guard investigation resulted in the
prosecution of officials of a fishing company for willful negligence.

Three years later, in April of 1994, fourteen officials of Arctic
Alaska were indicted by a federal grand jury in Seattle on more than
one hundred counts, including criminal negligence and manslaugh-
ter. The investigation by the Coast Guard and U.S. attorney's office
yielded evidence that the company had falsified records of the qualifications of its personnel, had covered up safety violations, and had
lied to federal investigators. The officers, including Mark Siemons,
the captain of the *Aleutian Enterprise,* and Francis Miller, the
founding owner of the company, faced hundreds of thousands of
dollars in fines and ten years each in prison.

One year later, on the eve of their trial, seven of the company's
thirteen key officers pleaded guilty to negligence and perjury. They
were subsequently fined and given three years' probation. The six
remaining officers followed suit shortly thereafter and were fined
and given probation as well. Francis Miller, however, chose to face
a jury. In the summer of 1996, the jury found him innocent.

Still, the *Aleutian Enterprise* case was a victory for safety advocates. Mark Siemons's license to operate a vessel the size of the
Aleutian Enterprise was forfeited, and he did not apply for reinstate-
ment. In supporting affidavits gathered in its investigation, the
Coast Guard had more evidence of the extent to which shipowners
falsified their records and hence further endangered the lives of
their crews.

The Arctic Alaska indictments and the publication and distribution of the safety law–enforcement act by the Coast Guard had immediate repercussions along the waterfront and at sea. In 1994, the year of the indictments, eighty fishermen died at sea, fourteen fewer than the previous year. In 1995 and 1996 the number of fatalities dropped to seventy-three and seventy-five respectively, and fell to fifty-four in 1997—among them Steve Brooks, an Anacortes captain and one of Brian Melvin's and Doug Knutson's best friends. With the exception of 1998, when a particularly bad winter led to forty fatalities during the first five months of the fishing and crabbing season, the great numbers of previous years had been reduced and the reduction seemed to be holding, although no one considered the numbers worth celebrating.

CHAPTER 20

On A Dark, Wet Morning In December 1994, Jeff Hendricks stood in the wheelhouse of the ten-thousand-ton *Alaska Ocean,* the largest factory trawler afloat. She was berthed at the giant Todd Shipyard in Seattle, undergoing final preparations for a season that would take her through the Bering Sea in winter and to Japan in the early spring. Longer than a football field and more than six stories high, the *Alaska Ocean* was capable of catching and processing one hundred tons of fish a day for sixty days without returning to port. She carried enough fresh water to sustain the entire town of Anacortes for over a week and generated enough electricity to illuminate the town of ten thousand day and night for an entire year. With a season's catch she could feed three successive generations of townsfolk, from birth to death. She was capable of working in any sea and in any weather. By fishermen's standards, her ninety-four-person crew experienced a comparatively comfortable ride and relatively luxurious working conditions. In the evolution of the commercial fishing industry, the *Alaska Ocean* was the essence of technology.

She had been assembled by a huge shipyard in Norway; under provisions of the Magnuson Act, which permitted only American-built vessels to fish within the two-hundred-mile U.S. limits, the *Alaska Ocean* would have been illegal. Hendricks, however, had found a loophole. For around $1 million, he purchased an aging U.S.-made "mud boat"—so-called because it had hauled mud to insulate the shafts of oil drills in the Gulf of Mexico—and scrapped all but a small portion of the keel, which he sent to a state-of-the-art conversion shipyard in Norway. There he commissioned a completely new vessel to be built around the keel, retaining just a piece, exposed and on display for inspectors. Technically, then, the *Alaska Ocean* was a converted vessel, not a new one. Carrying the remnant keel was as good as carrying a "Made in America" label. Soon, dozens of other seagoing entrepreneurs would follow his lead, igniting a strong backlash from none other than Don Young of Alaska, who claimed the practice was destined to put smaller, local Alaskan trawler–processors out of business.

In the meantime, Norwegian and Japanese banks were willing to finance the conversion of these vessels for U.S. fishermen for 150 percent of their ultimate book value, between $10 million and $20 million. Hendricks himself forged a joint venture with a Japanese holding company that put up the conversion money, and together they launched the *Alaska Ocean* in June of 1990 for the single purpose of harvesting and processing a huge biomass of protein—turning fish into fish paste called surimi—for the $100 million Japanese market, the largest in the world. That fall the vessel joined sixty other U.S. factory processors in Dutch Harbor to begin the hunt for huge schools of pollock and hake in the North Pacific and Bering Sea. Five years earlier there had not been one U.S.-flagged processor in the port.

At first there were dockside jokes about her: The *Alaska Ocean* had a fifty-seat movie theater and a 250-square-foot exercise room. Both rumors were true. The only thing her bronze-and-wood brasserie-style galley lacked was a maître d' and wine steward, jealous fishermen on other vessels said, knowing that Hendricks allowed no drinking on board. Her color-coordinated staterooms (eleven singles, thirty-one doubles, five for four persons) had piped-in stereos and Jacuzzi-style bathtubs. There were a paramedic and nurse on board and a separate housekeeping crew to clean the staterooms and tend to the crew's laundry. If this was a joint venture, the other fishermen joked, it must be with Carnival Cruise Lines.

At the Todd Shipyard, three other factory processors—the *Island Enterprise, Kodiak Enterprise,* and *Harvester Enterprise*—all owned by Tyson Foods, were moored nearby for repairs. "That's a four-billion-dollar company," Hendricks said, without disguising his contempt. "The largest fleet out there."

Tyson Foods was a chicken-processing giant based in Little Rock, Arkansas. In 1992 Tyson bought out Arctic Alaska, the owners of the ill-fated *Aleutian Enterprise,* for $233 million, even as the federal investigation was under way. Hendricks had been following the case closely; he knew of Arctic Alaska's reputation despite its public-relations campaign, but the Justice Department's prosecution of the company was unprecedented. He also reminded himself that the *Aleutian Enterprise* was neither the *Americus* nor the *Altair.* More than ten years had passed since he lost both brothers-in-law, a nephew, and eleven other crewmen, and still, when left alone with his own thoughts, the guilt would revisit him. Had he himself been negligent? Should he have insisted on new stability tests when the *Alyeska, Americus,* and *Altair* had been fitted with all that heavy trawling gear?

"Am I or am I not the cause of this tragedy?" he asked himself time after time. The question governed the tone of his voice, the rhythm of his moods, even his physical health. People in Anacortes often remarked how Hendricks seemed to have taken the entire tragedy upon himself.

"The obvious thing is that we had overconfidence in the boats," he said. "We should have reemphasized, redone the stability when we converted. But we didn't. It was a terrible mistake. It was certainly called for. Why wasn't it done? That's a valid question. It wasn't thought of by me.

"Things became more sophisticated in the late 1970s and 1980s," he said, explaining how the stakes had risen. "The whole way of life became more complicated. You had a lot of capital, and that bought a lot of technology. You could make things bigger and make them go faster. Who wouldn't do this?

"It's part of the race for the fish. Technology gets pushed by capital, and it exceeds the experience of the vessel and the crew. Technology gets out in front and . . . with technology, you get to a point where you begin having casualties. This is the point where we were, and the challenge was to tame the technology, turn it into opportunities."

The wheelhouse of the *Alaska Ocean* reflected Hendricks's obsessive vigilance. Amid the radar screens, plotters, and satellite monitoring devices, he could detect the beat of nearly every moving component of his vessel as it was propelled by a 6,250-horsepower engine. Here he could make strategic decisions that would affect both his crewmen's lives in the Bering Sea as well as the markets in Japan. He knew there were a good number of people whose truck payments or mortgages back in Anacortes depended on his leadership and that his company had provided training and jobs for hundreds of people, not just on board, but in ancillary positions in Anacortes as well. His success, at its peak with the *Alaska Ocean,* had become his means to make amends.

For Hendricks the *Alaska Ocean*'s wheelhouse had also become a political forum to promote safety and efficient working conditions on the high seas. By 1995, its tenth anniversary year, the North Pacific Vessel Owners Association's safety program had enlisted more than one hundred owners as members and enrolled more than thirteen thousand fishermen from Oregon to Dutch Harbor. Recently, one insurance company had given a boat owner a $9,000 rebate on the $12,000 the fishing company had spent on the safety training program. Since 1985 Hendricks had insisted that all prospective crew members undergo a mandatory Predictive Index test. Tailored to various jobs on board, the test was designed to disclose an individual's aptitude for risk orientation, leadership, drive, independence, and teamwork. The Predictive Index was even able to test a potential crew member's ability to cope with the monotony of working belowdecks in the fish-processing plant.

But Hendricks believed these measures alone were not enough. The government, by continuing to support the dangerously competitive Olympic system, was still retarding progress by forcing fishermen to race into life-threatening situations. In 1991 he had lost yet another boat, the *Andrew McGee,* which went aground near False Pass along the Alaskan Peninsula. Joey McKenzie, an Anacortes skipper, had made eight trips through the pass in seven days when he fell asleep in the wheelhouse and the boat ran pilotless into a shoal. Luckily, the whole crew had survived. It wasn't his young skipper alone that was to blame, Hendricks insisted, but the Olympic method itself. "We're all in a race for fish. One of the primary contributors to accidents is this attitude," he maintained.

The alternative to the free-for-all Olympic system, Hendricks argued, would be a system that would grant fishermen the right to catch allocated amounts of fish. This right would be based on a vessel's average catch over a number of seasons, and a limit per boat would be set. Known by industry advocates as "individual transferable quotas" (ITQs), they would stretch the season and give operators more discretion when and where they fished, thereby greatly reducing the breakneck competition of the current system. Not only would fishermen be protected, but theoretically the fishery itself would too, by limiting the number of vessels and size of the catch.

These ITQs could be purchased from the state of Alaska or from the federal government, and they could be resold to other fishermen. The quotas would be expensive, but Hendricks believed that those who couldn't afford them shouldn't be in the business in the first place. He could point to hundreds of boats similar to the *Western Sea,* the decrepit vessel that sent Peter Barry to his death; a quota system would keep boats like those at the dock.

Hendricks knew the system was far from perfect and he knew it would have its detractors, especially Alaskan fishermen who operated smaller vessels. Under a quota system these independent operators, the backbone of the Alaskan fleet for decades, could easily be bought out by larger, better-financed owners, especially syndicates and corporations that managed huge catcher–processors. Moreover, eliminating smaller vessels that delivered their catch to dockside in Kodiak and Dutch Harbor might cause the processing plants to shut down. Alaska could lose thousands of jobs to processors like Hendricks's *Alaska Ocean,* which could do everything from catching to canning fish without ever returning to port. Lastly, individual quotas could become a commodity unto themselves, creating a whole secondary market in fishing rights and paving the way for graft. Congressional opponents, including Don Young and others, argued that the character of one of Alaska's largest industries would disappear. Young had said flatly that he was against putting his state's resources into the hands of a few rich entrepreneurs—and outsiders, at that.

Hendricks had a sober reply. The industry was already killing itself off, he claimed. The romantic notion of fathers and sons plying Alaskan waters in their fifty-eight-foot wooden vessels, making it on guts and good instincts, had long since passed. The sea had proven how finite the industry was, claiming too many lives with too much competition for a catch that, like the king crab and halibut, could be within a season of dwindling away. The romance of the sea was being snatched away by the sea itself.

If he could take any personal solace it was in the rejuvenation of his company and his own standing in the industry, despite the losses of the *Americus* and *Altair*. There was another solace too; when Kevin Kirkpatrick, one of his key captains, was finally transported home from the hospital in Anchorage after the terrible accident in the Bering Sea, the crude prognosis was that, were he to live, he would do so as little more than a vegetable. Medical experts tried to explain the irreversible brain damage he'd suffered from the blow by the high-tension cable as delicately as possible to his friends and family without causing them to give up hope completely.

During Kevin's first days home, his wife, Krystal, stayed vigilantly by his side, squeezing his hand, talking gently to him, and looking for such telltale signs as a flicker of the eyelids or a rise in his blood pressure. Nearly every time she spoke, her husband's eyes responded, and, early on, that was enough. But as time wore on she demanded more of him, and somehow, Kevin's spirit began to answer back. His convalescence came slowly, after repeated surgeries and many uncertain months. He could see, but he could not hear or read. He could move, but he could not walk or care for himself.

Krystal stayed after him all the while, gently challenging him to match her own fortitude. She taught him to ride a large tricycle and then a bike and was there holding him when he took his first steps. She consulted therapists and became one herself, teaching him to mouth words and breathe them out so he could be heard clearly again. She taught him to read words and say them out loud so that he could prove to himself that he was getting better.

And he did get better. In town, Kevin's recovery was considered a miracle. When he left to go to sea again, only a couple of years after his accident, Hendricks was among those who saw him off at the dock, and shared the community's pride in reclaiming one of its own from the sea.

As July 1995 brought steady, even weather, Francis Barcott, age seventy-six, began spending more time down at the dock. When he came home there was a smattering of black paint on his pants. Ethel, his wife, didn't have to ask—he was getting the boat ready again. Even before she saw the *Veteran*'s black paint, she saw that look in her husband's eye and never once reminded him that he'd vowed the previous season would be the last time he'd take his boat into Puget Sound.

The commercial silver-salmon season had been shut down altogether by the state of Washington the year before, and the sockeye season had been considerably shortened. FOR SALE signs had begun to appear on boats at the docks from Seattle to Everett to Anacortes. Francis Barcott and his elderly four-man crew worried that this season would turn out to be the same. There had been talk that silvers would be put on the endangered-species list along with the Columbia River chinook, as king salmon were called locally. The *Veteran* had caught just three thousand salmon the year before, about twenty thousand fewer than previous years. Francis Barcott wondered whether this would be his last season, once and for all.

On the dock, though, he still enjoyed the old rituals of preparing for a new trip out on the sound. He and his crew spent their mornings and afternoons stretching the nets and mending frayed or broken meshes. Old friends and relatives would drop by to lend practiced hands, and Ethel eventually got around to bringing coffee and sandwiches. Occasionally, a tourist would take a snapshot of the men working at their nets. Neither Francis nor his crew would look up, but he could imagine himself being described somewhere down the line as "local color." It made him chuckle. Because it was true. If the tourists only knew—when he and Bill Lowman and the handful of other independent fishermen finally stopped fishing, there would be no more local color.

Around six he would come home for dinner, wash up, and tend to a few things before joining Ethel upstairs in their living room looking out onto the Guemes Channel. Deep into the night, if a cold north wind brought fog to the channel, he could hear the deep-throated foghorns sound, and he was certain his cousins Frank Barcott and Ivan Suryan could hear them too, in their houses up on the hill. He knew somewhere out there along the way, another horn would sound and another beacon would reveal the path to the fishing grounds. Thousands of days on deck had taught him how to steer a steady course home even in the wildest seas, even in his dreams.

Francis Barcott did take the *Veteran* out again late that summer to fish for salmon. He guided the boat clear of the Anacortes marina and the point at South Harbor Park, where a statue erected by the Port Commission would soon be dedicated. Barcott had been the project's chief advocate. The statue depicted a woman holding a lantern raised in one hand while resting the other on the child who clung to her skirt. The woman stood vigilantly, craning toward the sea. She would be dedicated to all those who had ever waited for a fisherman to come home.

Barcott enjoyed enough success that summer to mention to his wife that he was thinking of fishing the whole season, which, of course, would certainly be his last. Ethel listened patiently and said nothing.

Her husband fished through the end of the summer and into the fall. On the last day of October, on the water off Hood Canal in lower Puget Sound, while helping his crew pull a net laden with five hundred salmon aboard the *Veteran,* Francis Barcott died of a heart attack.

Within two weeks his name would be the 115th inscribed on the monument to the Anacortes fishermen who died at sea.

EPILOGUE

Having lived among fishermen and their families in Anacortes, I felt one more experience was necessary in order to complete this story.

I signed on as a crew member aboard the 130-foot crabber *Provider* for the winter season of 1995. She was out of Kodiak, Alaska, but had originated in Bellingham in 1974, some months before the *Alyeska* was built in the same boatyard. In fact, the hulls of the *Provider* and the *Alyeska* were nearly identical, with one difference: The *Provider* had been recently extended by about eight feet to create more deck and crab-tank space, and her wheelhouse was located in the stern.

The *Provider* had been designed by Jacob Fisker-Andersen, and to compound the irony, the vessel's skipper was Doug Knutson, the son-in-law of Ron Beirnes, skipper of the *Altair*. Also, during the fall and early winter of 1994, the *Provider* had undergone repairs at Dakota Creek, the Anacortes boatyard that built the *Americus* and *Altair* and retrofitted them with trawling gear. With the exception of George Johnson, a twenty-one-year-old greenhorn from Denver, and myself, the rest of the seven-member crew was from Anacortes.

On Saturday, New Year's Eve, we said our good-byes at the town dock and sailed under brilliant blue skies into the Guemes Channel. We swung north, hugging the leeward coastline of Vancouver Island, following the Inside Passage until we ran out of the protection of land. We would then sail across the Gulf of Alaska to Kodiak. There we would pick up a hundred crab pots and head to Dutch Harbor, where we would pick up more, before sailing to the Pribilofs. The second half of the trip would retrace the final voyages of the *Americus* and *Altair* twelve years before.

It would take nearly two weeks to reach Dutch Harbor. These relatively easy days offered me a chance to get my sea legs and become accustomed to the work routine on deck. Though it was understood that my primary motivation was to gather research, it was equally understood that if I was to be entitled to a share of the catch, I was to earn it working on deck. My main function, though, was to feed the captain and crew three meals a day. My job title was cook/deckhand.

The first third of the trip north was pleasure-boat perfect, with obliging weather and vistas bigger and more beautiful than those advertised in travel magazines. The work was tedious but light. When I remarked early on about the light work on deck, one of the crew members said it wasn't really work at all, just preparation. We rigged lines and knotted them and generally kibitzed, the crew amusing themselves by harassing George Johnson, the greenhorn, whom they called "Junior." They took turns loudly criticizing him, calling him "stupid," and wondering out loud whether or not he was gay. This was a time-honored protocol, I knew, but one I still found distracting and potentially dangerous—clearly the taunts only made Johnson feel insecure and isolated. When I asked why they continued to harass him, Bud Ryan, a veteran fisherman and the deck boss, said it was for his own good, implying that they were getting Johnson into a mental condition tough enough to handle the days ahead.

I was spared this ritual for one reason, I suspected. Not because I was chronicling the voyage, but because they had to eat what I prepared. There was something powerful about being in charge of the menu, the stove, and ten thousand dollars' worth of groceries, I soon learned, and was determined to leverage my position in any way in order to gain acceptance.

When we reached open water in the Gulf of Alaska, the seas got bigger, and I noticed that an overtone of violence and anger began to pervade my crewmates as they worked. Hammers and crowbars, tools that had been carefully tended earlier, were slammed to the deck where they would bounce or slide with each roll of the boat. Bait cans and crab-pot buoys were slung indignantly through the air. Coils of line and links of chain were slammed about, curses came more readily, and taunts became harsher. The crew, it seemed, was working itself into a state of violent equilibrium with the sea.

Things were becoming rough in the galley as well. As the seas came up and the *Provider* rolled more severely, the act of getting a ten-pound roast into the oven and slamming the door shut had become a major triumph. Opening the refrigerator door at the wrong moment, out of sync with the roll of the boat, would send the contents—milk, eggs, mayonnaise, tomato sauce—flying out like wild birds. The same would happen to a pot of boiling pasta water not held in place by rails on the stove, or a five-gallon container of olive oil that might explode on contact with the floor. To survive in the galley, I had to assume a siege mentality. Every can, every jar, pot, plate, or glass that wasn't secured might as well have been an artillery shell. The hours I spent back on deck working offered instant—albeit momentary—relief, even as the seas kept building and my time spent taking notes and transcribing them diminished.

By the time we reached Dutch Harbor, I began to notice a

change in the eyes of each crew member. When they straggled in drenched from the deck and gathered around the galley table, their talk was subdued, their eyes downcast and dull, much like combatants in war. During these times the cook must be tactful. This is the time when food is merely fuel, when the cold and hard work cause the body to crave calories and animal fat. Nothing fancy is required of the cook. Just get the food on the table; the less fanfare the better. It was a lesson I soon learned.

One night, after about two weeks at sea, I left the deck an hour before the rest of the crew and cooked an aromatic, spicy vegetarian dish on a foundation of basmati rice. It was 4:00 A.M., but the crew had just worked a nineteen-hour day and this was dinner. I liked to cook and had been saving this dish as a reward. But I made the mistake of informing my diners how difficult it was to prepare—chopping, sautéing, blending, and reducing to take full advantage of the basmati's superior absorption and succulence while the galley pitched with the force of an earthquake. I knew something about earthquakes and cooking, I reminded them. I came from San Francisco, located near the continent's great seismic faults and certainly one of America's gastronomic epicenters. I had friends who were chefs. As far as rice went, they offered no substitutes for basmati. The crew should be honored.

My presentation drew no response. The only sound was the clanking of forks on plates and the estimable "pass the hot sauce," from more than one crew member. I felt rage, owing somewhat to my own fatigue. But I deflected my emotions by pressing onward, lecturing the crew on the concept of grace under pressure and the heroic value of dining well under the worst possible conditions. I had presented an eloquent rebuke, I thought.

Finally, one crew member rose to the occasion. He was Dave Moe, the vessel's engineer, a blond man in his early twenties with a boyish face. From stories he told about himself, I gathered he had been somewhat of a hero as quarterback for the Anacortes Seahawks and something of a ladies' man as well. He raised his head slowly and put both hands on the galley table. Then he rose to his feet as if he were about to deliver a major address himself. I could still see the dull stare in his swollen, narrow eyes.

"Fuckin' rice is fuckin' rice," he said softly, and without clearing his plate he left the table. I assume he headed into his room to grab a few minutes' sleep before the work began again.

It was not long thereafter, on deck in the dead of the night, that I found myself spread-eagle and clinging for my life to the webbing of a seven-hundred-pound crab pot covered in ice. I could not halt my slide from the top of the stack of pots. Thirty feet below me the sea was in full and glorious rage. And in that single moment, when, according to the script, your life is supposed to flash before you, mine did. I laughed hysterically and screamed, "What the hell are you doing out here?" And realized immediately that everyone who ever sailed these waters had likely asked himself the same question.

Just after midnight sixteen days into our journey, not long after the *Provider* had slipped out of Dutch Harbor, past Priest Rock, and headed into the Bering Sea, the seas began to mount. All through the previous twenty-four hours the wind had been high and the snow had blown in a continuous drive across the deck as we loaded and stacked the crab pots. In the wheelhouse, the barometer began to drop. We listened to the weather report over the radio; Doug pulled a fax from the National Weather Service. Conditions were going to get worse, if anything. We could expect sixty-mile-an-hour winds and seas reaching thirty-five to forty feet. But because this was the opening day of tanner-crab season and the Olympic system was still in effect, we could not hesitate. We were already a day behind, due to some equipment problems. The commercial crab fleet—more than a hundred boats in all—was on the run north to the Pribilofs and beyond, and we were not with the front of the pack.

Around 2:00 A.M. we passed over the positions where everyone reckoned the *Americus* and *Altair* had gone down. I was in the wheelhouse with two other crew members. Doug had gone to bed, and nobody on board dared wake him. If the moment was to be acknowledged, its significance went unspoken.

Later, curled into a fetal position with my feet bracing the side of the bunk to keep from falling out, I felt the *Provider* working hard against the sea. I could hear the engine labor and the vessel's bones strain in ways I had not heard before. She rolled and snapped upright, rolled again and snapped back, nearly jarring me out of bed. This, I had been told, was the sign of a good boat, this inclination to roll and snap back quickly. It was also a sign that the seas were getting rougher. At times the boat would roll and dip so violently, I found myself suspended in midair before crashing back on the mattress. We had been at sea for more than two weeks, but this took some getting used to.

I gave up trying to sleep and went topside. In the captain's stateroom beneath the wheelhouse, Doug had dragged out the survival suits from the settee where they were stored and stacked them next to his bed. He wasn't preparing for a disaster, he said. He merely needed a safety net should he be rocked out of his bunk. On the one hand, I was reassured to see the suits; on the other, the sight of them confirmed my own fear.

I looked out the wheelhouse window to see the bow, the railings, the deck covered in pure, glistening whiteness. We were heading north, directly into the wind, and whenever our bow bucked into a wave, the spray flew all the way back and over our wheelhouse in the very aft. The spray was freezing before it reached the scuppers, the openings in the bulwark designed to flush water from the deck. This was known as "making ice," the dreaded condition I had been hearing about, the one seamen fear most. If not eliminated, ice can come close to doubling the tonnage of a vessel, heightening its center of gravity to the point of capsizing.

Bud Ryan, the relief skipper, who had been standing watch in the wheelhouse, said we had been making ice all night.

I began to imagine the *Provider* growing sluggish under the added weight. How long would it be before we would be on deck banging away with sledgehammers and ax handles just to stay afloat?

"Er, how long before we should be concerned?" I asked, clearing my throat.

"Sometime before we sink, I guess," Ryan answered.

This did not set well with me.

"I asked you a goddamn straightforward question," I stammered. "I expect a straightforward answer."

He was silent for a long time, considering my alarm and anger. "I don't know. Not for a while. But sometime."

Knutson had awakened by now and came up into the wheelhouse. He looked out the windshield and lowered our speed from ten knots to eight, slightly altering our course so we weren't taking the waves head on, then lowered our speed again. He did this silently, the expression on his face grim. We had planned to deposit our pots about halfway between St. Paul Island and St. Matthew, nearly two hundred miles farther on. In this storm, it seemed to me, it would take an eternity.

We bucked the weather over the next twelve hours; the bow of the *Provider* rose and fell and made crazy figure-eights as though she were trying to shake loose from the harness of ice and the waves that bore down upon us.

About 2:00 P.M., and still about one hundred miles southeast of the Pribilofs, we picked up a MAYDAY relayed by the Coast Guard. A vessel was reported capsized. The Coast Guard had picked up the position: *58 degrees 22.9 minutes north latitude, 173 degrees 53.7 minutes west longitude*. Doug plotted the numbers on the chart and fixed the position at about 140 miles northwest of St. Paul, but closer to St. Matthew Island. Even in the best of conditions it was at least a full day ahead of us. Still, we changed our own course and set out for the overturned vessel. But the weather pushed back harder than ever.

Hours passed before the Coast Guard sent an advisory confirming that the MAYDAY had been sent from the *Northwest Mariner,* a 120-foot Seattle-based crabbing vessel with a reputation for being well-equipped and well-maintained. Nearly everyone on the *Provider* knew the vessel and her crew and agreed she was first-class. The owner, Kevin Kaldestadt, a cousin of Jeff Hendricks, insisted that his crews take safety classes and conduct safety drills. The skipper, Jim Foster, thirty-seven, was a highly regarded veteran with fifteen years of experience, and the crew had been together for many years and were all competent and safety-conscious. The vessel had left Dutch Harbor twelve hours ahead of us but had stopped on its way to the crabbing grounds to clear the decks of ice.

The Coast Guard advisory said the vessel had capsized and sunk, and that four crew members were likely trapped in the hull. Two others were reportedly picked up by the fishing vessel *Alaska Trojan*. They were found floating in a life raft. They were wearing no survival gear and they had no vital signs.

Through the night we could hear the radio traffic between the *Alaska Trojan* and the Coast Guard. There was still no trace of the *Northwest Mariner,* and there had been no witnesses. The skipper of the *Alaska Trojan* was pleading with the Coast Guard to send a helicopter to lift the two bodies off the deck. The Coast Guard declined. The weather was too rough.

The captain of the *Alaska Trojan* finally told the Coast Guard that he would put the bodies in the frozen-bait locker and return to St. Paul, when another voice came on the radio. He identified himself as Craig Forde, a crew member on the *Aleutian Mariner,* a sister vessel to the *Northwest Mariner.* The vessel was about two hours behind the *Northwest Mariner* and *Alaskan Trojan* when it picked up the MAYDAY. Forde's brother Bruce had been one of the crewmen on the downed vessel.

"Do what you have to," Craig Forde told the captain of the *Alaska Trojan.*

On the *Provider* there was little time to acknowledge the solemnity of the radio traffic or indulge in sympathy. The weather wouldn't allow it. Doug announced that we were not going to buck the seas much longer. We spent the better part of the next twenty-four hours searching for a hole in the storm, running at low speeds in the ditch between thirty-foot waves. It was nearly impossible to stand up; we could not even sit without holding on to whatever was stationary nearby. An emergency call from another vessel came over the radio. A crewman had been thrown out of a chair, and the others on board feared he had broken his back. As if anyone needed another cautionary note.

Finally, on the morning of the eighteenth, Doug swung the *Provider* back into the wind and we began baiting and dumping crab pots over a spot that he conceded was far from ideal. We had already lost too much time, he said; we had to get our pots into the water. The temperature was approximately twenty-five degrees below zero. The wind whipped our faces, tearing into our foul-weather gear. We used duct tape to strengthen the seal around our necks, ankles, and hands. We used the high-pressure hose to clear the deck of frozen fish slime after every pot was dumped to prevent more ice from buiding up. After each pot was launched, a new one was dragged across the deck by a crane and readied for the next launch. We worked quickly, if for no other reason than to give ourselves an extra minute to duck under an overhang on the bow, out of the wind and spray. We'd pull off our rubber work gloves and hold our hands, still in their soggy wool liners, up to a butane heater to try to thaw them. We devoured candy bars and swilled half-frozen cans of soda. We leaned against heavy chains or immovable pieces of equipment and grabbed thirty-second naps, falling asleep before Doug sounded the *Provider*'s horn to signal us to prepare to dump another pot. Each blast of the horn would summon a curse from one of us, and then we'd be back on deck ready to launch. I felt vaguely inhuman, not part of anything except the routine and conscious only of the cold stabbing my face and gripping my hands and feet. As we worked, grim silence prevailed among all six of us, unless something went wrong.

We had been working eighteen straight days and were midway

into what would be a twenty-hour shift when someone screamed: "Watch the hook!"

I looked up to see the two-foot-long, fifteen-pound, stainless-steel snare for lifting crab pots swinging wildly across the deck. I saw George Johnson, the greenhorn, react as if he'd just been awakened from a stupor. Slowly, listlessly, he turned and stepped into the path of the big steel claw as it swung from the crane. The moment of impact is frozen in my memory. The snare grazed George right between the eyes at what had to have been the precise millisecond it had reached the end of its arc and started to swing away. Still, the force of the blow knocked him on his back. Work stopped. Someone captured the runaway hook and lashed it down. George climbed to his feet looking dazed, but no more so than the rest of us had looked for the past forty-eight hours. Ryan, the deck boss, cursed once at him and work resumed. There wasn't time to dwell on how close he'd come to having his skull split because of greenhorn inattention. It could have happened to anyone, though no one else on board would admit it.

When there were only a few more pots to go, Doug ordered me into the galley. I lurched off the deck and leaned against the handle of the hatchway, opening it just as a wave caused the boat to roll and the hatch door to fly open, flinging me against the bulkhead that separated my body from the sea. My vision blurred and I felt sick, sliding on my back toward the unlatched hatch door as the boat rolled the other way. I reached for it and held on, wobbling to my feet just as another wave rolled the boat and the two-hundred-pound door swung back on me, slamming me against the steel cabin. With the next roll I was flung back toward the open hatch, and then somehow I was launched through the threshold into the cabin. The hatch slammed behind me. Had I been caught halfway, with one foot in and one out, my backbone would have been snapped, or an ankle at the very least.

I staggered into the head, where the sink, toilet, and shower were located, and turned on the hot water to thaw my hands and face. As I did, I got a glimpse in the mirror above the sink of what I supposed I'd come to the Bering Sea to experience. My eyes were swollen into slits. Ice hung from my eyebrows, mustache, and beard. I was shrouded in steam and looked very old; I felt no sense of duty, only the need to sleep.

The sound of the hatch opening and the crew staggering in snapped me out of semiconsciousness, and I somehow found myself in the galley scrambling eggs, turning bacon, and making coffee. But most of the crew paid no attention. They just shuffled to their bunks, falling in without even removing their foul-weather overalls. Only George lingered. He said he guessed he knew how lucky he was to be alive and sitting in the galley at that particular moment. Having witnessed his near miss on deck and barely avoiding a mishap myself, I was able to affirm his feelings. He said he wasn't so certain he was cut out for this; I said I sure as hell knew I wasn't. I don't think it made George feel any better. I do not remember if this was night or day; my notes do not say. But they do say that we left our stateroom doors open as we slept and that we made certain we had a straight path to Doug's stateroom and the survival suits.

It seemed that I had just gotten to sleep when Doug idled the engines and sent one of the crew members who'd been on watch to wake us. There was too much ice, he said. The *Provider* was in a risky condition. The ice would have to come off before we ran any further. We took baseball bats and ax handles and assaulted the ice, working as hard as but with more purpose than we had at any time since leaving port. Eight hours later the foredeck and railings were clear enough to satisfy Doug that we had a fair chance of making it back to St. Paul Island for more pots. He ran slowly, but the sea was behind us now, pushing us along, and it had come down some.

We made the harbor in St. Paul in the early-morning darkness of January 20. The *Alaska Trojan* was tied up just ahead of us, eerie in the dock lights. We were told that the bodies of the two *Northwest Mariner* crewmen were still on board. Several crewmen were telling the captain that they would not go back out until the Coast

Guard arrived and took the bodies away. Even then, the crewmen said they might be reluctant to go back on board. It was too rough out there and too spooky. Already the relief captain could be heard interviewing a couple of prospective crew members within earshot of everyone on the dock, including the crewmen who refused to board until the bodies were taken off.

No cause for the *Northwest Mariner*'s capsizing could immediately be determined. As was so often the case, there were no surviving witnesses. Two weeks later, during the memorial service in Seattle, the captain's sister, Nancy Thurston, would tell reporters that Jim Foster, her brother, had announced at Christmas that this would be his last season. "He told us the risks were just getting too high," she said.

After we had loaded more pots onto the *Provider,* Doug set the course northward again. As we sat in the wheelhouse on the way out, the thirty-eight-year-old captain, who'd been fishing for half his life, said glumly that he was getting too old for this: "This is it. This is the last year. I just want to stay home and be with my kids."

At the end of January, four weeks after I boarded her, I left the *Provider* according to our prior agreement and flew home to San Francisco. We had made one more round trip to Dutch Harbor and to the Pribilofs, meaning I had crossed the Bering Sea, from the Aleutians to the Pribilofs, three times. During the last trip north from St. Paul Island, the temperatures hovered at zero, but the seas subsided. This was not a good sign. The Coast Guard advisories warned us that a large ice pack was starting down from the Bering Straits, moving south twenty miles a day. As it moved, the ice calmed the sea in its path. With the approaching ice in mind we dropped our pots and retrieved others previously dropped forty-eight hours before. The catch was small and the crew disappointed.

It was forty-five below zero the evening the small turboprop plane lifted off from the little airfield built on the highest point of St. Paul

Island. There was a full moon, and in the light I could see the ice begin to form in the harbor. As we ascended, the ice pack came into view north of the island. It must have been a hundred miles wide.

Doug and the crew returned safely to Anacortes in late February. He told me the rest of the season had been pretty much like the beginning. The U.S. Weather Service and the Coast Guard confirmed what everybody already knew—the weather had been the worst in twenty years. Fourteen people had died during the three-month crabbing season. The *Provider* had lost sixty crab pots worth nearly $42,000 to the ice and suffered equipment problems because of the cold. Bud Ryan's hands had cramped up on him and so had George Johnson's. For the final week they had been unable to do much heavy work. Each crew member earned less than $25,000. The season had been one to try to forget, a season to send even a veteran fisherman home believing in his heart that he was home for good.

Doug said he was done with the *Provider,* and I congratulated him on making good on his word and for putting his family ahead of this terrible way of life.

A long silence followed.

He wasn't quitting, he said. He had found another boat to run, the *Pacific Monarch,* a 190-foot trawler. It was a much better boat, much better equipped than the *Provider*. He could make some money on this one. Maybe even take it all the way to Russia for the king-crab season. He was planning to head back up to Dutch Harbor just after Christmas. This time along with Nate, his eighteen-year-old son.

One year later, Doug returned to the Bering Sea without his son. After experiencing the lethal potential of one season, Nate had had enough.

About the Author

Patrick Dillon grew up among commercial fishermen on an island in Puget Sound. Formerly an editor and columnist for the *San Jose Mercury News,* and a journalist for over 25 years, he has won numerous national journalism awards, including a share of the Pulitzer Prize. His columns and essays have appeared in the *Los Angeles Times, Chicago Tribune,* and *Fast Company* magazine, among other publications. He lives in San Francisco with his wife, photographer Anne Dowie, and his two children, Pete and Tess.

Acknowledgments

The names of those to whom I owe the greatest debt of gratitude appear throughout this book. Many are the people of the town of Anacortes. Many suffered the worst losses imaginable. They received me hospitably and directly, if for no other reason than to help me tell their story clearly, within the fullest human context. Thanks also to Joel Fishman, my literary agent, for championing their story, and to Susan Kamil, my great editor, and her assistant Carla Riccio, for respectfully and painstakingly steering my thoughts and emotions along a true and frank course from beginning to end. I am thankful for having two patient and trusting kids, Pete and Tess, for allowing me to sacrifice our time together for the sake of a story they recognized to be at times dangerous to get and interminably difficult to tell. Finally, to my wife, Annie, whose clear head and compassion for the people of this book led me to prevail where I know I would not have alone.

LOST AT SEA

1. Tracing the decline of the Pacific Northwest fisheries and commercial fishing, the author follows fishermen northward toward Alaska, into bigger, more dangerous waters that hold potentially bigger, more lucrative catches. Does your view of the fishermen's lives change as you follow this journey from the relatively safe, close-in waters of Puget Sound to the treacherous Alaskan seas? Do you become more or less empathetic? Do you think the economic imperatives facing the fishermen justify the greater risks they take?

2. What did you learn about the changing stakes in today's fishing industry? Do you view the rise of heavily bankrolled commercial fishing, with larger, more efficient, and potentially safer boats, as a positive force? Or do you thnk that its focus on financial reward transcends the romance of the sea and shows that money is at the root of these and other sea tragedies?

3. As the story unfolds, the families on the dock say good-bye to their sons, brothers, and husbands. Can you put yourself in their places? Given the previous year's multimillion-dollar losses, would you have encouraged your own son, brother, or husband to take a berth on one of Jeff Hendricks's boats? Was the economic incentive worth the risk?

4. When he gets word that the *Americus* is down, Brian Melvin, a rookie skipper on the sister ship *Alyeska,* turns his boat around and begins jettisoning 700-pound crab pots. "We might [have been] sitting on a time bomb ourselves," he says. Do you think he had an inkling the *Americus* was overloaded and that his own boat might be unseaworthy as well?

5. At home in Anacortes, hearing the word from Dutch Harbor that the *Americus* is down and the *Altair* is missing, Jeff Hendricks is shocked. His first instinct is to charter a plane and leave immediately for Alaska, yet ultimately he stays and begins phoning his neighbors with the bad news. Do you think Hendricks should have gone to Alaska to aid in whatever rescue there might have been? Do you think his instinct to help was genu-

ine or do you think he feared having to stand and answer to the fathers, mothers, sisters, and wives of those crewing for him? Hendricks expresses self-loathing and guilt for not going to Alaska, but do you think there was anything he could have done at that point? Is his guilt justified, or did he do the right thing?

6. Later, Hendricks admits to being astounded to learn that the boats apparently weighed more than their blueprints said they weighed. Do you think the author explained this inconsistency clearly enough? Or do you think it was plausible that anyone, even someone as talented as Hendricks or his boat designer, could be wrong about such an important feature?

7. Who do you think is most to blame for the colossal mistake about the boats' weight? Hendricks? Jacob Fisker-Andersen, the boats' designer? The principal partners at Dakota Creek, the boatyard that built and tested the hulls? The skippers? Anyone else?

8. The Coast Guard spent nearly two years investigating the tragedy, summoning the expertise of a marine engineering professor who was able only to give his opinion. Without the vessel remains, the professor had only the statistics of similar vessels and software probability compilations to work with. Do you think this was a sufficient investigation? Do you agree with the findings? Could anything else have contributed to his conclusions?

9. No actual blame was assigned by the Coast Guard, and consequently no recommendations or materials for indictment were passed along to a U.S. attorney. There was no grand jury investigation, therefore no case of criminal negligence. Do you agree that the case should have stopped where it did, with the Coast Guard's conclusion that the fault rested specifically with the skippers? Do you agree with the Coast Guard that any guilt was due to ignorance on the part of the boat owner, builder, and designer? Or do you think there was at least enough evidence to seat a grand jury to examine allegations of possible criminal negligence?

10. Do you think civil liabilities should have been pursued after criminal negligence was ruled out? A $1 million lawsuit was originally filed and then dropped on the advice of Shannon Stafford, the attorney for the plaintiffs. Did Stafford pursue this case hard enough? Should the plaintiffs have had their day in court? Would the book have been richer (a la *A Civil Action*) had the case gone to court?

11. The case did go to the U.S. Coast Guard Commandant's office for review. Those who worked on the case (Captain John De Carteret, in particular) felt the Coast Guard had enough ammunition to push for new, strict regulations governing vessel stability and captain and crew proficiency, but none was forthcoming. Were you disappointed? Outraged? Does this give you any insight as to why the commercial fishing industry remains America's deadliest occupation?

12. Should government officials have taken a more proactive role in enforcing safety on the high seas? Was it possible to regulate safety and enforce it?

Or was the tragedy simply a reality check, a grim reminder of the inherent dangers fishermen have undertaken for ages?

13. During a congressional hearing on safety regulation, Don Young, a congressman from Alaska and fishing industry advocate, reminded anyone who would listen of the dangers fishermen face. Yet, he strongly opposed regulations. Do you think of him as an advocate for the fishermen? What reason might he have for his laissez-faire approach to the fishing industry?

14. In the end, a new law governing safety on the high seas was considered and ultimately a watered-down version was passed. This was largely due to the persistence of one mother, Peggy Barry, whose son died two years after the fourteen crew members died on the *Altair* and *Americus*. In fact, no one representing the *Altair* and *Americus* crews came forward to advocate for safety. Why do you think that was? Did it have anything to do with the strictures of living in a small town? Or was it because Peggy Barry lived in Washington, D.C., was a diplomat's wife, and had access to the seats of power that propelled the first-ever safety law in the history of the United States?

15. What was your overall reaction to this event and its aftermath? Where does the true tragedy in *Lost at Sea* lie?

Discover more reading group guides online! Browse our complete list of guides and download them for free at **www.simonsays.com/reading _guides.html.**